ROUTLEDGE LIBRARY EDITIONS: METAPHYSICS

Volume 2

REALITY AND VALUE

REALITY AND VALUE
An Introduction to Metaphysics and an
Essay on the Theory of Value

ARTHUR CAMPBELL GARNETT

LONDON AND NEW YORK

First published in 1937 by Allen & Unwin

This edition first published in 2019
by Routledge
2 Park Square, Milton Park, Abingdon, Oxon OX14 4RN

and by Routledge
52 Vanderbilt Avenue, New York, NY 10017

Routledge is an imprint of the Taylor & Francis Group, an informa business

© 1937 Arthur Campbell Garnett

All rights reserved. No part of this book may be reprinted or reproduced or utilised in any form or by any electronic, mechanical, or other means, now known or hereafter invented, including photocopying and recording, or in any information storage or retrieval system, without permission in writing from the publishers.

Trademark notice: Product or corporate names may be trademarks or registered trademarks, and are used only for identification and explanation without intent to infringe.

British Library Cataloguing in Publication Data
A catalogue record for this book is available from the British Library

ISBN: 978-0-367-19087-3 (Set)
ISBN: 978-0-429-20029-8 (Set) (ebk)
ISBN: 978-0-367-19387-4 (Volume 2) (hbk)
ISBN: 978-0-367-19403-1 (Volume 2) (pbk)
ISBN: 978-0-429-20210-0 (Volume 2) (ebk)

Publisher's Note
The publisher has gone to great lengths to ensure the quality of this reprint but points out that some imperfections in the original copies may be apparent.

Disclaimer
The publisher has made every effort to trace copyright holders and would welcome correspondence from those they have been unable to trace.

REALITY AND VALUE
AN INTRODUCTION TO METAPHYSICS AND AN ESSAY ON THE THEORY OF VALUE

by

A. CAMPBELL GARNETT
M.A., LITT.D. (MELBOURNE)
*Associate Professor of Philosophy in the
University of Wisconsin*

LONDON
GEORGE ALLEN & UNWIN LTD
MUSEUM STREET

FIRST PUBLISHED IN 1937

All rights reserved
PRINTED IN GREAT BRITAIN BY
UNWIN BROTHERS LTD., WOKING

CONTENTS

CHAPTER		PAGE
	Preface	9
I	Subject and Object	13
II	Structure and Process: Objective	44
III	Structure and Process: Subjective	73
IV	Appearance and Reality	100
V	The Self and the World	124
VI	Value: Subjective and Objective	154
VII	Value and Will	181
VIII	Value and Will—*continued*	203
IX	Truth	228
X	Beauty	249
XI	Moral Values	273
XII	Conclusion	304
	Index	318

PREFACE

THE centre of interest in philosophical discussion has transferred itself, in recent years, from the theory of knowledge to the theory of value. In an age when traditional values are so much called in question this movement was inevitable. Yet it is something more than a response to the spirit of the times. The battle between Rationalism and Empiricism, which passed over into that between Idealism and Realism, has involved a thorough exploration of most of the possibilities in the former field. It has not led to agreement, but it has clarified the issues and brought the contestants closer together. But, more important still, it has brought about a growing realization that the most fundamental problem of philosophy is not that of the nature of sense data or of logical universals, but that of the status of values. Are values a recent and perhaps temporary product of an evolving, changing world, or are they stable elements within the flux, the Alpha and Omega of its being? Religion has always given the latter answer. Few, even of the opponents of institutional religion, go so far as to deny that somehow the values are eternally "there." But how do we discover them? Why do we mistake them? In what sense are they "there" when we fail to recognize them?

These are the great philosophical questions of all time. But never was the nature of the problems clearer, nor the demand for an answer more insistent, than it is to-day. It is only by discussion that the answer can be found; and it is as a contribution to that discussion that this book is written. It is my hope that it may contain something original and constructive—something that even those deeply versed in the problems may find worth while. But I have not written it solely with the advanced student in mind. Works on philosophy can never be easy if they are to say much that is true and valuable, for they must delve into realms of thought not familiar to everyday life. But I see no reason why they should ever be beyond the understanding of the really intelligent beginner, for the data to be discussed are a part of every man's experience. The problems dealt with in this book are such as every intelligent person wishes to understand; and it is vitally important to the rest of the world that intelligent and educated people should understand them. I have therefore striven to write in a way intelligible to the beginner in philosophy, explaining technical terms and not overburdening the pages with questions of historical interest. The book, I hope, may be found useful by some teachers as an introduction to metaphysics as well as a work of reference on the problems it discusses. But still more I hope that it may be found of use and interest, outside the classroom, by many others who are trying, amid the prevailing intellectual stresses, to work out a stable and significant philosophy of life.

It is with some reluctance that I have begun, in the first few chapters, with questions of epistemology, for these, to the uninitiated, always seem to be the least interesting and most academic problems in the whole field of philosophy. But the essential contention of the book is that we are aware of the reality of values in just the same way as we are aware of the reality of other things and that our knowledge of mind is as direct and reliable as our knowledge of the physical world. It therefore seemed advisable to begin with an analysis of the process of knowledge itself. The epistemology developed is a type of critical Realism akin to the views of Kemp Smith, Stout, and Whitehead. But by showing that this epistemology applies equally to subject and object we are lead directly to an ontology akin to the systems of the great Idealists. Most important of all, we discover that our knowledge of the good and of God rests upon a direct acquaintance as unequivocal as in the case of our knowledge of the self and the world.

The range of philosophical problems that have necessarily come under review in this discussion is such as to have made anything like adequate treatment in many cases quite impossible without such an extension of the size of the book as to make the task of reading it too great for any but the special student. I have tried, however, as far as possible, always to indicate the more important alternative views and state some reasons for the positions adopted. For the rest, I hope that the solutions presented may commend themselves by their consistency with the argument as a whole. My aim has been to discuss with reasonable fullness the main issues in the theory of value and to render the solutions advocated more intelligible and acceptable by presenting them in consistent relation to a general metaphysical background. That is a sufficiently large programme for a book no bigger than this. The layman, I know, will forgive me for not making it larger. The teacher of philosophy will probably find it no disadvantage if I have raised more problems than I have solved, providing I have raised them in a way that stimulates discussion. The special student who finds my treatment often inadequate I must ask to be content with the suggestion of interpretations for his critical consideration.

In the preparation of this book I owe a great deal to stimulating discussions with Professors W. M. Urban, W. H. Sheldon, and D. C. Macintosh at Yale, and Professor N. Kemp Smith at Edinburgh. Professors Urban and Sheldon have read the whole of the manuscript and I have benefited greatly from their criticisms, coming, as they do, from points of view to the right and left of my own. Professor Kemp Smith also helped me with critical suggestions after reading the manuscript of an earlier draft of certain chapters. I would also like to pay my tribute here to my earlier teachers of philosophy, the late Professor W. R. Boyce Gibson and Professor J. McKellar Stewart, both formerly of the University of Melbourne, and to Professor F. Aveling, under whom I studied psychology at King's College, London. Another stimulus to my thought has been that of frequent discussions with Professor E. Jordan, my former colleague at Butler University, and Professor D. S. Robinson, of Indiana University. This close contact with both British and American thinkers has, I feel, been a special advantage in the attempt to form a balanced judgment on problems of such recent philosophical development as many of those involved in the general theory of value.

My thanks are also due to Yale University for according me the privileges of an Honorary Fellowship during the Spring semester of 1936, when the greater portion of this volume was written, and to the editors of *Philosophy*, London, and *The Australasian Journal of Psychology and Philosophy*, Sydney, for permission to incorporate portions of articles formerly published in those journals.

A. CAMPBELL GARNETT

TRANSYLVANIA UNIVERSITY
LEXINGTON, KENTUCKY
September, 1936

REALITY AND VALUE

CHAPTER I

SUBJECT AND OBJECT

PHILOSOPHY is distinguished from other departments of human knowledge and inquiry by the kind of questions it raises and its method of solving them, rather than by its subject-matter. There are no facts which do not come within the province of philosophy, no matter to what particular science they belong. It is the business of science to describe the data accurately, to classify them, and to formulate the general laws of their occurrence. But in order to do this science must use language; and the exact use of the language requires the definition of terms; and terms can only be defined by careful reflective analysis of the experience which gives them meaning and by critical comparison with each other. Science begins with the concepts and terms developed by unreflective common sense and refines their meaning as it proceeds. This reflective analysis and critical comparison of its fundamental concepts is the philosophy of science. It is not a seeking to know more, but a seeking to know better, to know more clearly, what is known already. To perform this philosophical part of his task the scientist has to step beyond the boundaries of his own particular science, for many of his concepts are common to several sciences. Further, even the concepts peculiar to his own science must not be defined in such a way that they have implications which conflict with those of other sciences. Where such conflict arises one or other is wrong and each must re-examine his concepts.

The difficulty of securing clear and distinct concepts, free from contradictions, increases as we pass from the purely physical sciences to the biological and from them to the psychological or sciences of the spiritual life, such as Ethics or Aesthetics. It is for this reason that all studies which are primarily concerned with the mind's own inner experience are usually grouped together as philosophical. With them our chief problem is to know more clearly what we know already; with the natural sciences the chief problem is to discover what is not yet known at all. The distinction, however, is only one of emphasis. Natural science has its philosophical problems which can only be solved by the philosophical method of reflective analysis of the experience and critical comparison of concepts. And philosophical studies cannot dispense with the collection and classification of facts and their formulation, where possible, in general laws.

The philosophical problem has sometimes been divided into two, known as Critical Philosophy and Synoptic Philosophy, the former consisting in the task of analysis and critical comparison which we have described, and the latter in the effort to bring together in a world view the ultimate results of all the sciences. This division, however, is not really necessary. The former task inevitably leads to the latter and is incomplete without it. Neither is there any approach to the latter problem except by the method which involves the former. Reflective analysis of the experience underlying our concepts and the critical comparison of all our concepts can never be complete until every concept has found its place in relation to every other. The task inevitably involves us in the working out of a world view. We can never see the world with complete clarity until we see it whole.

The task of philosophy may then be considered as the analysis of experience with the aim of clarifying all distinctions within it, the descriptive definition of those distinctions, and the critical comparison of all the concepts thus derived so that they may fit together without contradiction in a view of the world as a whole. In this task our greatest difficulties are concerned with the analysis and description of our experience of values and their relation to the rest of our world. In recent years the conviction has been growing among philosophers that Ethics, Aesthetics, Logic, and the philosophy of religion have certain fundamental features in common—that underlying them all there is a common problem of the nature of value. Thus the general theory of value has come to the fore as a distinctive and fundamental philosophical problem. Yet this problem cannot be isolated from other problems. Values are something of which we have knowledge. They are involved in the inter-relation of other things that we experience. And they are somehow vitally related to our activity. The theory of value needs must, therefore, find its place in a general metaphysic. It is that part of the whole metaphysical problem which to-day calls most loudly for study and it is to this problem that the major portion of this book is devoted. But because of the excessive confusion which still reigns in this department of philosophy it will probably be better to begin elsewhere. We shall commence, therefore, with the most general possible analysis of experience and take up the specific examination of the problems of value when we have found some data on which to base a preliminary view of its place within the whole.

Experience is so multifarious that when we set out to analyse it our first problem is to know where to begin. Somewhere or other we must thrust in the dissecting knife of thought and carve out some distinction. But the texture of experience has proved to be an extremely delicate and intricate fabric, and philosophical experiments in its analysis have often carved it up in such fashion that it has been found impossible to put it together as a working model again. For instance, we may begin as did Descartes, the father of modern philosophy, by distinguishing between matter and mind, defining the former as that which occupies space but has no thought or experience and the latter as that which has thought or experience but does not occupy space. Then we discover that we have made such a crude dissection that we can find no way in which two such entities could possibly work together in the same world. So defined they have nothing in common. So to explain how they do, as a matter of fact, belong and work together, resort has to be made to some hypothetical invention. Something that is not actually experienced in this connection has to be imagined and dragged in to fill the gap created by a clumsy act of analytical thought. Malebranche, Leibniz, and Spinoza, the three great successors of Descartes, each in a different way called in the idea of God to bridge the chasm. Later philosophers, taking warning from the difficulties discovered in this line of thought, have sought to avoid making so complete a cleavage. There is a difference between the mental and the physical; but it is not so complete, nor quite so easily distinguished, as it at first seems to be.

Another of the dangers in the analysis of experience is that of overlooking that which is too familiar to strike attention, that which is taken for granted in all experience. This has led to a tendency to overlook the part that the experiencer himself plays in all his experience.[1] Attention is concentrated on the object, and it is this changing world of objects alone that is analysed. We seem to look out through our eyes, as through a window, at things that are out there in the world beyond us; and with our other senses we seem to do much the same. In all this we seem, at first

---

[1] The distinction between the act of being aware and the object of awareness has only become clearly recognized by philosophers since the publication of Professor G. E. Moore's now famous article on "The Refutation of Idealism," in *Mind*, N.S., 1903.

sight, to be mere passive observers of the world—a world which, of course, includes our own bodies. Movements and other changes go on in this world and seem simply to impinge themselves on our experience. Apart from the fact that we seem to be able to control somewhat the movements of our own bodies (and through them of other things) and to order to some extent our own thoughts and imaginings, our minds seem to be mere mirrors held up to Nature to reflect what goes on there.

But if we thus neglect to observe at the outset that our minds are active in all experience then the fates take a peculiar revenge upon us. Either our own mind or the whole independent world of its objects has a disconcerting way of slipping out of the picture. It becomes extraordinarily difficult to hold them together in the world of our experience because we have neglected one of the vital factors that go to make experience what it is.[1] The objective world, we find, possesses two very distinct types of characteristic, sensory and dynamic, e.g. colours, sounds, smells, on the one hand, and shape,[2] mass, movement on the other. Now our increasing knowledge of the world is concerned chiefly with these dynamic characters; and because we know so much about them we are inclined to think that whatever else may be dubitable in our experience these must be real. Then we begin to take note of the fact that our senses often deceive us. Not only are there dreams and hallucinations and vivid visual imagery, but our normal waking senses play peculiar tricks upon us. Green hills turn blue as we travel further away from them; railway lines appear to draw together in the distance; a stick seems to bend as we thrust

[1] This statement has no reference to the question as to whether, or how far, our minds have something to do with making the *perceptual object*, as such, what it is. It merely denies that our minds are passive in experiencing the object.

[2] Shape, though apparently something static, is defined by dynamic processes.

it into water; our own faces appear to be behind the mirror; tepid water feels hot to our cold feet and only mildly warm to our warm hands.

Further, we learn something of the physics and physiology of these perceptions and discover that the apparently motionless solid table is really composed of millions of swirling particles of energy moving at relatively great distances from each other; that light is radiant energy of a certain periodicity; that our perception of colour depends upon an elaborate series of physiological events consisting, firstly, of a chemical process in the retina of the eye caused by this energy falling upon it, second, a wave of chemical change passing up the optic nerve, and thirdly, a process of some kind in the brain cells. And our other sense experience turns out to be similarly complicated and almost or quite as far removed from the physical object which it seems to qualify.

Having discovered this distinction between the sensory and the dynamic characters of the objective world the problem is next to say how they are related. The most plausible possibility, at first sight, seems to be that they are brought together through the inter-relation of the body and mind of the person who perceives them. The physical objects may be believed to have the dynamic characters they seem to have; and these make their impact upon the percipient's body, which, of course, has similar dynamic characters. Then, on account of some unknown relation between body and mind, when the appropriate physical processes have been thus caused in the brain, the sense experiences also occur. The data of sense are thus purely mental and exist only in the mind of the person who perceives them. We each see our own private green and brown when we look at a tree. But because our visual experience is conditioned by the physical or dynamic character of the tree, which exists quite independently of our minds, these sensory experiences enable us to infer, more or less accurately, the existence and structure of the physical object. Thus from our private worlds of sense we pass to the knowledge of a common, or objective, world of physical objects. The inference involved is, of course, recognized as not explicitly performed, except in cases of special difficulty or doubt. The animal and the child respond to their sensations instinctively with movements; and these, taken in conjunction with the spatial character of sensation, especially vision and touch, are regarded as suggesting irresistibly the notions of three-dimensional shape, mass, and movement.

This is the doctrine of *representative perception*. Its distinctive feature is the view that the objects of our immediate experience are all simply contents of our own minds. The physical world, which is not regarded as a content of our minds, is viewed as known only inferentially. The occasionally delusive character of sense experience is thus explicable as due to mistaken inferences. The sensory and dynamic characters of objects, separated in the philosophical analysis of experience, are brought into relation to each other in the psychophysical organism of the percipient. This theory, with varying explanations of the ultimate remaining mystery of the relation of body and mind, dominated the early period of the history of modern philosophy, from Descartes to Kant, and is still probably the popular assumption among scientists and other educated people who have had no training in philosophy.

But the theory has repercussions that are disastrous. It ends in the destruction of all knowledge. If all our knowledge depends upon sensations, and sensations are merely occurrences in our own minds, then can we trust this inference that we make (following some infantile assumption) that these sensations are conditioned by, and thus represent, objects extended in a three-dimensional spatial world? Obviously, there are many other possibilities. When we dream we seem to live and move in a world similar to that of our waking hours. May not life be one long dream, a delusion, as some Indian religious thinkers have believed? Or might not our experience be thrust upon us, not by a physical world, but by some other mind greater than our own, as Berkeley suggested? Perhaps such speculations may seem bizarre. But would they seem so strange if we had not grown accustomed to the interpretation of the world in terms of physical objects? In any case, all real assurance of the existence of a physical world, or of other human beings, or of anything but the mental processes of the present moment, is lost if we once adopt a representative theory of perception. Our world of immediate experience is then purely subjective. There is no distinction of subject and object. All our awareness is a mere succession of our own mental processes and we have no guarantee that it is anything more.

To escape this impasse many thinkers, while still neglecting to recognize the essential activity of mind in all experience, have sought to deal differently with the problem presented by the distinction between the sensory and the dynamic characters of the world. Instead of passing the sensory elements over to mind (and so leaving their relations to the physical, or dynamic, as part of the problem of the relation of body and mind) they have sought to retain that objective and material character of these elements which they seem on first acquaintance to possess. In the simple form of the view of naïve common sense, however, this theory is very difficult to maintain. If it is contended that colours, for example, are spread out over the surface of objects, as they seem to be, then we must admit that an extraordinary number of different colours are spread out over the same object. One person sees pure red spread on the surface of a given object. Another, who is colour blind, sees grey there. Another who has taken santonin, sees there a yellowish tinge.

Yet another, who is wearing blue spectacles, sees it as purple. In fact there is no end to the colours that must, on such a view, be spread out on that surface. Now, of course, it is not impossible that this may be the case. But it is very difficult to believe. And the situation becomes worse when we remember the effects of time and motion. We never hear or see any event at the time at which it occurs, for it takes time for light or sound waves to reach us and for the chemical processes in the sense organ and nerve to work up the stimulus and transmit it to the brain. The case of the distant star which we seem to see occupying a position in the heavens from which it moved long ago is only an extreme instance of this sort. Added to these difficulties are those of dreams and hallucinations, where colours seem to be spread out in space where no corresponding physical objects exist. Thus the theory of the spatial identity of sensory data and physical things becomes extremely difficult to believe. And though it seems to be demanded by common sense most Realists have come to agree with C. D. Broad that "in face of the facts we can only advise common sense to follow the example of Judas Iscariot and 'go out and hang itself.'"[1] Thus the attempt to defend naïve realism is given up.

If the data of sense are not simple qualities of the physical objects which they seem to characterize, and if they yet are to be regarded as having an existence independent of the perceiving mind, then they must be regarded as entities of a distinct type. They are not merely the *qualities* of physical things; and they are not merely sense *data*, having their existence in being *given* to the percipient. So they have been called "sensa," or have been spoken of as parts of a "sensory continuum," and are thus given a distinctive status as entities of the objective world, which make their appearance in our experience according to discoverable physical and

[1] C. D. Broad: *Mind and Its Place in Nature*, p. 186.

physiological laws, but which are not to be identified with the colourless, soundless, atoms and other entities which science discovers as conditioning these sensory appearances. To call them "material," however, can mean only that they are regarded as non-mental.

So far so good, although much is left to be explained. But suppose we neglect to take account of any distinctive *activity* of mind in our becoming aware of these appearances, then we are on that slippery downward path whereby, as it has been said, a certain type of psychology first lost its soul, then its mind, and finally it lost consciousness. For if all the stuff that dreams are made of is the same kind of stuff that waking reality is made of, and if this kind of stuff exists independently of anybody dreaming it or observing it, then mind is seen to have no claim on a great empire which once was regarded as its peculiar domain. The scientist no longer needs mind as the rubbish heap into which to throw all the stuff of his experience (colours, images, feelings, etc.) for which he has no use in constructing his physical world. And people have been so used to thinking of mind in terms of this rubbish heap, as the limbo where the old memories dwell, the shady realm where thoughts and fancies play, that when these things are all cast forth into the material world they have not noticed that there is anything left. In brief, if we lose sight of the mental *act*, and think of mind only in terms of *content*, then it is fatally easy (by just a little further blurring of distinctions) to resolve thoughts into associations of ideas, ideas into images, desires and emotions into sensations, will into desire, memory into imagery, and images into sensa. Thus the whole content of consciousness is resolved into sensa and their relations and cast out into the material world. And what is "consciousness" if it is neither mental act nor content?

A serious attempt to formulate such a theory was made by some of the American New Realists,[1] following up suggestions put forward in a, now famous, essay of William James.[2] There is no mind, they argued, as distinct from the brain; and it and the nervous system are merely a delicate mechanism, tuned to react or vibrate selectively to the impact of the outside world. The world has all the colours and other features it seems to have, and just where they seem to be. Consciousness is simply constituted of the collection of the characters of the objects to which the cerebrum reacts. Somehow (they were not quite clear or united on this) this cerebral motion gathers up for the organism, not merely the physical effects, but also the qualities and relations of sense resident in the outside world. This is very mysterious, but was supposed to be explained by calling it a "cross-section" of the world. The brain selects or cuts this cross-section; and we call it mind. But there is nothing distinctively mental. Consequently it had to be recognized that all sorts of queer things, like round squares and centaurs and dream faces and logical fallacies, have a peculiar being of their own, called "subsistence," and the brain also somehow gets these into its cross-section.

Difficulties of this kind caused Lord Russell, who at first was inclined to follow the American movement, to transfer all the perceived qualities of the world to the brain that perceives them. They are then still regarded as merely qualities of physical processes, but of the changes going on in the brain, not of the things where they seem to be. Sense and value (interpreted as a relation) are thus an *internal* aspect of matter; and our brains are not peculiar in having what we call "contents of consciousness." This overcomes the problem of error without introducing anything that is distinctive of mind. But the theory has peculiar difficulties

[1] E. B. Holt and others: *The New Realism.*
[2] "Does Consciousness Exist?" in *Essays in Radical Empiricism.*

of its own which we shall take up later.[1] However, the most important objection, to both this theory and that of the American group, is that of its failure to recognize the distinction between the act of experiencing and that which is experienced.

This criticism is very forcefully and clearly expressed by Professor Alexander in a reference to Holt and, coming from so unbiassed a source, it deserves quoting in full, for it applies equally to every form of Pan-objectivism, i.e. to every doctrine that denies the distinctive existence of the perceiver in perception. "If I am unable to accept a doctrine which goes beyond my own but is so simple and apparently so close to facts, and to which I find myself perpetually being drawn back and persuaded to adopt it, I am bound to state the reason why. It is that the doctrine fails to account for a vital feature in the cognitive situation, as we experience it, namely, that in being aware of the fire, the fire is before *me*, or it is *I* who see it, or it is in a sense *my* fire. This is easy to understand if the response to the fire is an act of consciousness, for then not only is there a fire, but the response is not merely something which is there alongside the fire which it selects as its object and so is for itself, but something which experiences itself. For every act of consciousness is then self-consciousness, not in the sense of containing a reflection on itself, . . . but in the sense that whenever we know we know that we know, or that knowing and knowing that we know are one and the same thing. Now if consciousness belongs not to the neural response but to the cross-section itself which it makes, as a totality, how can any object be *my* object? And yet experience says that it is."[2]

Consciousness, then, must be recognized as involving a

[1] These are the problems raised by psychic fusion, psychic blindness, and the unity of consciousness, which we discuss in connection with the theory of Professor Drake. By refusing to recognize the distinctive act of consciousness Russell makes these problems more difficult still.

[2] S. Alexander: *Space, Time and Deity*, Vol. II, pp. 111-12.

definite and distinctive reaction occurring in all awareness of objects. If no such act were discoverable by experience it would be necessary to postulate its existence. But there is no need to do this, for the awareness of such an act is implicit in all our discourse. It is somewhat elusive when we try to introspect it for, being the common content of every moment of experience, it is taken for granted and overlooked in giving attention to the changing objective content. But there is this duality in every moment of experience between the act of thinking, perceiving, willing, or feeling and that which is thought, perceived, willed, or felt. We express insight into this duality by use of the personal pronoun "I," saying "I see," "I think," etc. And this suggests that we are aware of the "I" as an entity just as distinct as the rose which is seen or its relation to the garden which is thought about. It was David Hume who first drew attention to the fact that this is an overstatement of the case. He pointed out that if we look within ourselves for some object which we can regard as the permanent ego or self we do not find it. Our supposed awareness of the self tends to dissipate into awareness of feelings of muscular tension and other bodily states.[1] Recent careful experimental investigations seem to show, however, that Hume was not entirely right in this.[2] With adequate training in introspection it does seem to be possible to discern the self as active. But whether this be so or not, it is certain that Hume went too far in denying awareness of anything but particular presentations—sensations, images, etc. He overlooked the dual nature of all such awareness. There is not merely an object, but there is an awareness of the object. I am not merely aware of a lamp on my table, but that I see the lamp. The fact that I am not aware of the "I" as I am aware of a sensum or a pleasure or a relation or other

[1] David Hume: *A Treatise of Human Nature*, Book I, Part IV.
[2] F. Aveling: *Personality and Will*, Chapter V.

content of thought, and that I am not aware of the "I see" as something that can be known in isolation or in abstraction from the object seen, does not alter the fact that there is something in my experience indicated by the words "I see" as well as something indicated by the word "lamp." And this that is indicated by "I see" is something different in kind from that which is indicated by "lamp." It is not just another sensum, such as one of eye-strain, compresent with the light sensum. It is something equally present, and present in the same way, in my awareness of *both* light and eye-strain; and it gathers them into the unity of a *single* experience.

Here we have, indeed, one essential function of this subjective act. It is that which gathers up the multifarious data of any moment and gives to them the unity of a single experience, the experience of a single individual, gathered within the order of a certain focus of attention, their various spatial positions ordered within a particular spatial perspective and their slightly differing times held within the duration of a single moment of experience.

This achievement with regard to time is one of the most remarkable facts about the act of experiencing; and it is this that makes possible the other great achievement of the subject, the act of intention or purpose. In our experience of time we actually gather up a *stretch* of duration, inclusive of a series of successive events, and experience them together in one transaction of conscious life. Thus we are aware of what otherwise we could never know—the fact of transition, of change, of the passage of what was into what is and what will be. William James did philosophy and psychology the service of calling attention to this in his own inimitably graphic way: "The practically cognized present is no knife-edge, but a saddle-back with a certain breadth of its own, and from which we look in two directions into time. The unit of composition of our perception of time is a *duration* with a bow and stern, as it were a rearward—and forward-looking end."[1] But James also did us the dis-service of calling this the "specious present," as though it were a mere appearance, as though the experience of transition, the actual *passing* of what was into what is and what is to be were something really impossible, something logically inconceivable because it would involve the being of the experient in two points of time in the one experience.

Now there is a phase of experience which is rightly described as the specious present; and it is variable in apparent duration. It is due to the facts of immediate memory and anticipation. True memory involves recall. Events pass out of consciousness and are, in a sense, brought back again in memory. But events also remain in consciousness for some little time after they have happened, so that they are there as data, or conscious content, for comparison with other data, without having to be specifically recalled. The beginning of a normal sentence does not have to be specifically recalled, after the last word has been heard, in order to grasp its meaning as a whole. A phrase of music is heard as a whole, though with perfectly distinguishable succession of its parts. Whatever is thus retained in primary memory is thus felt as, in a sense, still present; and the more vivid experiences tend thus to remain longer than others in this specious present. In a slightly less realistic sense the events of the immediately anticipated future are also incorporated in this specious present so that, as James says, it possesses both a "rearward—and forward-looking end."

But it is not this mere compresence of the consciousness of a series of events occurring at successive instants that constitutes our consciousness of time. So far as the sense experience of the earlier notes of a phrase still lingers as a *sensation* (due to the "lag" of the physical process) it mingles with the later notes now being heard to form a

[1] William James: *Principles of Psychology*, Vol. 1.

composite tone in the *present*. So far as it lingers as a mental image in immediate memory it is also a content of the *present*. If this mere experience of *present* sensation and *present* imagery were all that we are aware of we could never be aware of a past and we could never anticipate a future. Neither could we recognize objects of recall as belonging to the past. They would be present imaginal content and that is all. In brief, the compresence of sensory and imaginal content due to a succession of sense stimuli and mental acts does not itself explain our distinction of them as successive. Immediate memory and the *specious* present offer no adequate explanation of our knowledge of real time.

To be aware of past as past and present as present and of the relation and distinction between them the two must be held together in a peculiar kind of unity—the unity of an *act*. An act is something that cannot be simply instantaneous. A snapshot of a racing horse that presents its movement as it *is* at a certain instant presents all the spatial relations so far as two dimensions are concerned. But it leaves out the movement. It is an action photograph, but the action is left out. It is an attempt to present action *at* an instant. But the very essence of action is that it occupies successive instants. It is this that is achieved by the act of awareness or consciousness. It grasps the changing sensa and other data *together with the change*. In doing so it occupies successive instants, uniting them in its own peculiar unity, and is thus an awareness of succession as well as an awareness of data—an awareness of data in succession.

If there is any difficulty in conceiving this persistent unity of the single act through a stretch of time, this real intuition of a present moment which includes a succession of moments, it is probably due, as Bergson[1] suggests, to our habit of thinking of time in terms of space. We then think of the

[1] Henri Bergson: *Time and Freewill* (London: George Allen & Unwin Ltd.).

immediate present as equivalent to a point in space; and as the ideal geometrical point has no extension, but merely position, so the ideal present instant has no duration, but only position on the time line. It is the ideal point dividing the past from the future. Any duration can be analysed by thought into past and future without remainder, so that the logical or mathematical present does not *occupy* time; it simply divides time as the geometrical point divides a line without occupying any part of it. As such, it does not really exist. It is merely a logical abstraction. For nothing can be said to exist that does not occupy time. But if the present does not exist, nothing exists. For the past has ceased to exist and the future does not exist yet. Thus our logically conceptualized picture of time is seen not to be a true picture.[1] It reduces itself to an absurdity. It rests upon the same false reification of mere abstractly conceived points or instants as did the famous paradoxes with which Zeno the Eleatic used to puzzle his contemporaries. Such a picture of time must not be set up as a logical objection to our description of the intuition of time as depending on an act in which a succession of distinguishable events is grasped within the unity of a single experience. Every experience must *endure* or it could not *be*.

It is this act wherein time is intuited that carries with it the element of intention in experience. It is essentially forward-looking. Intuiting the *passage* of time, the events of

[1] Even for physics the theory of an instantaneous present is proving unsatisfactory, and efforts are being made to reconstruct it. Thus Professor Whitehead, after criticizing this theory, says: "The theory which I am urging admits a greater ultimate mystery and a deeper ignorance. The past and future meet and mingle in an ill-defined present. The passage of nature, which is only another name for the creative force of existence, has no narrow ledge of definite instantaneous present within which to operate. Its operative presence which is now urging nature forward must be sought for throughout the whole, in the remotest past as well as in the narrowest breadth of any present duration. Perhaps also in the unrealized future."—*The Concept of Nature*, p. 73.

past and present experience of which the subject is aware are, for it, signs of anticipated future experience, including that of its own future activity and bodily response. In its minimum expression it involves the awareness of objects as such, with a minimum of temporal and qualitative distinction from each other. In its fuller expressions it is at one and the same time the act of *attention* whereby, among the multiplicity of data for consciousness, some few are, as we say, singled out, concentrated upon, so that their character becomes clearer; it is the act of *cognition* (perception, thought, or judgment) whereby the given datum is seen as part of an interrelated whole, thus acquiring meaning, arousing expectation; and also it is *intention* (conation, purposive striving) for the conscious act constantly moves from the grasp of the present to the anticipation of the future, bent on moulding that future, or at least, selectively enjoying it.

We are apt to create for ourselves a logical difficulty in conceiving the awareness of the subjective act, or subject, by a wrong way of regarding this act. It must not be thought of as an act like a blow with a hammer on a gong, in which the hammer passes over to its object and does something to it, pushing or vibrating it. So conceived it becomes difficult to think of how the subject may be aware of itself. Can a hammer strike itself, or perform upon itself any act comparable to that which it performs on the gong? Of course not. So how can the subject know itself? At best, so the argument runs, it can only be some retrospective aspect of itself that it knows, something that has ceased to be a subject and becomes now an object. But this is to misunderstand the whole situation. To be aware of an object is not something that a subject does to an object. Awareness, or consciousness, is the compresence of subjective process and objective process in a unique kind of relation.[1] To put it

---

[1] I do not say, as does Professor Alexander, their compresence in the one space-time.—*Op. cit.*, Vol. II, p. 81.

SUBJECT AND OBJECT

another way, experience is the polarization of being into subject and object. The subjective process or event and the objective are both contained in the experience, which is experience of the one by the other, thus constituting what Ward calls "the duality of subject and object within the unity of experience."[1]

The other view, which would make the subject's self-awareness unintelligible, arises from the confusion of knowing with attending. The total content of experience is complex, especially on the side of the object, and some features of this content tend to have a greater vividness than others, a distinction which does seem to be due to some modification on the side of the subjective act. But in those acts wherein we are most clearly aware of the object we are also most clearly aware of the act of cognition. In cognition the intensification of presentation of the subjective and objective sides go together. This is attention, which, strictly defined,[2] is cognitive in aim. Where the aim is practical intensification of effort seems to lessen rather than increase the clarity of presentation of both subjective and objective factors. It is in these cases that introspection is most difficult. But always the subjective and objective are presented together, their clarity as mere presentations varying concomitantly.

Introspection, on this view, is not a case of one act of mind observing another act of mind. That interpretation has led to all sorts of paradoxes. August Comte argued that we can never observe our own mental acts because to do so the act to be observed must give place to the act of observing it; and that would leave nothing to be observed. William James somewhat grudgingly acknowledged that introspection must always be a post-mortem examination.

---

[1] James Ward: *Psychological Principles*.
[2] G. F. Stout: *Manual of Psychology*, fourth edition, pp. 157–8: "Attention is simply conation so far as it requires for its satisfaction fuller cognition of its object without other change in it."

But if once we recognize that attention is not a new and distinct act of awareness, but simply the degree of vigour or intensity of the cognitive act, the difficulties disappear. In our complex human mental processes it is impossible that all mental acts should be equally vigorous. There could be no singleness of direction if that were the case. A few co-ordinated acts are performed with maximum, or a high degree of intensity, and the others shade off into the marginal and subconscious. In those cognitive acts which enjoy the highest degree of attention both subjective and objective processes attain the maximum degree of clearness.

The difficulty in introspection is not that of securing clear awareness of subjective act and object together, for we cannot intensify the presentation of the one without doing the same to the other. The difficulty arises in the second step of the cognitive process—always in practice inseparable from the former—whereby we are not only aware of a presentation but know something *about* it. Every act of cognition passes from presentation to meaning. Only so is there a complete perception, for perception involves the grasping of a presentation in a content of meaning. Now ordinarily we pass from awareness of the object to its meaning; i.e. the *object* is allowed to direct the cognitive aim and thus the course of further thought. It is only when we seek to understand ourselves that we allow the awareness of the *subjective act* to become directive of cognitive aim and thus pass from awareness of it to its meaning; i.e. become not merely barely aware of it, but actually *perceive* it. It is not difficult to pursue such a process of subjective examination when we are content to do that alone. But psychological introspection involves the attempt to pursue a line of cognitive activity directed by the object and at the same time grasp the meaning of each subjective act. It can only be done, of course, by swift transitions of cognitive aim; and these tend to interfere with the normal course of the objectively directed activity. But these difficulties of psychological introspection are not present in ordinary self-examination. The only difficulty there is to explicate all the implicit ramifications of purpose underlying the subjective act. But that act itself is as clear as daylight.

Now the important thing about this subjective activity involved in consciousness is that it is a response to the *qualitative* characters of events, to sensa and whatever else of qualitative character enters into experience. In this it is unique among the reactions of the organism. All physico-chemical reactions, including those in our brains, if, or so far as, they are purely physico-chemical, are reactions to the dynamic character of related objects alone. A wave of chemical change passing up the optic nerve as the result of stimulation of the retina by a beam of red light is not a response to the colour red, but an effect of the impact of radiant energy of a certain intensity and periodicity. But "seeing a red light" is, if it is anything at all, a response to the colour quality of a sensum.

Now it is probably true that whenever the event "seeing a red light" occurs there also occur certain dynamic reactions in the visual nervous system. Assuming this to be the case some thinkers, in too great haste to reduce everything to the kind of terms they regard as "scientific," have thought that the unique feature of the complex of events, the mental act of seeing red, even if its existence needs must be recognized, may still be ignored so far as the practical explanation of behaviour is concerned. Thus they have asserted that consciousness of an object is nothing more than a complex physico-chemical event in the cortex accompanied by the appearance of concomitant sensa and values which, however, have nothing to do with the course of the process or its effects.

But if this is the case then some strange results must be admitted. It means that consciousness plays no part in conduct; that men and animals would avoid wounds and burns just as they do if they had never felt pain; that Turner would have painted his pictures just the same if he had never seen colour; that Wagner would have written his operas and Melba and Caruso would have sung them to applauding thousands just the same if no one had ever heard a sound; that the whole course of history would have gone the same way, with its struggles for power and for liberty, if no one had been able to enjoy fame or appreciate freedom; that men and women would have slain each other and died for each other just the same if they had never known the pangs of jealousy or the joy and sweetness of a strong affection. If the dynamic characters of the world, the push and pull of particles of energy, in the brain and out of it, are alone effective in human conduct then this nonsense would be sober truth. Somehow, therefore, even though we are unable to see how, it must be the case that the reaction we call consciousness, or awareness, must be a reaction to the qualitative characters of objective reality, i.e. to sensa and whatever other qualities may be discovered on the further analysis of experience. And it must be the case that this reaction, such as the *seeing* of red, the *feeling* of pleasure, makes a difference to the subsequent course of the dynamic processes that go on in the brain and issue from it in conduct.

Yet, such is the force of the habit of thought inculcated by our modern scientific outlook, that some philosophers, even though they recognize the distinctive existence of the act of consciousness, still try to interpret it on physical principles. This means that the objective qualities have to be recognized as the psychic accompaniment of one set of physical processes, but the awareness of this psychic accompaniment has to be interpreted as due to another. The implications of this type of theory have been thoroughly worked out by Professor Drake. He certainly does not

SUBJECT AND OBJECT 35

attempt to meet the general consequences of mechanism which we have referred to above, but he clearly states the nature of the psycho-physical problem involved. Consciousness he regards as simply a "unitary cerebral process" by which the organism is "adjusted . . . to this or that object."[1] Very definitely he recognizes that "Consciousness is not the mere existence of sentience. Consciousness involves transcendence; it is awareness *of* something else; it implies a relation between a *here* and a *there*, a *now* and a *then*."[2] Yet he nevertheless asserts that "All the existents conserved in a case of consciousness can be described (that is, could be if we had enough physical and physiological knowledge) in physical terms."[3]

This attempt to interpret the act whereby sensation is endowed with meaning for the direction of conduct as merely a cerebral "reaction-system" or "set of motor responses" means that the dynamic characters of cerebral events are alone effective in the direction of behaviour. It is all merely a matter of attraction and repulsion of molecules. It is quite in vain that Professor Drake points out that, on his theory, "the psychic states aroused in the cerebrum are a sign to the organism of that thing whose presence the organism is taking into account."[4] The psychic

[1] Durant Drake: *Mind and Its Place in Nature*, p. 175.
[2] *Op. cit.*, p. 173.
[3] *Op. cit.*, p. 186. Note: On Professor Drake's theory the contents of consciousness are imaginal not existent.
[4] *Op. cit.*, p. 176. Note: Professor Drake suggests that his view does not *necessarily* involve mechanism (pp. 252 ff.) because our ignorance prevents us from asserting that there are no independent variables or irregularities in the cerebral processes. He sees no reason, however, for assuming that there are such gaps in the mechanical explanation and several reasons for cautiously refusing to do so. The ether, he thinks, an existent "more pervasive than matter," provides room for anyone's "will to believe" in forms of life other than the material. But in that he treats consciousness, the experience of the qualitative aspect of events, as having no effect upon behaviour his position is characteristically mechanistic.

state and the awareness that they are a sign of some real thing have, on his theory, nothing to do with how the organism will take account of it. Man is like a person in an aeroplane that is entirely mechanically controlled. He can look out of the windows and see the passing scenery, with its beauties and dangers, and he can see the direction he wants to go, but he might as well be asleep for ought he can do to direct the course of the machine. Colour has nothing to do with the behaviour of the artist, nor sound with that of the musician, nor was it ever pain that extracted the confession from the tortured sufferer on the wrack. This is the kind of view that, with all due respect to its numerous brilliant exponents, we earlier described as nonsense. It is very learned, and often very cleverly argued, nonsense. But it is so contrary to that well tried interpretation of human behaviour in terms of experience and motive, by which human beings have understood each other so well as to develop a civilization, that it just does not make good sense.

Further, it is impossible to make any theory of the reaction of a unitary system of sensory-motor arcs explain the distinction between mere sentience and consciousness as we know it. Professor Drake is more fully aware of both the philosophical and the psychological difficulties here than are most mechanistic writers on the problem and that is why we select his exposition for criticism.[1] There are two types of fact which he regards as most definitely necessitating the recognition of consciousness as act or process additional to the cortical processes of the sensory areas which are accompanied by sentience. These are the unity

[1] Professor Alexander, in *Space, Time and Deity*, also duly recognizes the significance of this problem; but his theory of emergents enables him to escape the real difficulties of it. This theory, however, whereby mind, life, colour, etc., are miraculously produced from nowhere, as the conjurer produces rabbits from a hat, must fail to satisfy anyone who lacks the "natural piety" to believe that they were not somehow there all the time.

of consciousness and the facts of psychic fusion. The physical processes in the brain are enormously complex. Yet the contents of consciousness are relatively simple and have a peculiar kind of unity. They belong together in a single field, are gathered up in a more or less completely unified totality of meaning, and are sorted out with varying degrees of clearness in relation to a single focus of attention. Further, data that, under conditions of relatively close scrutiny, are distinct and qualitatively different fuse together under conditions of more distant or more rapid appearance, or of less keen attention; and the resultant fusion is often very different, qualitatively, from the same data observed in distinction. The facts of psychic fusion are worth illustrating in some detail. Thus, the sound of an orchestra is different when we relaxedly listen to it as a whole and when we attentively pick out a single instrument.' A hill that is a uniform green in the distance becomes a variety of greens and other colours on closer inspection. The spokes of a rotating wheel fuse into a single, apparently solid, object. A garment of black and white spots appears a uniform grey at a distance.

One of the most remarkable instances of fusion, which Professor McDougall has emphasized[1] as a case which could have no possible neural counterpart, is that experienced when to one eye is held a blue glass and to the other a red. The resulting colour percept may be either red or blue or purple. Where only one of the two given colours is seen this must be explained as a case of psychic blindness—the sensum being presented but not perceived. Cases of this kind show very definitely that consciousness of an object requires something more than presentation of an adequate

[1] W. McDougall, *Body and Mind*. In a footnote to p. 290 he adds: "The problem may be presented in a form rather more striking perhaps, but more complicated, by substituting a bluish-green glass for the blue one. The subject A will then see a white spot, though his left eye is stimulated by red light and his right eye by blue-green light."

stimulus to an efficient sense organ of a wide-awake person; and such cases can be multiplied indefinitely from psychopathology, where psychic blindness, deafness, and anaesthesia are commonly recognized phenomena. But when purple results in the above-mentioned experiment we have a very instructive case of psychic fusion. The optic nerves convey the two different colour impressions to the two different (and opposite) hemispheres of the brain. There seems to be no possibility of a final physiological fusion of the two stimuli in the stimulation of common brain cells.[1] The cortical processes that, if first one and then the other eye is closed, condition the awareness of first blue and then red must now both occur together. Yet neither red nor blue is seen, but a different colour, purple. Now the two pictures seen by the two eyes are, we know from the stereopticon, though each slightly different in perspective, normally fused together, the differences that enter into the fusion helping to give us the impression of a third dimension. This is remarkable enough; but here, from the fusion of two differently coloured pictures, a new colour emerges, for which we cannot even conjecture a process in the sensory areas of the cortex distinct from the two separate processes which, each occurring alone, condition the perception of red and blue. Obviously there is *some* kind of further reaction needed to explain the emergence of the purple by fusion.

McDougall argued that no physiological process could be suggested which might reasonably be supposed to perform this function and the similar one indicated by all cases of psychic fusion and by the unity of consciousness in general. Drake attempts to meet this difficulty. "Two steps," says he, "seem to be necessary—and sufficient—if we are to *explain* the appearance of simple data to consciousness. First, we must admit that the units which make up the complex

[1] McDougall enumerates seven experimental results and physiological acts which show the impossibility of this.—*Body and Mind*, pp. 290–3.

which is apprehended as simple, in introspection, or used as a means for such apprehension in perception, are 'psychic' —i.e. are units of sentience."[1] . . . But since "our mental life, as introspectively known, seems far too simple to be the inner, or substantial, aspect of anything so complex as any cerebral process must be,"[2] the question arises "How is the 'condensation' or 'contraction' effected?" "We must then take our second step which is to recognize the rôle that the motor adjustment plays in conditioning consciousness."[3] "When a blue patch is presented to one eye and a red patch to the other eye, simultaneously, the usual result is that one of the two sensory areas produces the motor response, and we see one of the two colours above. The sensory excitement in the other hemisphere is able to produce no response, and consequently evokes no consciousness. But it sometimes happens that the two sensory areas cooperate to produce a joint motor response, and the result is . . . an awareness of purple."[4]

It is then, on this theory, the motor response of the organism to the stimulation of the sensory areas of the cortex that finally produces awareness of sense qualities; and the unity of consciousness is explained by the fact that this is normally a unified reaction of the organism as a whole. Our psychic life is really just as complex as the physical processes of the cortex. But the vast majority of the psychic events accompanying those physical processes are extremely transient and slight. The strong, vivid mental events which are distinct elements of our consciousness are the psychic aspect of the activity of those cerebral structures which condition our sensori-motor responses. These are organized into an elaborate system of connections, some congenital, others developed in the course of experience. "Resistances are lowered here and heightened there, we form mental ruts. . . . The plastic child forms habits, gets set in its ways,

[1] *Op. cit.*, p. 123.   [2] Page 105.   [3] Page 124.   [4] Page 126.

becomes a developed self."[1] This same structure is the basis of memory and accounts for the fact that only those psychic events which have played a part within the activity of this structure have any chance of permanence and recall. The rest have their brief being outside the main stream of responses and so attain no distinctive vividness and cannot be recalled.

This theory has some important defects and one crucial objection. The sensum, e.g. the purple resulting from the red and blue glasses, has to be regarded as the psychic accompaniment of the *motor* response or adjustment of the organism instead of being that of the visual area of the cortex which receives the stimulus. Yet artificial stimulation of the sensory areas evokes sensation and artificial stimulation of the motor or any other areas does not. Further, since it is the unified reaction to a multiplicity of cerebral events that produces the simplified quality of which we are conscious, and since the qualitative aspect of this cerebral reaction gains its predominance over other sensitivity by reason of its belonging to the main system of habits or tendencies of the developed self, we should expect that habitual reactions should have the most marked conscious accompaniment, but this is the reverse of the facts. If, on the other hand, what is meant is that the sensum is the psychic aspect of the cerebral process in the *sensory* area of the cortex (in which sense stimulation culminates) and that the motor reaction or organic adjustment simply gives this psychic state predominance, then, though this would explain discriminative attention, it certainly does not explain psychic fusion. If the experience of purple in our crucial case is really merely the psychic aspect of a physical process then it is the aspect of some *other* process than those which occur separately for red and blue, and which must occur when a different coloured glass is put to each eye.

[1] *Op. cit.*, p. 120.

SUBJECT AND OBJECT

The attempt to give a physiological account of the activity that accounts for psychic blindness, psychic fusion, and the unity of consciousness is, then, far from satisfactory. But the really decisive objection to it is that such a physiological response must be a merely mechanical reaction, the effect of the dynamic processes alone, so that the qualitative aspect of reality has to be regarded as having no function whatever in the scheme of things. All would have gone on just the same if the stuff of the universe had contained no qualities (and no qualitative potentialities) providing the dynamic characters, the attraction and repulsion of units of energy, had remained the same. Such a view, instead of being one which we ought to feel obliged to defend as scientific, should be regarded, like Solipsism, as the *reductio ad absurdum* of any theory that leads us to it. It should be recognized as implying the necessity of starting again and searching for something that has been missed that would explain how (or at least some theory that would suggest how) every aspect of the universe, qualitative and dynamic or quantitative, plays its part in the process of things.

The plea that we must adopt Mechanism or cease to be scientific is quite unsound.[1] The ultimate aim of science must be to give an account of the whole of experience; and that account is not complete until qualitative changes are brought into functional relation with quantitative. That may be ultimately beyond the possibility of our knowledge and the two-aspect theory may be the last word. But, even so, it is certainly not an *a priori* demand of the logic of science that it *must* be the last word, that no theory of functional inter-relation of the two features of reality can

[1] For a strong statement to the contrary by an eminent physicist, based on consideration of recent discoveries, we may refer to the following from A. A. Eddington: *The Nature of the Physical World*, p. 313, "It seems that we must attribute to the mind power not only to decide the behaviour of atoms, but to affect systematically large groups—in fact to tamper with the odds on atomic behaviour."

be entertained. It is sometimes urged that if psychic events are regarded as affecting the course of behaviour then we have admitted an incalculable factor which will forever make impossible the completion of the scientific account of conduct. But if behaviour is entirely dependent upon the chemistry of the living brain then does any one suppose that science will ever be able to give a complete account of it? Indeed, in that case, it must forever remain a mystery. As a matter of fact nearly all the understanding of human conduct that man has ever achieved, or is likely to achieve, has to be put in terms of felt experience and motivation, love, pain, and longing, rather than physics and bio-chemistry. And even in biology such concepts as the struggle for existence and the self-adjusting tendencies of the organism are found exceedingly valuable. It would, of course, be unscientific to rest content in referring a process to psychic agency and cease to look for a physical cause where there may be one. But it is equally unscientific to rule out *a priori* the possibility of psychic processes affecting, in any way, the course of conduct.

Since, therefore, we have already seen the necessity of recognizing an act or process operative in consciousness distinct from the changing qualities (sensa, etc.) which we call its objective content we shall not be deterred from considering the possibility that this act may be something different in kind from the physical processes which, we recognize, also condition their appearance. And if it is possible to conceive this subjective act as something responsive to the changing qualitative character of the objective content, and also having an effect upon the course of physical processes in the cerebrum, then we shall have discovered a link which may connect the qualitative features of experience with our motor response to them. It would not be necessary, as has often been pointed out, that such a factor should introduce energy into or subtract it from the cortex of the brain, but only that it should constitute a change in the medium in which physical processes occur (perhaps a medium of which physical energy is a peculiar form) such that the transition from potential to kinetic and *vice versa* may be facilitated or retarded.

In any case we must be grateful to Professor Drake for having so clearly shown the necessity of recognizing the distinction of seeing and that which is seen, of knower and the character known, of subject and object. This distinction Mechanists have been loath to recognize. Yet it is one which has been admitted or vigorously asserted by philosophers of almost all shades of opinion throughout history. Lord Russell frankly states that though Mach, James, Dewey, and the American New Realists, stand with him in rejecting it, the great majority of philosophical opinion is on the other side. The fact of the matter is that the adoption of this view derives almost wholly from the influence of one man, William James, whose versatile and highly original genius seems to have fathered or fostered more fallacies[1] than any philosopher since Descartes. And it is worth noting that the fallacies of both great thinkers were due to the desire to shape philosophy in accordance with what in their respective times was regarded as being "scientific."

[1] I would so regard the Pragmatist theory of truth, the pan-objectivist epistemology of New Realism, the Behaviourist psychology without consciousness, the Pluralist theory of a finite deity, and the effort to find the foundations of religion in the subconscious mind.

CHAPTER II

STRUCTURE AND PROCESS: OBJECTIVE

HAVING drawn attention to the way in which experience is initially polarized into subject and object we can now pass on to the examination of another distinction which is discoverable within each. This is the difference between structure and process. On both sides we have a flux of changes but through them all a certain continuity and order, a structure that is relatively permanent amid the temporary and sometimes fleeting processes. This distinction is to be recognized on both sides, but for the present we shall confine ourselves to its manifestation on the side of the object. The fluctuating character of objective appearances is, of course, in part due to the instability of the subjective activity which observes them. But they also change of themselves, independently of the subject. Some features of the object are, of course, much more enduring than others. The houses in the street and the hills we visit in the summer seem to outlast many observations—and many observers. Still we know they change. They all manifest the transitional, ephemeral character of *process*.

Yet amid all the flux of process there is some degree of continuity and order. And it is by this continuity and order amid the flux that we distinguish things or structures. On the side of the object this is, of course, readily recognized. The will-o'-the-wisp that flutters over the marshes at night and is gone, the rainbow and the mirage which retreat as we approach and tantalizingly appear and disappear, we hesitate to say are any*thing* at all. But the faithful stars that follow their appointed courses we never doubt, though we can never catch them. A thing may change, as the hailstones do when we bring them inside the house. But so long

STRUCTURE AND PROCESS: OBJECTIVE

as there is continuity and order about the changes of a thing we never doubt its thinghood. The coal that burns and turns to ashes in the grate, though it changes in all its qualities, is yet a single thing for common sense because of the continuity and order of the change. The structure of the thing is nothing more than the continuity and order of its processes. The processes and these relations between them are all that is there to be observed. Together they constitute all that is immediately given of the objects or things we know.

This knowledge has its foundations in direct acquaintance both in regard to structure and process. But direct acquaintance is, of course, limited to the present moment. The further building up of our knowledge, including our knowledge of the continued existence of things not presently experienced, is a matter of inference. The logical principles of inference, and the psychological principles of memory and primary acquirement of meaning with which they must co-operate, are part of the structure disclosed within subjective process. A full examination of these principles would take us far away from our main theme into the provinces of logic and psychology, so we will not attempt it. But we must return to this matter of subjective structure, for a brief analysis, in the next chapter. Our first task, however, shall be the examination of the main outlines of structure and process on the side of the object. This examination must begin with an analysis of all the kinds of difference manifested in the objective world and then proceed to discover the ways in which these differences are united together to form structural wholes. We shall find three main types of diversity, with a number of subsidiary features under each, and three categories of unity whereby the diversities have their character of structure, are unified into things and the things into larger wholes.

The first of the three main types of diversity among objective processes is that of sensory quality. We put it first for the reason that it is the most obvious. Sensa[1] seem to pervade our whole objective world. But they are transitory, coming and going and changing in correlation with our movements and movements of our objects. They are something *sui generis*. We can explain their occurrence, and to some extent control it, by reference to movements. But that does not mean that we *reduce* colour to motion of the ether or pain to molecular changes in the brain cells. Physics and chemistry can therefore never hope to give a complete account of our world, for sensa are entirely beyond their scope, and yet any account of the world without them misses out that which is the key to all the rest, for, even though we do have some intuition of motion that is non-sensory, it is far too fragmentary to have made physics and chemistry possible except for its correlation with sensa. How this correlation occurs is the difficult problem to which we must next give our attention. First, however, it is necessary simply to note the obvious fact of sense appearance and differentiation.

Sensa differentiate themselves, in the first place, according to "quality." This term applies both to distinctions *within* the one kind of sense data, e.g. distinctions of colour within the visual field, and to distinctions *between* the different kinds of sense data, e.g. that between sound and smell. All these are distinctions of "quality." But sensa also differ in intensity, in protensity (the effect due to differences of duration) and in quantity, voluminousness or extensity. Closely allied with sensa, too, we must recognize mental images. They distinguish themselves from sensa chiefly as being more or less within deliberate control and not so directly correlated with physical objects. But they are fundamentally sensory nevertheless. There is no need to regard them as a distinct type of objective process.

[1] This is the technical term for the colours, sounds, warmths, etc., with which we become acquainted in sensation.

STRUCTURE AND PROCESS: OBJECTIVE

The second main type of diversity is that which includes all spatial distinctions, i.e. distinctions of dimension, direction, plane, size, shape, etc., and of movement, or progressive change of these distinctions. We are, of course, more accustomed to thinking of spatial relations as connections than as diversifications and, indeed, when a spatial relation is taken together with its terms to constitute a whole, it does form the connecting link between them, as when, in looking at a puzzle picture, we happen upon those relations between certain lines which form those lines into the picture of a human face which had to be found. But here it is the particularization, limitation, or definition of the relations which forms the whole out of the comparatively discrete elements. Those very elements had to be differentiated spatially as placed in the picture in order to appear as separate elements at all. Space is presented as differentiation of position. Without this differentiation there would be no space. The various spatial *relations* are therefore primarily spatial *differentiations* and only as limited or defined between terms do they become connections within wholes. Even then it is really more correct to say that the distinctive and particular whole is constituted by the *limitation* of the spatial relations between the terms than by the introduction of them. As the *Gestalt* psychology has emphasized, perception seems to move from the whole to the differentiation of the parts. It is the higher cognitive process of constructive thought that takes terms and relations in abstraction and puts them together in new wholes. The space of our developed thought is, certainly, of this conceptual order. But this is not space as primarily given. In that perceptual space, therefore, which is the foundation of our knowledge of space, spatial relations are differentiations of the given, not given connections within it.

If spatial relations are diversities, differentiations, of what are they diversities? Not of colour. Diversities of colour are red, blue, etc. Are they the diversities of that peculiar character of some sensa which we call their quantity, voluminousness or extensity? Or are they differentiations of non-sensorially intuited motions? At first thought we are inclined to the former answer, and this has always been the popular view even among philosophers. Our own conviction, however, is that this is wrong and that this natural mistake is the source of many of our difficulties in the theory of knowledge. It must, of course, be granted that in our developed perception we are aware of space through sight and touch. But much of what is grasped in developed perception is acquired meaning, not immediate sensory presentation. Much of this acquired meaning is so firmly fixed that even trained introspection cannot entirely disentangle it from the purely sensorial. Of this the facts of perspective are the best illustration. This filling out of the perceptual datum with associations and acquired meaning so closely related to the sensum that they seem to be a part of it, is technically known as "complication." In addition to perspective other familiar examples are the "hard" appearance of polished steel, the "cold" appearance of ice, the "warmth" of certain colours, the "rough" look of a piece of sandpaper, and so forth.

Now it is generally recognized that the third dimension, or distance, apparently perceived in visual space, is in this sense a complication from acquaintance with distance acquired in touch and movement. Vision depends upon impression upon the retina; and no possible difference in the stimulus of light waves could be due to the distance from which they had come. The impression of seeing a third dimension, which is so vivid and inextinguishable a part of our visual experience, must therefore be due to acquired experience, either that of the individual or the race, but chiefly, if not entirely, of the individual. It depends upon the relative size of the objects in the visual field, upon

STRUCTURE AND PROCESS: OBJECTIVE

differences of perspective of the two eyes, and upon sensations from the adaptation of the lens and the varying clearness of focus of objects at different distances which results from lens adaptation. The illusions of perspective created by the painter and the stereoscope depend upon taking advantage of the two former factors.

For the explanation of our primary awareness of the third dimension in space we are thrown back, therefore, to the examination of tactual and motor perception. Now so-called motor sensations are not really sensations of movement at all and only possess an extremely vague voluminousness. And even this voluminousness varies with intensity, as in hard pushing, not with distance moved. The voluminousness of motor sensa therefore cannot give us our primary awareness of space. And as they are really only peculiar tactual sensations in the joints, muscles, and tendons, and contain within themselves no distinctions of apartness or transition, they could not, of themselves, give us our awareness of spatial extensity and movement of muscles and limbs. They do enable us to perceive the position and movement of the various parts of the body; but a little examination and consideration of their nature will suffice to show that this must be due to a complication from some other source of awareness, as is the third dimension of visual experience.

We come, then, to that form of tactual perception whereby we distinguish spatial relations on the surface of the skin. Different parts of the skin vary in capacity for spatial discrimination, but to some degree this capacity is distributed over the whole surface of the body. Here we have plain discrimination of spatial relations and movements in two dimensions. But what of the third? We certainly *perceive* three dimensions when we grasp a ball in the hand, or place our hand over the corner of the table, or run a pencil down and round the wrist. But how much is sensum and how much is complication? Suppose we did not know already that the wrist was round, or that the fingers were bent round the ball or the corner of the table, could any such distinctions as are merely sensorially given make us aware that a third dimension of space was involved in the order of these sense data? It seems fairly obvious, upon consideration, that it could not. Without an accompanying awareness of the shape and position of our limbs (which would involve awareness of the third dimension) the mere apartness and sense of transition on the skin surface could not give us awareness of the third dimension. Neither the two-dimensional spatial awareness of cutaneous sensations nor the so-called motor sensations could, taken severally, give us awareness of three-dimensional space.

We ask next, then, could these two achieve it working together and with the help of the two-dimensional visual field? This is the view usually taken, and such a statement as the following would be regarded by many as an entirely sufficient explanation. "Our acquaintance with the shape and size of our own body and limbs and with the positions and distances of different parts of our skin relatively to each other is not due, in the first instance, merely to muscle, joint, and tendon sensations. Primarily, we obtain this definite spatial apprehension of our body, partly by experiences arising from the mutual contact and mutual exploration of the different parts of the skin, as when the hands rub against each other, or one of them passes over the surface of the face or leg; partly again, by seeing our body and its parts at rest and in motion."[1] This statement, however, is later qualified by this same authority by recognition that along with the sense factor there goes something that is called an "activity factor,"[2] and that the development of our knowledge of the material world depends on these "two main conditions." Before examining this activity factor, however, let us return to the question whether the third

[1] G. F. Stout: *Op. cit.*, p. 259.   [2] *Op. cit.*, p. 408.

STRUCTURE AND PROCESS: OBJECTIVE

dimension of space could possibly be perceived by the sense factor alone.

We have now narrowed this down to the question whether cutaneous and motor sensations, working together in the way described in the above quotation, could give us three dimensions. When we rub the hand around the face or around the other hand we certainly *perceive* three dimensions; but it is equally clear that we do not *sense* them. Since one skin surface only presents us with two-dimensional extensity and movement the mere duplication of this from contact of skin with skin does not give us three. Neither could the correlation of these changing two-dimensional cutaneous sensations with the vague (and quite distinctly different) muscle, joint, and tendon sensations present a third dimension. We conclude, therefore, that no single sensum, and no combination of sensa, could possibly account for our perception of space as three-dimensional. If we possessed sense perception alone we might have instinctively performed three-dimensional movements in response to variations of sensa due to the third dimension (e.g. variation of visual size according to distance), but we could have had no thought (even in the most elementary sense of that term) of three dimensions. We could never have come to perceive space as three-dimensional. Or, at least, we could never have done so until after some genius had conceived the notion of an unperceived third dimension of space as an explanation of the behaviour of our sensa—an achievement of the scientific imagination which would rank far above those of Copernicus and Einstein. Instead of that we begin, from our earliest experience, so far as we can remember, to perceive our world as extended in its three directions around us.

This fact is commonly attributed to some kind of innately-determined interpretation; i.e. the tri-dimensional character of perceived space is recognized as not sensorially given but as a complication determined by racial heredity. This, I think, must be recognized as to some extent true. But it does not eliminate the necessity of recognizing a source of experience of the physical world other than the sensory; i.e. a direct intuition of its spatial-dynamic character. For a racially inherited *interpretation* must be rooted in racial *experience*. It is not enough that instinctive *reactions* should have become adapted to the variations in sense data due to the tri-dimensional character of the world. The question is not that of how we come to *react* in and to three-dimensional space, but how we come to *know* it. It forms a part of our primary awareness and must therefore be derived from immediate experience. As it is not sensorially given it must be intuited in some other way. And this intuition must still be part of the developed consciousness. Ancestral experience could not provide the notion of space itself, but only as association tendency whereby the vaguely given motion and extensity are interpreted. We must therefore either recognize the direct awareness of space as a distinctive primary element of experience or revert to the crude form of the doctrine of innate ideas castigated long ago by John Locke.

Having discovered that the third dimension of perceptual space is not merely sensorial but is a complication of the sensory due to independent spatial intuition, it becomes probable that this is also true of the two dimensions of our cutaneous and visual sensa, i.e. that even visual and tactual sensa possess only a quantitative character, not genuine extension. This view is adopted by Professor Alexander[1] and is endorsed and developed by Professor Kemp Smith.[2] If space is known by direct intuition it is certainly intuited

[1] "When I see a blue patch I see its blue quality, but I have an intuition of its extent. I do not see a blue which *possesses an extent* but I intuite an extent of space which I see blue."—*Space, Time and Deity*, Vol. II, p. 164.
[2] N. Kemp Smith: *Prolegomena to an Idealist Theory of Knowledge*.

STRUCTURE AND PROCESS: OBJECTIVE

in the same act whereby we become aware of the sensum, so that the quantitative character of the sensum is grasped in a spatial setting and the qualitative variety of the sensory field becomes a perception of spatial relationship through complication with the intuited spatial continuum.

Now the act of awareness, as we have already seen, must be a response to physical processes in the cerebral cortex. Such processes must occur in the sensory cortical areas as the central termination of the stimulus which began in the end organ of sense, e.g. touch spot or retina. This stimulus may be conceived as upsetting the normal chemical equilibrium of certain brain cells, upon which there must supervene that constructive, recuperative reaction which is at once typical of organic processes and distinctive of them.[1] It is, apparently, while this process is in progress that the sensum may be perceived. It is not necessarily then perceived, as the facts of psychic blindness show. Nor is it (even occurring unperceived) merely a correlate or character of this reintegrative, organic process; otherwise the facts of psychic fusion would be inexplicable. Nevertheless, it is while this reintegrative organic process is going on that the act of awareness of a sensum is possible—a fact indicated by all the data relating to positive and negative after images and the lag of sensation behind the process of actual stimulation.

If, as everyone who is not a Mechanist must believe, there is something in the nature of an organism as a whole that is more than the sum of its physical parts, then this "something more" is in operation when the reintegrative process sets in, in a sensory cell in the cortex, after its equilibrium has been upset by a sense stimulus. The act of awareness of a sensum must therefore be itself a response (taking account of psychic fusion) to a complex of such higher organic operations. What our analysis shows is that this act of

[1] See Chapter III, pp. 85 ff.

awareness intuits the bodily, four-dimensional, spatio-temporal character of this higher organic operation together with the sensum. This intuition of moving body must be extremely vague. It certainly is not an awareness of the shape and arrangement of the cells of the cortex involved in the sensory cortical process. Yet it must be a primitive awareness, such as perhaps even a single-celled organism might have, of the nature, essence, or stuff of space-time.

It is very important to realize that motion as intuited is not the mere abstract extensity and duration of our thought. Experienced motion has a concreteness which our thought of it leaves out, reducing it at last to mathematical symbols. But as given in intuition it is not merely the distances, directions, and durations we abstract from it. It has the concreteness of pressure, energy, resistance, and inertia. Where else could we obtain these notions if not in the direct intuition of motion? The content of these terms is no more nearly given in the cutaneous and bodily sensa experienced when a weight presses upon us than is motion given in "motor" sensa. It requires very little effort of introspection to isolate the sense quality from the "complication" which gives it its significance. Whence, then, this significance, if motion, as intuited, does not include experience of the concrete reality? The mere transitions of visual and cutaneous motion have no such content; the "motor" sensa only have it by complication. Certainly conation, as experienced, offers a somewhat similar content. But yet there is a very real difference between our own experience of effort and that of the concreteness of the body that presses upon us or resists us. There is also something much more in the notion than any concept that could be built up out of the observed spatio-temporal relations of sensa.

There is no other explanation, therefore, of the origin of this notion of physical energy, power, resistance, pressure, inertia, than in the recognition of its direct intuition in

STRUCTURE AND PROCESS: OBJECTIVE

motion. Motion must be intuited as concrete, moving body. And together with this goes the intuition of sense quality so that, so far as this quality has a quantitative character, it is linked with the quantitative character of space intuited with it. Thus in visual sensation the space intuited has colour, and in tactual sensation it has the various cutaneous feelings distinctive of it.

The great importance for epistemology of this recognition of our direct intuition of space-time is, as pointed out by Alexander and Kemp Smith, that it shows that we have direct acquaintance with the physical world. If it is supposed that we depend upon the extensity of sensa for our awareness of space, and so of physical objects, then the deceptiveness of sensa casts a doubt upon the whole existence of an objective world. When, however, it is recognized that space and sensa are cognized together, but independently, then the illusions of sense cannot affect the validity of the intuition of space and yet, at the same time, we can see how the correlation of the sensory and spatial in our experience makes the former a good, though not a perfect, guide to knowledge of the differentiations of the latter.

The primitive, direct intuition of space-time, or bodily movement, is, of course, extremely limited. Its meaning, as presenting an external world beyond our bodies (and, indeed, as presenting a body beyond the part of the brain concerned), must depend upon associations due to acquired experience both of the physical connections of movements and of their association with sensa—and at our stage of development, even in our earliest experience, the formation of these associations must be due, chiefly, to racially inherited tendencies. Let us keep, for the moment, to tactual space. Physical impacts from outside the body reach the brain by way of a wave of chemical change up an efferent nerve and bring about that complicated reaction which is awareness-of-sensum-and-space. But, because of inherited associations, the space thus intuited, with the sensum, carries with it the meaning of being located, in relation to other spaces similarly intuited at the same time, at the end of that efferent nerve, where it is developed into a touch spot. The tactual experience of the infant must be a vague mass of sense-filled spaces to which he reacts instinctively, reducing them to conceptual order, locating them in his thought on the surface of his body and within it, and thus building up, more or less accurately, the notion of his body as a three-dimensional shape. A fuller discussion of this subject, however, and also the questions of how thought transcends the limits of the body, and how visual and auditory sensa come to be located in distant spaces, we must leave until we have discussed the categories of structure.

It is a further question whether there is any intuition of space in the act which initiates physical movement. It is quite certain that there is no "sense of innervation." But having recognized that intuition of motion does not depend upon sensa it remains possible that we are immediately aware of the effort to move, not merely as an effort, conation (which is certain), but as an effort to *move*. Introspection rather persistently indicates that this intuition does occur. But, since in all conscious movement there must be at least an implicit thought of space-to-be-moved-into, it might be the case that this is the explanation of our introspective experience. A more important consideration, however, arises from the question as to how we come to associate movement with the "motor" sensa of joints, muscles, and tendons. It may be argued that this might arise from their concomitance with visual perception of the movement of our limbs. But the significance of motor sensa seems to be too immediate and primitive to have been slowly acquired in that way and the solution is scarcely applicable to awareness of movement of the jaw! Further, and most important of all, it is difficult to see how, in our earliest experience, we could be aware of the connection between movement and conation if this knowledge had to be built up from external perceptions of our movements. Once we recognize that sensation affords no primary awareness of motion or space we seem driven to recognize that intuition of these must occur in the mental acts concerned both in the reception of stimuli and in motor response. These conclusions we shall find further supported when we come to discuss the categories whereby the diversities of our experience are unified into knowledge of a world.

The third main diversification of objective processes is that of value. At the lowest level, that of sensory pleasantness and unpleasantness, value experience is very difficult to distinguish from sense quality. Particularly is this the case with the physical pain sensum. However, even sensations ordinarily regarded as pains, such as the sting of a blow, can, when we are in vigorous spirits, if of low intensity, be pleasantly stimulating without losing their distinctive quality. This in itself indicates a real distinction. And all through the range of sense experience we find pleasantness and unpleasantness vary independently of the quality and other characteristics of the sensation. In the higher types of pleasure and pain—the kind perhaps better described as satisfactions and dissatisfactions, and often called "mental" pleasures and pains—the distinction seems plainer. The pleasure or satisfaction of obtaining social distinction or the unpleasantness or dissatisfaction of a disappointment seem quite distinctly non-sensory. Efforts have been made to reduce all these to the effect of vague masses of visceral, motor, and skin sensations; and certainly such sensations are always to be found accompanying them. But the intensity of feeling frequently reached in such experiences is altogether too great to be explained as *consisting in* such vague complexes of bodily sensation. These so-called "mental" pleasures and pains can be far more intense and moving than the "physical," so to attribute them to vague conglomerations of the "physical" is entirely inadequate. They must therefore be recognized as something *sui generis*, quite distinct from sensa. And when this new category of objective processes has once been recognized it will probably be agreed that the hedonic tone of sensation should be included in it, rather than among the characteristics of sensation itself.

There are sure to be protests against inclusion of hedonic tone (pleasure-unpleasure, sensory and "mental") among the *objective* processes. Surely, it will be said, they are purely subjective. Now from the epistemological standpoint, where the problem boils down to the question as to whether everybody experiences his own private data or whether some data are common to two or more experients, the theory which we shall develop is that we all experience different particular views of the same qualities and entities. But the emergence of a quality (e.g. a blue or its pleasantness) as a datum of experience is a particular objective process; and particular objective processes are parts of the perspective of some act of awareness and, as such, are private. In that sense the colours we see and the pleasures we experience are equally subjective. But in the sense in which we have used the terms subjective and objective in the last chapter both sensa and value qualities (including pleasures) are equally objective. We there distinguished the act of awareness from that of which we are aware. The former is a subjective process; it belongs somehow to the subject. The latter is an objective process; it belongs somehow to the object. Pleasure and other values are not part of the act of awareness, but part of that of which we are aware. In that most important sense they are as objective as anything else.[1]

[1] James Ward's emphasis on the common-sense distinction between "I know some*thing*" and "I feel some*how*" is quite irrelevant. Common sense says "I feel somehow" when it means "I feel cold, or warm, or

STRUCTURE AND PROCESS: OBJECTIVE 59

There is, however, an important fact which lends colour to the view that values, particularly pleasures, are subjective (characters belonging to the mental act). This is the fact that the nature of the value process (e.g. its degree of pleasantness or even its being pleasant at all) depends much more on the nature of the subjective activity of the moment than does the nature of the sensum. The kind of sensum we experience depends almost entirely on the character of other objective processes, especially physical movements. Yet even so, it is modified somewhat by subjective activity, e.g. the revival of acquired meaning. And imagery, of course, is very much dependent on subjective activity. So, although the character of our value experience is modified by changes of intention and subjective effort almost as much as by changes of physical processes and sensa, that does not justify us in calling the experienced values subjective in any sense in which the experienced sensa and movements are not also subjective.

Another feature of our description of this third type of process to which objection is likely to be taken is our inclusion of pleasures, even sensory pleasures, in the same category with the higher values, with beauty and truth and moral and religious values. But this objection, I hope, will disappear as the exposition proceeds.[1] It is not meant to reduce these higher values to mere pleasures after the fashion of the Hedonists. The distinction between higher and lower forms of value is very real and important. But the distinction is one of degree and scale and of the conditions and kinds of mental activity under which the dif-

hungry, or sick," whenever, in brief, it refers the datum to the empirical self, which includes body and mind. This argument would therefore make all these sensa subjective, as well as hedonic tone. Cf. *Psychological Principles*, by James Ward.

[1] The fuller discussion of distinctions of value, and of the nature of the acts upon which our awareness of values depend, will be found in later chapters.

ferent kinds of value experience emerge. And there are certain features of subjective activity common to all levels of value experience and quite distinctive of it. All this will appear as we proceed. Meantime, we need simply to draw attention to the fact that objective processes include value as a distinct type of object, co-ordinate with space-time and sensa.

These diversifications of the object, however, could never present to us a *world*. They do no more than differentiate a multiplicity of distinct processes. Even the spatial relations do not so much relate together their terms as separate them from each other. Paying attention to the processes and types of diversity alone David Hume declared that all our impressions come to us "loose and separate,"[1] and denied any logical justification for that linking of them together into a world order which is performed by both science and common sense. Immanuel Kant, shocked by this shattering of the world of reason, yet convinced by Hume that the categories which link our world together are not deliverances of experience, argued that they must be "forms of the understanding,"[2] principles of the mind's own constitution, which impose themselves upon what is filtered through them in the way of knowledge. It is our contention that the ground of these categories of unity *is* to be found in experience, though not in sense experience but in the non-sensory intuition of motion. The discovery of the roots of our constructive thought in this intuition will constitute a further demonstration, if any is needed, of the necessity of recognizing its existence. It will thus help in two ways to lay the foundations of a realistic epistemology; first, by strengthening the contention that we have direct acquaintance with physical objects; second, by providing empirical justification

[1] David Hume: *Enquiry Concerning Human Understanding*, Section 7, Part 2.
[2] Immanuel Kant: *Critique of Pure Reason*.

STRUCTURE AND PROCESS: OBJECTIVE 61

for the categorial forms of thought by which we pass beyond what is immediately intuited to the vast constructions which we recognize as mediate knowledge.

The first of the characteristics of structural unity in the objective world is that which has been designated the category of totality or "whole and part." Experience comes to us, not as a congeries of discrete sensations and other data, but as a world whole within which diversities are discriminable. As the *Gestalt* psychology has emphasized, we pass from the whole to the part, not from the part to the whole. And, as Professor Kemp Smith has pointed out,[1] every perception of space and time transcends itself. We grasp every time as something with a before and after, as coming from a time before it and passing on toward a time beyond it. And every space is grasped as part of a larger space. We simply cannot think space as coming to an end somewhere, with no space beyond it.

With regard to time we have already shown the reason for this in arguing that in the subjective act of awareness there is intuition of real time as containing before and after within itself. So that, though the finite subjective act does not grasp the *whole* of time within itself, it nevertheless grasps the nature of time as successive. Thus that which it grasps, being by nature successive implies its being in succession, having time before and after it not grasped in the finite act.

But why do we do the same with space? As Professor Stout puts it: "The process of immediate experience ... is in its intrinsic nature so essentially incomplete that to know it, or any part of it, is to know it as continued in ways determined by its own constitution, into a world process which transcends and includes it."[2] Now, what gives it this character of incompleteness? Why, in particular, do we apprehend every space as contained within a larger space? It is not the character of extensity that belongs to visual

[1] *Op. cit.*   [2] G. F. Stout: *Mind and Matter*, p. 310.

and tactual sensa that contributes this to our thought, for it is of the very nature of such spaces that they should be particular and limited. The visual continuum, for example, contains parts within it. But there is nothing within its nature to suggest that it is not complete within itself, that it (or even its bare extensity) *needs must* be continued beyond itself. No! It is not of sensory, but of motor space that we necessarily think this. It is not even of tactually and visually observed movements that we think it, for these always are particular, limited. It is only the intuited act of movement itself that necessarily implies space beyond itself. The very act of movement implies some rudimentary thought (if it is a conscious act) of space to move into. So if movement is intuited it must involve the intuition, not only of space in which the movement occurs, but of space beyond it; and as movement may occur in any direction this must involve the intuition of three-dimensional space.

Thus the intuition of time in all activity, and the intuition of time and space together in the activity of movement, will explain the operation of the category of whole and part in our thinking. In movement, space and time are grasped as, respectively, extensive and durational in nature, and so implying, by their nature, their character as finite parts of an unlimited whole. Without such an intuition we might, indeed, have observed that the whole of that which is presented is divisible into parts, and then, having further observed that new presentational wholes are constantly appearing, have hit upon the happy thought that all presentational wholes are really but parts of some larger whole. Such a hypothesis, once adopted, would be found to work very well; and it might be argued that, some primitive infra-human ancestor having once hit upon it, it could later become the universal inheritance of the race. But it is difficult to take seriously such a suggestion in explanation of the origin of one of the fundamental forms in which,

STRUCTURE AND PROCESS: OBJECTIVE 63

from the beginning, we interpret all our experience. And further, such an explanation would constitute no real justification of the category and would still fail to explain that *necessity* which we feel about the thought that space and time stretch beyond the limits of our experience. It would fall short too of the conviction that in their essential nature they are limitless. The category of totality, therefore, seems to demand for its explanation, the recognition of the direct intuition of the nature of space and time.

The second and most important of the categories of structure is that of causation. Our world is a whole, above all, in the sense that it is a causally related whole. Indeed, if we cannot conceive of causal relation between two entities or sets of entities, as, on some theories, we cannot with regard to the mental and physical, then we feel we are left, not with one world, but two. Everywhere we look for causes; and where there is diversity without apparent cause we assume that there is there a cause to be sought. Yet, obviously, experience presents us with many diversities without apparent cause. It is by no means as a generalization from the greatness of the proportion of cases where the cause is known that we conclude that in the unknown cases there still must be a cause. It is rather that we bring to bear the idea of necessary connection, in the first instance, upon the interpretation of experience. It is a general category with which we greet all experience, not a hypothesis arrived at after consideration of numerous particular cases.

The category of causation is therefore either a general principle of the operation of our minds, a "form of the understanding" in Kant's phrase, or it is a relation intuited in our most fundamental experience and so applied naturally and inevitably to other experiences. If this were the case we could understand how its success in the interpretation of experience and control of events would fix it in the dawning, growing intelligence of every child as the universal principle of interconnection of its world, so that, where there was no apparent cause observed one would be assumed, and where it was thought that there was no causal relation possible the world would be bifurcated into two.

Now if we look for such an intuition of the causal relation, as Hume did, among the phenomena of sense and the categories of diversity that obtain among them, we certainly shall not find it. Not only, as already indicated, is it only in occasional cases that we observe an *apparent* cause, but, as the great sceptic was the first to point out, we never *really* observe a cause at all. When one billiard ball strikes another and causes it to move we do not observe causation, or *necessary* connection, but only contiguity and the succession of events. Contiguity and regular succession are as near as sensory phenomena can get to presenting us with experience of causation. They reveal a connection, but not that which is the essence of the notion of cause, a *necessary* connection.

But if we recognize the reality of the intuition of movement the case is very different. Physical science to-day teaches us to regard the necessary continuity of motion as the essence of causation. As Professor Alexander puts it: "Space-Time or the system of motion is a continuous system, and any motion within it is continuous with some other motion. This relation of continuity between two different motions *is causality*, the motion which precedes that into which it is continued in the order of time being the cause and the other the effect."[1] The intuition of motion, therefore, including, as it necessarily would, this continuity of one motion into another, would involve the intuition of the causal relation. Motion meets with motion, is resisted and diverted, so that awareness of motion could never be confined to awareness of one single motion only at a time, but necessarily of motions passing into each other, causally

[1] *Op. cit.*, p. 279.

affecting each other. Thus a self, aware of its own motion, could not but be aware of other motions passing beyond it. The intuition of motion must therefore involve the intuition of the self, as embodied, in causal relations with the not-self. And as such causal activity is regularly correlated with changes in experiences of sense and value we can also understand the inevitable development whereby the intuitions of sense and value are complicated with acquired meaning from this causal-motor experience.[1] Thus the category of causation would be brought to bear upon the interpretation of all the diversities of experience and would justify itself by its success. Here again, then, the recognition of the intuition of motion reveals the source of the categories of structure. There is no need to resort to the desperate expedient of Kant, upon which so much Phenomenalism and Idealism has been based, nor yet does the adoption of Realism involve any *tour de force* to escape the risk of slipping back into the Scepticism of David Hume.

The third of the unifying categories that bind our world together is that indicated by the traditional notion of Substance. This is something that to common sense appears the plainest of facts, and yet philosophy has found it one of the most elusive and variable concepts with which it has to deal. Historically, the notion has taken at least six distinct forms. First, that of essence, the essential, or necessary and most important character of a thing. Second, that of the concrete individual, the ultimate unit of which things are formed. Third, the generalized reality, of which the variety of particular existents are diverse manifestations. Fourth, the underlying reality to which various properties

[1] A very similar view is expressed by Professor A. N. Whitehead. "The world given in sense experience is not the aboriginal experience of the lower organisms, later to be sophisticated by the inference to causal efficacy. The contrary is the case. First the causal side of experience is dominating, then the sense presentation gains in subtility. . . ."—*Symbolism: Its Meaning and Effect*, p. 49.

belong or that in which attributes inhere and of which they are appearances. Fifth, that substance is the permanent which persists through change. This was the interpretation of Kant, although he qualifies it by applying it only to the existents we know. The true substance seems to have been, for him, the ultimate logical subject which, itself, remains entirely unknown. Sixth, a notion akin to the Kantian Transcendental Subject, that of the Absolute, more or less truly manifested in the variety of the world's appearances.

Now why, we may ask, do we find this persistent attempt of philosophers to posit the existence of a reality which most of them are constrained to admit remains unknown? Why can they not be content to construct their interpretation of the world out of that which is actually given? In reply we point to the persistent demand of common sense for a reality that is substantial and say that, since none of the particular entities recognized by common sense as given facts conforms to the requirements of the notion of substance, philosophy is merely trying to meet the demands of common sense by inventing one that does. But is this justifiable? Is it not the business of philosophy to criticize common sense, and point out its errors, instead of just yielding to its prejudices? Yes, but this notion of substance proves to be more than a prejudice. It is something that is required to make the world *intelligible*. And that is why, when the analysis of experience has been carried to its limit, and nothing that fits the notion of substance has been found, philosophers have still posited its reality.

This situation suggests three questions. First, why is it that the notion of substance is required to make the world intelligible? Second, since philosophical analysis of experience does not reveal anything adequate to the notion as a fact, how has common sense arrived at the conception? It could not have been invented as sheer logical hypothesis to make the unintelligible intelligible. So is there any feature

STRUCTURE AND PROCESS: OBJECTIVE 67

of experience, which is sufficiently substantial so far as it goes, to have suggested the more adequate principle? Thirdly, can any adequate definition of substance be given?

We may approach the first question by asking what are the common features of the various interpretations of substance, for since these have been developed in the effort to render experience intelligible they must all, if they are successful, contain the elements of meaning necessary to that purpose. Upon examination we find two features common to all these notions of substance. They are the concepts of permanence and continuity. The essence or most important feature of a thing is that which it always possesses, however else it may change; other characters may disappear and reappear, but not its essence; or it is no longer the same thing. The concrete individual, e.g. the ultimate atom or monad, likewise has permanence and continuity; it may pass in and out of various combinations, but it still exists; and there are no gaps in its nature which require a further principle to unite them. The third conception of substance, likewise, is but a way of expressing the conviction that diversities are not ultimate; they are merely diversifications of the real and there is continuity in the changes; the most familiar example of the notion of substance in this form is the attempt of modern science to render physical nature intelligible by interpreting all its diversities as forms of motion. The fourth, which is the classical doctrine of substance, reveals its aims in Descartes' famous illustration of the piece of wax; when it is melted all its qualities change; colour, shape, smell, etc., are all different; yet we say it is the same piece of wax; we mean by this that the substance is the same; substance is thus presented as that which has permanence through all the changes, and which constitutes a continuity holding together its varied appearances. Kant's doctrine of substance definitely emphasizes permanence as the content of the notion;

and his further recognition of the ultimate logical subject as, after all, its only proper definition reveals the need he felt of something that would form the basis of continuity between the diverse phases of the object. The doctrine of the Absolute and its appearances, likewise, is a way of meeting this double demand for continuity and permanence to be found somewhere if the world is to be rendered intelligible.[1]

What is the ground, then, of these two requirements of intelligibility? We must answer that they arise from the very nature of thought, to which we have frequently to recur. Even in its simplest form cognition is more than the simple awareness of a particular datum. It is essentially a temporal act. It grasps that which is presented with an outlook toward that which is to come; and its expectation of what is to come is formed of that which is retained, and to some extent revived, of the experience of the past. It is this present expectation, formed of past experience, that constitutes the meaning of that which is presented. And the fundamental cognitive act is the grasp of a presentation with its meaning. The higher cognitive acts are only elaborations of this process.

All understanding of meaning, therefore, presupposes the continuity of past, present, and future. It presupposes a continuity between experiences of sense and spatial relation, between these and future (and present) experiences of value, between conation and objective experience, between antecedent and subsequent experience; it presupposes, too, the permanence of these continuities, as otherwise the past could never have meaning for the future. Every act of experience, therefore, assumes that all the variety of its

[1] I do not suggest that *spatio-temporal* continuity and permanence are the only requirements of an intelligible world, for meaning is never complete until it also incorporates the idea of value. This is the important truth emphasized by Professor Urban in *The Intelligible World* (George Allen & Unwin Ltd.).

STRUCTURE AND PROCESS: OBJECTIVE

experience belongs together in a permanent world continuum. Nothing has any meaning for us except the meaning it derives from belonging in that world continuum. The continuity of any object with the world continuum, and the permanence of its place in that continuum, are therefore conditions of the intelligibility of that object. The understanding of a thing consists in the discovery of its place in the continuum—a continuum of subjective activity, space, time, sense, and value.

But the place of each object in that continuum is by no means obvious; and there are some aspects of it which are extremely difficult to relate. How is thought related to material things? How are sensory data related to the push and pull of the physical? How is value related to all else? So far as relations are discovered, objects of these kinds are intelligible. So far as their place in the world remains obscure, objects are unintelligible. Yet the intelligibility of the world requires that there must be relations even where we can find none. So common sense posits that all things needs must be related, that its world really *is* a permanent continuum in which all its objects have a place. But things that are absolutely and entirely different cannot be related. If they belong to a common continuum they must have some nature in common. So, if the world is to be intelligible, then, even where there is no common nature discoverable between things, it must still be there.

This is the doctrine of substance. All things must be ultimately interpretable as diversifications of some common nature. Only then are they intelligible. The various historical theories of substance are attempts to explain what that common nature might be. One can go a long way with the notion that it is physical energy, but values stubbornly refuse to be incorporated in this way. Much progress may be made with a dualism of two substances, matter, and mind; but unless these can eventually be brought together in a more ultimate substance the universe remains finally unintelligible. The pluralistic theory that the common nature is that of a multitude of atoms or monads, whose qualities differ only in degree, not in kind, works very well until we come to the problem of explaining the order manifested by this crowd; then we have to go deeper. In one way or another, Descartes, Spinoza, Leibniz, and nearly every other thinker who has studied the problem, have come to the conclusion that since space, time, sense, value, intelligence, and will must all be regarded as diversifications of some ultimate common nature, that nature must be worthy of the name of God. But some of their interpretations of what the nature of the Ultimate Substance, or God, then must be, have been very far from what religion means by the same name.

We have seen, then, the way in which the reflective mind is driven to adopt the notion of a universal substance, in which we must believe even where we cannot see. The implicit notion of common sense is, of course, far short of this. But neither is it by any process of reflection on the requirements for intelligibility that common sense has arrived at its notion of substance, such as it is. Our next task, therefore, is to explain the origin of this category as one of the implicit assumptions of common sense.

It is here that the recognition of the intuition of motion again comes to our aid. Motions must needs be intuited in relation to each other, and so, as diversifications of a spatio-temporal continuum. But motion as intuited is something concrete. It is not mere extension and duration. These are abstractions from the concrete reality. One of the reasons for failure to recognize that motion is intuited, independently of sensa, is that our very notion of the substantial concreteness of reality makes us recognize that, in the words of Professor Stout, "bare extension is an absurdity."[1] And so, though Stout clearly recognizes that experience of activity plays an essential part in our awareness of the objective world, he feels impelled to say that it can only do so in conjunction with sensation. Consequently he maintains that sensa are somehow properties of physical things. Thus he falls into line with the contention of Mr. Bradley that "extension without secondary qualities is inconceivable."[2]

But we are not thus faced with the dilemma of trying to conceive of bare extensity or else filling space with sensa and trying to persuade ourselves that this flimsy content makes intelligible the rough and tumble of the physical world. Motion, as we have already seen, is intuited as concrete, as, not merely space and time, but space-time, as pressure, energy, resistance, and inertia. The intuition of motion is the intuition of the dynamic character of physical reality, of concrete movements which, in their relationship, form material bodies.

It is the continuity and permanence of the physical, as thus intuited, that is the foundation of the primitive, common-sense notion of substance. And this category, together with those of causation and whole and part, provides the logical framework whereby we build up our notion of the structure of the physical world. Further, since sensa are intuited together with the physical—and in such close relation that sensa come to *mean* physical objects—this physical structure provides common sense with what it needs for thought of a substantial basis for the continuity and permanence of sensa. The physical also, together with experience of conation, provides sufficient notion of permanence and continuity underlying values. Thus, for unreflective common sense, the substantial means the physical, even when the concept is also applied to the idea of the inner

[1] *Op. cit.*, p. 280.
[2] F. H. Bradley: *Appearance and Reality*, p. 16.

self or soul. Thus this third category is revealed to have the same intuitive basis as the others. And it is only enlightened reflection that reveals the fact that this basis needs to be extended if we are to make intelligible our view of the world as a whole.

CHAPTER III

STRUCTURE AND PROCESS: SUBJECTIVE

On the side of the subject, as on that of the object, we are able to discern both diversities of process and the unity which is structure. On neither side is structure a matter of direct acquaintance except so far as, in the immediacy of the present, processes manifest a certain relationship to each other, a transitory, but quite definite, continuity and order. It is this that, as we have seen on the side of the object, provides the ground for the inferential elaboration of our knowledge of the structure of the physical world. So, too, on the side of the subject, our knowledge of structure is almost entirely inferential; and yet, having its ground in immediate acquaintance with the continuity and order of subjective activity, is as well founded as our knowledge of physical structure.

The processes discoverable on the side of the subject are acts. They are less easily discerned than the objective processes of sense, but far clearer than those of physical (as distinct from sensory) movement and, as it is only by recognition of these last-named that we are able to justify our belief in a physical world, there is therefore some truth in the claim that we know the real existence of the mind with more certainty than we do that of matter. On the other hand, because of the correlation of sensory processes with physical, we are able, having once justified the acceptance of sense as revealing a material world, to build up a great deal of knowledge about it with a high degree of certainty. Having admitted the justification of its basis it must then be recognized that we can gain a great deal more, and more certain, knowledge about the physical world than the mental for the simple reason that observable physical processes are mechanical. Given the same circumstances they can be relied upon to repeat themselves and so can be treated mathematically. Mental processes, on the other hand, never repeat themselves, for after the performance of an act the subject is never the same again. Each act contributes to a growing structure. Psychology may gather statistical data which have a certain relevance due to the general similarity of different subjects. But the fact of memory makes it forever impossible for psychology to be an exact science. Nevertheless, because, as just remarked, there is a general similarity among different subjects, it is possible to learn much about the growing structure of minds. This, however, can only be achieved by the introspective examination of our own mental activity, helped to some extent by interpretation of our observation of others.

The question of the possibility of introspection we have already discussed[1] and we have seen that its difficulties are not insuperable. We have also seen that even these difficulties do not apply to the bare fact of awareness of subjective process, but only to the effort to know something further about it. Experience is a bi-polar unity and within that unity both poles, subject, and object, equally, simply *appear*.

Our awareness of both structure and process, therefore, on the side of the subject, is exactly on all fours with our awareness of structure and process on the side of the object, the only difference being that the cognitive aim is normally directed to the elucidation of the objective content, while the subjective tends to be little more than barely presented. Yet the convictions of common sense show that it is not overlooked. We are normally as fully convinced of the continued existence of the psychological self as we are of the physical object. Nor is this conviction due to any lingering religious beliefs in a substantial soul. Rather, the belief in souls, found throughout the human race, is a

[1] Chapter 1.

substantialization of the experienced structure of the subject, the self.[1] We have the same kind of knowledge, therefore, of both subject and object, of the self and the world.

The diversities of subjective activity have, from the time of Immanuel Kant, been classified into the three categories of Cognition, Conation, and Feeling. But it must not be thought that these are three distinct kinds of act. What lends them distinction is rather the three kinds of object discovered in the subject's activity—the sensa and the world revealed through sense, the subject's own body as intuited from within in control of its movement and, thirdly, the whole hierarchy of values.

At the most primitive level at which we can conceive consciousness to exist there needs must be conation, the effort to control the movement of the primitive body. But there can be no effort to control the body without some awareness of the body, which is awareness of movement, of space-time. And there could be no effort to control unless this apprehension of bodily process included the forward look—as indeed, the apprehension of time must do—thus apprehending the situation as alterable. Here then, we have the essential minimum of cognition, the grasp of the present situation with an outlook upon the future. Mere awareness does not constitute cognition and never occurs as mere awareness. Conation presents the primitive object—body. But cognition grasps what is thus presented and reaches forward toward the future. It grasps the presentation with expectation. And, as expectation is informed by retention of the after effects of past experience, this definite, or formed, expectation constitutes the meaning of the object perceived. Thus, because of the nature of time experience, the most primitive awareness of

[1] Tylor's ingenious theory that belief in souls is due to dreams is open to three great objections: (1) It attributes too great inventiveness to the primitive. (2) It explains a universal belief as arising out of a very rare one. (3) It ignores the fact that the vivid visual imagery of savages suggested readily the true explanation.—E. B. Tylor, *Primitive Culture*.

an object must be an awareness of an object-and-something-more. And because of the preservation in present experience of the after effects of past experience this "something more" takes a more or less definite form. Thus every thought[1] of an object is also a thought of something about it. That polarization into subject and object which constitutes experience involves something in the nature of primitive judgment, the awareness in relation of elements which may be later explicated as logical subject[2] and predicate in a proposition. There could, if our discussion above is well grounded, be no presentation of either body or sensum without conation. Neither is conation intelligible without awareness of an object. It is fruitless to ask which came first. Both are involved in the very nature of experience as polarization into subject and object.

The next point that we should note is that the presence of feeling must turn the "logical predicate" of the primitive "judgment" into an objective. That which is thought *about* the primitive psychological object receives its form and content from retention of the after effects of past experience. Thus the smallest beginnings of feeling, even the vaguest consciousness of bodily comfort or discomfort, must tend to colour the meaning of that which is presented. And conation responds to the feeling element in meaning by seeking to maintain the conditions which present a prospective feeling tone of a positive nature and to change those which promise the reverse. Thus the values discovered in experience are, from the first, directive of conduct. Tentatively and erringly, but nevertheless persistently, the finite individual is, from the beginning, oriented toward the good. The capacity to discriminate degrees and scale of values, and

[1] The term "thought" is here used in the broadest possible sense. Cf. G. F. Stout: *Manual of Psychology* (Fourth Edition), p. 98.
[2] It should be noted that logical subject and predicate are both part of the psychological object.

to understand the conditions upon which their realization depends, has, throughout history, unsteadily made progress.

Having distinguished the three features which are omnipresent in subjective process we should next note the enormous elaboration which takes place, particularly in cognition. Somewhere in the course of development (just where we do not know, but perhaps with the beginnings of a nervous system), the effort at bodily control presents a sensum as well as the body. It may be, of course, that some form of sensum is presented to the most primitive consciousness; but the connection of sensa with special organs, and with the subjective reaction to a number of cells shown in psychic fusion, suggests that they are only discovered after a certain development of the organism and its subjective activity has taken place. This is not the place to inquire into the status of sensa in relation to the rest of the world, although we may, in passing, note that felt values and sensed sensa are as definitely part of the objective world as intuited space-time. What we are here concerned with is the elaboration of subjective processes whereby sensa are sensed. We have seen that the re-integrative process of the brain cells following upon stimulation is the physiological pre-requisite to sensation. But the facts of psychic fusion showed us that it could not depend on this alone. The simplest process upon which it could occur is some co-ordinating subjective reaction to a number of these re-integrative cortical processes together, a re-action which would intuit the bodily character of the cortical processes as well. But the facts of psychic blindness indicate that *awareness* of the sensum (and of body) require a further subjective reaction, which, in its cognitive character, grasps the presented sensum and intuition of body in their temporal relation as about to be followed by some further presentations, not necessarily different. The sensum thus acquires its character of extensity and its physical significance and is, of course, further complicated by its association with value experience.

Sensing thus indicates the operation of one subjective activity superposed upon another and co-ordinated in definite relation with it and with subsequent conation. Such elaboration of subjective activity having a definite order only becomes intelligible as a manifestation of definite structure on the side of the subject. There must be a relationship between subjective acts which is as truly causal as that between physical processes. And yet this causal relation is not mechanical, for the processes connected are not physical. Language imposes upon us physical metaphors, but it is not a physical act that "grasps" a sensum or value, nor a mechanical connection that can cause this act to respond then in some definite way to what is thus grasped. The interconnection of subjective activity, however, definitely does demand the recognition of psychical, or subjective, structure. No entirely undifferentiated, structureless, simple soul could be made to account for what actually occurs. Still less, could an explanation be given entirely in terms of physical structure. The elaboration of physical structure which makes sensation possible requires an elaboration of psychical structure in order that there may be awareness of sensa.

This same principle must be pursued throughout the development of brain and mind. In man the enormous development of the cerebral cortex has made possible a great elaboration of mental processes. From mere awareness of sensa in their physical setting there has been enormous advance, including development of the capacity to abstract a datum from the perceptual situation, to recall explicitly the past, to isolate relations, to generalize what is thus abstracted, to build up new concepts out of these elements, to connect these into universal and particular judgments, and to draw inferences. Probably none of these processes

STRUCTURE AND PROCESS: SUBJECTIVE

goes on without cerebral activity. That would seem to be indicated by the dependence of memory and thinking upon the physical fitness of the brain, as well as by the apparent dependence of consciousness itself upon some degree of such cerebral activity.[1] But since the simplest process of awareness involves subjective act as well as physical change these higher levels must involve further elaborations of mental process into complex forms, one depending upon another, to some extent, as well as upon the physical development.

Many attempts have been made to argue from this elaboration of cognitive acts, and particularly from the fact of self-consciousness, to the existence of cognitive acts which are entirely independent of any physical basis. Such theories, however, are opposed by the stubborn facts of the dependence of all forms of consciousness upon the functioning of the brain. We are faced, apparently, by these two facts, not easy to reconcile. First, that subjective structure seems to be independent of the brain. Its activity, though a response to the physical, is not merely an effect of the physical. There should therefore be no reason why such activity should not occur independently of the physical. On the other hand, subjective activity apparently ceases when the appropriate physical processes are stopped by poisoning, starving, or disintegration of the brain. And they are adversely affected by partial brain injuries of a like character. It seems fairly clear, therefore, that all subjective activity operates upon the brain and derives its data from cerebral reaction. If there is any survival of personality after death, therefore, it does not seem likely that it could be a mental existence entirely independent of any physical medium. Further, as we have shown that in every cognitive act both subject and object appear, there is no justification for adducing any transcendent self to account for self-con-

[1] A discussion of the implication of these facts for the doctrine of immortality will be found in Chapter v.

sciousness. All we need to recognize is the elaboration of processes on both the side of the subject and that of the object.

Instead of being able to show that mental process may go on in a medium of "consciousness" independent of the physical we are faced with facts which show that a great deal of apparently mental activity may go on unconsciously. Here we have to recognize two explanatory conditions. First, that psychic blindness to sensa is explicable in view of the fact that an act of awareness must be performed before there can be awareness of a sensum. Normally this act follows so regularly upon the conditions which present the sensum that in sensation we seem to be merely passive recipients of impressions. They impinge themselves upon us, and in our normal frame of mind we cannot shut them out. What the psychology of the unconscious shows, however, is that in abnormal conditions they are shut out. The normal reaction of sensing simply is not performed. And yet conative tendencies which have customarily followed upon observation of such sensory data may still occur. Now, normally, the conation is to be understood as a response to the sensum. But these facts of unconscious reaction indicate that when a reaction has become established it may occur without perception of the sensum or explicit awareness of conation. It is habitual, learned, established reactions that function automatically. The value of the normal consciousness of the sensum is that it makes possible a controlled re-adaptation to the data. Unconscious reactions to sense stimuli therefore do not prove that normal awareness of sensa has no effect upon conduct.

Secondly, we have to consider the facts of non-sensory cognitive processes (quite elaborate thought processes) which may go on subconsciously. Now thinking involves the interaction of brain processes with conative acts having a cognitive aim. The conative acts, in addition to being themselves presented to consciousness, tend to present values and sensory images. The latter, like sensa, probably function as signs which assist in guiding the selective activity of motor control of brain processes, but seem to be of little importance in thinking, especially when thought moves in familiar channels. So it is not surprising that subconscious thinking can dispense with them. The awareness of the act of thinking, also, need play no part in directing the course of thought. It is only when occasion arises for *redirecting* a train of association that it would ever seem to be important that we should be distinctly aware of our thought as our own. Likewise the awareness of the value element does not seem to be necessary in order that a set conative tendency should go on toward its goal. There is therefore no element in the whole thought process that *needs must* be clearly conscious in order for thought to go on. All that is necessary is that, a certain cognitive aim having been adopted, conative control of brain process should proceed. The aim is normally forgotten half the time in such cases, and self-consciousness is not necessary at any time.

It will be asked then what function does consciousness play in thought? And the answer is that consciousness of our thoughts is not a link that connects our thoughts together. They function perfectly well without it. But it is only in consciousness that conation and cognition are linked with value, as it is only in consciousness that conation and feeling are linked with sensation and sensory images. The subconscious mental process goes on automatically so long as it is able to use worn pathways, customary connections. To some extent it may go on more efficiently because unrelated to any sense of value, as many persons have found out who have slept over their problems and awakened to find them solved. But without consciousness of our thinking we could never direct it toward the ends we feel of value. We could never re-direct our trains of association as we found them wandering in useless or worse than useless trails. And we could never drive a new line of thought, purposively and stubbornly holding to that which is difficult to think; for subconscious thinking is sure to take the path of least resistance. The function of consciousness is therefore clear without trying to tear our mental processes loose from the brain in a way which the facts do not justify.

Cognitive processes have involved rather a long discussion. We can be briefer with what we need to say just now about conation and feeling. Every cognitive process is, of course, also an effort, a striving, a conation. And every conation carries with it, more or less distinctly, its feeling tone. But there is a psychic blindness possible toward feeling which is as definite as it can be in the case of sense. Even highly painful sensations can be completely ignored. Now pain is an objective quality, not merely a subjective process. If it were merely a subjective process, like thinking, the failure to observe it might be explained as due to the shutting of this process far away from the limelight of attention. Pain, and all forms of value and disvalue, however, are not something the subject is doing, which it may attend to or not, but something presented to the subject which, like a sensum, requires a subjective act for there to be awareness of it. Normally, pleasures and other values are thus felt, as sensa normally are sensed. But in abnormal cases this act may be withheld, as sometimes occurs with sensa. In the case of sensory pleasure and pain-values this is rare. But in the case of the higher values it is common, for the very emergence of these within the realm of possible experience is a relatively late development; and it is quite possible to go through life blind, or almost completely blind, to some of them.

The dependence of feeling upon conation is plain in all cases except the lowest. To bring that, sensory pleasantness and pain, within the orbit of conation we have to extend

STRUCTURE AND PROCESS: SUBJECTIVE 85

from the philosophy of biology and from experimental psychology. In regard to the former, it is becoming increasingly clear that something of the nature of will is the essential differentia of the animate from the inanimate. Even where consciousness is not actually present organic processes distinguish themselves definitely from inorganic; they tend toward a maintenance of structural form in a way quite different from the merely mechanical. And this apparent domination by an established order, instead of tending toward dissolution and chaos, is the distinctive characteristic of will. That this feature of will should manifest itself so far down the scale of vital processes is a fact of the first philosophical importance.

But here we need to guard against being misunderstood. Biology has been rejoicing for nearly three-quarters of a century in its emancipation from "vital forces" supposed to fill the gaps in physiological processes which did not seem explicable in purely physico-chemical terms. And no mere philosopher is qualified to suggest that any such entities should be reintroduced into the science. Nevertheless many biologists who vigorously repudiate Vitalism equally declare that purely physico-chemical principles are insufficient to explain organic phenomena. Notable among these is Professor J. S. Haldane, and the intermediate concept which he adopts is that of a prevailing form or order of the whole—something which seems to be closely akin to what we have conceived as a form of will.

The conclusions of this eminent scientist, which are not dissimilar from those of many other biologists, may be indicated by the following quotations. "The nearer we approach to a centre of living activity the more clearly does it appear to us that the molecules, atoms, and electrons present on the physical interpretation are behaving as if they were taking part in a co-ordinated dance, for which there can be no physical interpretation, and which differs entirely from the free chaotic movements of the molecules in a gas, the mutually confined movements in a liquid or the still more confined movements in a solid."[1]

Toward the end of the book the argument is summed up thus. "It is, moreover, quite impossible to return to vitalism. What the observations necessitate is nothing less than an abandonment of the physical interpretation of visible reality, substituting for it the conclusion that in the phenomena of life we have the manifestation of a unity within which physical bodies as such, with their corresponding spatial externality, do not exist, and which includes the environment as well as the bodies of organisms. This unity persists just as do the 'bodies' of the physical interpretation; but its persistence is active, since it is only through activity that it manifests itself. The structure which it displays is the expression of activity, and the activity is an expression of the structure. This is the unity which we call life."[2]

It is, definitely, not the alleged gaps in the physico-chemical explanation that lead Haldane to this view, but the fact of the peculiar co-ordination of physical processes in living organisms, a co-ordination which manifests itself in more elaborate form at the psychological level in the pursuit of interests and values. And as these values culminate in supra-individual values he concludes that the ultimate order culminates in the will of God. The mechanical order of the physical world is therefore interpreted as a mere appearance, valid within its own limits, but not an interpretation that needs must be carried over into the biological sphere. The order of the organic world, higher than the physical, but still apparently blind and uninfluenced by values, is also valid in its own sphere but seen to be incompletely real when we pass to the psychological realm where the ordering of life in the interest of values becomes mani-

[1] J. S. Haldane: *The Sciences and Philosophy*.   [2] *Op. cit.*, pp. 325–6.

STRUCTURE AND PROCESS: SUBJECTIVE 87

fest. But even this order, displaying as it does contradictions of interest and value, cannot be entirely real. Ultimate reality can only reside in the "one spiritual universe." "God is thus the only final reality, and individual interest or personality has its only reality in God. . . . We identify our own wills with God's will when we strive for what presents itself to each of us as his or her own particular duty."[1]

The will of God is thus presented as the omnipresent form within which all human purpose, all biological adjustment, and all physical process occurs. Physical and biological and psychological laws are a part of this eternal will and such conflicts as there may seem to us to be are unreal.

But is it necessary, we may ask, thus to brand the physical, biological and psychological as unreal? This part of Haldane's philosophy is due to the conviction that in the will of God there must be perfect harmony, that the several grades of order discoverable in the world are expressions of the will of God, and that the apparent conflicts within and between these levels of order are therefore only explicable on the ground that our knowledge of those orders, even so far as it goes, is essentially defective. But this relapse into scepticism is not the only escape from the apparent contradiction. Must we assume that there is no plasticity within the Supreme Will? Let us drop for the present the description of it as God, for our argument thus far is not sufficient to justify that interpretation. But let us grant, as Haldane does, that the order discoverable in life and mind is one which cannot be accounted for in physico-chemical terms (not because of proven gaps in that explanation but because the merely physical tends toward a different kind of order—or disorder). Let us grant further that these higher orders are oriented toward the maintenance of organic life and the realization of values. Is it then necessary that these higher orders should be so controlled under a Supreme Will

[1] *Op. cit.*, p. 333.

that any apparent orientation toward conflicting value must be unreal and that there could be no genuine modifications of the order of organic life in response to these lower and conflicting values?

It is obvious that any objections to such plasticity of the orders must be philosophical, not scientific. Once it is recognized that biological processes conform to principles of order not attributable to the type of causation (or order, for such is physical causation, as modern physics has shown) found below the organic level, then the requirements of the physical order can no longer be cited to show that the biological order must needs be rigid. And, of course, empirically, it appears anything but rigid. Neither biology nor physics and chemistry, therefore, can be cited as requiring that there must needs be no *real* plasticity in organic processes. It is only a philosophical conception that can then suggest that the apparent conflicts in animal striving and its organic basis must be only apparent. This philosophical conception is that which interprets the higher orders found at the level of life as an orientation toward ultimate values. But even this does not necessitate the unreality of the apparent plasticity and conflict within the higher order unless we are convinced that the real existence of such plasticity and conflict is incompatible with their being any value at all. But that would only be the case if all values must depend upon a single will and if that will could find no ultimate value in the relatively independent, and sometimes conflicting, purposes of its offspring. Whether that is the case we cannot decide at this stage of our inquiry. But as we are here dealing merely with the interpretation of scientific data we shall not hamper ourselves with the preconception that the form manifested by organic activities must needs be the form of the Absolute will. We shall accept the testimony of Professor Haldane that in the phenomena of life there is manifested a peculiar form of "unity," which "persists" and is "active" and displays its own "structure." We shall call this structure a form of will, which name is appropriate to the description given it. But we shall assume that this will may be both plastic and ultimately real unless later philosophical considerations lead us to decide otherwise.

Our doctrine of the primacy of will is therefore confirmed by the indication that will is the fundamental differentia of the organic from the inorganic. This doctrine, however, has been vigorously attacked by Professor Laird. Yet the form in which it is here advocated, is not dealt with very convincingly. He quotes with approval Professor Stout's assertion, and limitation, of the presence of conscious purpose in the instinctive activity of animal organisms. "It is only necessary to assume an awareness of the present state as transitional—as something which not merely *is* but *is to be*. Such rudimentary reference to the future is not wholly indeterminate; it is specific inasmuch as it is concerned with the further development of a specific situation and, more particularly, of certain selected factors within it. It is vague inasmuch as the animal has no clue to the particular nature of the changes which are to take place. The important point is that the situation is apprehended as alterable. This is enough to make conation possible."[1] Upon this, Laird comments: "If then the part which purpose, even in the dimmest sense, plays in instinct is very restricted, how much more is it restricted in ordinary processes of growth, alimentation and the like. Why do we need the 'psychoid' for all biological explanation?"[2]

Now if by "psychoid" is meant something like the old "vital force," conceived as supplementing physical energy by filling gaps between purely physical processes, then we hold no brief for it. But if what is meant is something of

[1] G. F. Stout: *Manual of Psychology*, third edition, p. 355.
[2] John Laird: *Problems of the Self*, p. 144.

the nature of a form of will to which physical processes, by their own nature, conform, then it seems that biology cannot dispense with it, while philosophy must demand that it be recognized as having a certain plasticity. And Laird's argument against the recognition of such a form is not difficult to meet. Most of that argument is devoted to objections to forms of the doctrine of primacy of will not advocated here and to answers to arguments for it which we are content to leave to the biologists to decide. The contention put forward in the above quotation, however, does seem to be relevant to our position; and we must meet it. It admits the operation of conscious purpose at the instinctive level, but claims that it is so slight that, at the still lower level of "growth, alimentation, and the like," purpose must be absent altogether.

In the first place it should be pointed out that modern studies of single-celled organisms[1] have shown that they manifest the same three characteristic types of behaviour on which Stout grounds his contention that instinctive action is consciously purposive, i.e. selective and prospective attention, persistency with varied effort, and capacity to profit by experience. There is every justification, therefore, for recognizing the operation of conscious purpose this low in the scale. Secondly, our bodies are simply colonies of highly differentiated single-celled organisms, with regular habits of reaction to their physical environment in the body. "Growth and alimentation and the like" are simply the activities of these cells. The fact that we are not conscious of their strivings in no way indicates that they cannot be in any degree aware of their own. They are probably too highly specialized to show much of that adaptability which, to the external observer, is the hall-mark of conscious purpose; but that does not show they are devoid of it.

[1] E.g. H. S. Jennings: *Contributions to the Study of the Behaviour of the Lower Organisms.*

STRUCTURE AND PROCESS: SUBJECTIVE

Indeed, the organic bodies in the blood stream, particularly the white corpuscles, show remarkable capacities for adaptation. Though Mechnikov's famous theory that the technique of immunization depends on the capacity of the leucocytes to adapt themselves, in a process of training, to the attack on noxious organisms has been much modified and restricted by later investigations the essential point seems to be established. These defensive agents seem to acquire added efficiency in the combating of certain disease organisms in the course of their attack upon them; and such adaptability is difficult to separate from a process of learning by experience.

To this it will be objected that growth requires for its explanation a co-ordinating process which will explain the progressive differentiation of the cells themselves and their adaptation to specific functions; and to attribute this to the purposive activity of the individual cells would overstrain the notion of such foresight as they may possess. This is true, but we have not eliminated the idea of a higher directive agency, over and above that of the single cells, in the purposive control of the body by an inherited psychoplasm consisting of established forms of will. To this it will be replied that we are entirely unconscious of any such directive activity during our growing period as children. But this brings us to our third point. When once the lines of purposive activity have become set in fixed habit it sinks into unconsciousness. And the lines of development of our bodily growth have all become well fixed before we are born. We could not, therefore, expect ever to be conscious of the strivings which have set those lines. They must remain forever in the limbo of things forgotten.

We may conclude, therefore, that that minimum of consciousness which Stout has shown to be requisite for all purposive striving may well be present in all living organisms and provide the explanation of that which differentiates the course of organic processes from inorganic, even down to such apparently unconscious processes as growth and alimentation. And, as already stated, if the subject be regarded as simply a peculiar differentiation of that universal stuff (essence or nature), of which matter is itself another peculiar differentiation, then the existence of such a relation between subjective activity (the activity of life and mind, or will) and physical objective processes becomes sufficiently intelligible, even though we are not able to state what kind of a differentiation of the universal stuff each of them is.[1]

This recognition of the fact of conscious purpose or conation as the distinctive characteristic of life and mind and the central feature of subjective activity is, finally, further supported by reference to recent experimental investigations of choice and volition. Researches on these subjects, as described by Professor Aveling, show very clearly the distinction between conation, as effort, and phenomena of sense and feeling which are (so far as experimental data can show) effortlessly perceived. But further, a distinction has been found between conation as effort and the formation of a decision or *fiat* of will, which is effortless, though clearly discriminated by the trained observer. Will, in the sense of resolution or choice, is thus distinguished from striving and Aveling confines the term "conation" to the latter. Whether we follow this verbal precedent or not the distinction must be maintained. Will is a "set" or "form" taken by the personality and a new task is only undertaken by a change in this "set" or "form." It is this change which these careful introspectors have distinguished as the "act" of will. From this elaborate series of experiments, carried out in four countries over a long series of years, it is of great importance to have the conclusion expressed: "It is clear that all the researches upon the will to which reference has

[1] An approach to the solution of this problem is made below in our discussion of Time.

been made point to an immediate experience of self-activity as constituting the experience of willing; and whether this experience be phenomenal only, in the sense that the self thus known may not be the self as it really is, or whether the knowing and known self are identical in the experience, the self as will emerges as the core and central nucleus of human personality."[1] This conclusion will help us to understand the development of the common-sense notion of the structure of the self and to defend its essential validity.

The first of these features of structural unity recognized by common sense on the side of the subject, then, is that of personal identity. Here again arises the shade of David Hume to deny the validity of the conception. "For my part, when I enter most intimately into what I call *myself*, I always stumble on some particular perception or other, of heat or cold, light or shade, love or hatred, pain or pleasure. I never can catch *myself* at any time without a perception, and never can observe anything but the perception."[2] But once again, Hume is looking amid the diversities of process for that which is manifest only as a unity of structure. Further, he also failed to distinguish between the act of awareness and that of which it is aware. It is a certain unity in the structure of this subjective activity that impresses us with the notion of personal identity. Two other factors are, of course, of tremendous importance, i.e. the continuing structure of the body and the accumulated resources of memory. But though the law maintains identity of personality to be associated with identity of the *corpus*, common sense has always regarded this as, in some cases, little more than a legal fiction. A man may so change that he seems to be a different person. He may have the same face; but he has not the same personality. We do not say that he is a different personality merely because he has lost

---

[1] F. Aveling: *Personality and Will*, p. 97.
[2] David Hume: *A Treatise of Human Nature*.

his memory, but only when (as often accompanies loss of memory) the structure of his purposive life has changed, when he manifests in his conduct a different *form of will*.

Our private consciousness of personal identity from moment to moment plainly depends upon the purposive continuity of will. Every mental act, as we have already seen, looks to a future beyond itself. It carries its past with it, too, and that, not as a mere qualitative modification of the present, but as a recognized succession of past experiences. And these illuminate the outlook on the future, colouring the expectations of what is to come. Thus past, present, and future are held together within the identity of a single present purpose; and that purpose of the present act is linked up in the larger purpose of a series of acts of which it is a part, and to which larger purpose it serves as a means. Thus it is continuity of purpose that gives connectedness to the passing moments of the subjective life and it is consciousness of this continuity that constitutes our awareness of personal identity. The abiding structural identity of an individual person is rooted in the fixity of purposes, in the permanence of the forms of will.

Even to himself a man may feel himself a different person if he undergoes a sudden transformation of his purposive nature, as sometimes happens in religious conversion; and at other times, usually with accompanying loss of memory, in the cases known as "alternating personality." If he has merely lost his memory a man may say to himself "Who am I?" He is seeking the connection of his present self with the identity which he believes persists. But if he has undergone a far-reaching change of will he says "I am a different man." He has the same body and the same memories. But there is a discontinuity of his purposes which convinces him that, for good or ill, the old man is dead within him and he is a new creature. On the other hand, when we wake up in the morning after an interval of unconsciousness the

STRUCTURE AND PROCESS: SUBJECTIVE 95

break in cognitive processes and volitional activity does not suggest to us that we are different individuals. We recognize the continuity of the self in the continuity of the purposes which disclose themselves as consciousness returns. The continuity of personal identity is known as a continuity of conational structure, the continuity of a form of will.

Now it is important to ask whether this continuity of purposes is really broken in those cases where personality undergoes drastic changes. Here we should recognize a distinction between the personality, in the sense of *persona*, the formal appearance of the self to itself and to others, and the underlying continuity of volitional processes which constitutes genuine personal identity. In the cases of sudden conversion and alternating personality, as in the slower changes of personality from youth to age, the former has changed, but the latter kind of continuity has been maintained. Every personality is a complex of numerous, often conflicting aims, usually ordered more or less systematically under some dominating motives. In abnormal cases the dominating motives may so repress some of the subordinate ones that the person never becomes clearly conscious of their presence. But such abnormal conditions are essentially unstable and liable to sudden and violent change in which the formerly repressed motives become dominant and, as usually happens in revolutions, fling their former masters into the dungeons whence they themselves have just issued. This is what happens in cases of alternating personality and sudden religious conversion. There is no real break in volitional continuity, only a drastic change of emphasis. Personal identity does not mean that will does not change its form, otherwise there would be no personal development. It means only that there is volitional continuity about the changes that occur. Normally we are aware of this continuity and do not doubt our personal identity when we "change our minds." It is only when this normally manifest continuity is obscured by the suddenness, violence, or abnormal character of the change that the expressions about "change of personality" or "becoming a new man" are ever thought to be anything more than vigorous metaphor.

The really important question is whether this continuity of mental structure, or form of will, is rooted in some genuine structural feature or form on the side of the subject, or whether it can be explained as due merely to structural modifications of the cerebral cortex. Now since conation, as already pointed out, is responsive to sensa and values it cannot itself be merely a physical process. That redness, or pleasure, or a guilty conscience should directly affect the molecular processes of the brain is just the unintelligible conception that has driven so many thinkers to mechanism. It is the conation, or effort of will, that responds to these objective processes; and we have already seen that a reasonable interpretation of the nature of both material and conative process is to be found which makes intelligible the notion of some degree of control of the former by the latter, as well as the reverse process whereby physical events necessitate fresh conative effort in order to maintain the purposes of the individual. But can we intelligibly conceive of a relatively permanent condition, or fixed form of will, which might remain in existence when the conative act is not in progress, and become effective, or operative, in control of bodily movement or other conations when the occasion arose, e.g. in response to a certain objective appearance or some other conation in some way contrary to it?

Such a conception, admittedly, is not easy, for imagery and language are so bound down to the spatial and sensory that we can form no adequate mental picture even of a process, still less of a structure, that is not spatial or sensory. But it is less difficult, it seems to me, to think of will as

STRUCTURE AND PROCESS: SUBJECTIVE

maintaining a definite, but non-physical, form than it is to believe in a structure composed of such diaphanous entities as thoughts; and this may be accounted a further advantage in the recognition of the primacy of will. But, unless we are to relapse into the worse unintelligibilities of Mechanism, we are driven to recognize the existence of relatively permanent forms of will as constituting a definite and elaborate structure on the side of the subject. Consciousness itself is too broken and too fleeting a thing to be regarded as maintaining the continuous identity of so elaborate a structure as that of personality. A form of will is something capable of increasing elaboration in the course of experience, and is also something that may remain temporarily inactive, and therefore unconscious, as in sleep.

The second feature of structural unity on the side of the subject is that of causal agency. It is obviously not as simple as causal efficiency on the side of the object, which consists in the sheer continuity of motion and the relation between kinetic and potential energy. Causal agency on the part of the subject involves the mystery of the subjective control of transition from kinetic to potential energy, and vice versa, within the cortex; and also it involves the problem of the complex relation between conation, cognition of sensa and their physical complications and implications, and value experience. These relationships are open to introspective examination, so that they can be fairly completely described; but the ultimate relation remains none the less mysterious. What we have to say about these relations will be better postponed to a later chapter,[1] together with the question of freedom, which is also here involved. All that is necessary at present is to point out that these causal relations, whatever they may be, and different though they are from the mechanical, are an important feature of the structural unity which binds the subjective processes together.

[1] Chapter v.

Finally, we come again to the question of substance. As objective processes seem logically to demand recognition of the existence of an objective stuff, so subjective activity seems to demand recognition of an active subject, a self or soul which is more than the sum of its processes. Such a concept we have, indeed, already been forced to adopt implicitly in discussing personal identity, for a form of will cannot be bare form. It must be a form or differentiation of some stuff, essence, or nature. And we have already suggested that continuity between the mental and physical will be rendered intelligible if we regard it as a differentiation of the universal stuff of which matter may also be regarded as another differentiation. Yet the notion of the self as substantial goes further than does the notion of personal identity. The distinction is the same as that on the side of the object between substance and totality and causality. Causality on both sides is recognized as a connection linking up the successive processes. Totality and personal identity imply that the present set of processes is but a part of a larger whole. But substance is the concept that every process is the manifestation of an enduring reality which is something more than the transient event.

The substance most clearly revealed by sensa, as we have seen, is space-time, or motion, which is also revealed in direct intuition with its content of the nature of resistance, energy, or inertia. And motion, on account of the categories of totality and causality, takes form in our thought as the structure of the physical world, which gives the element of continuity to the notion of physical substance. Similarly, as we shall see, values are a manifestation of conative activity, which is itself intuited as effort or striving. And conation, on account of the categories of purposive agency and personal identity, takes form in our thought as the structure of the self, which gives the element of continuity to the notion of spiritual substance, or soul. Physical sub-

STRUCTURE AND PROCESS: SUBJECTIVE

stance is thus known immediately as kinetic energy (or motion) and inferentially as potential energy (as structure or form). And spiritual substance, likewise, is known immediately as conation, and inferentially as structure, a fixed purpose or form of will. Soul and body are known together; and our knowledge of them is dependent, in precisely the same way in each case, upon direct intuition and categorial thinking.

CHAPTER IV

APPEARANCE AND REALITY

THE last two chapters have outlined for us the data of our experience. We have seen its two-sided character as revealing subjective activity and a world of objects. And we have seen that process and structure "appear," in precisely the same sense, on both sides. They constitute the content of this bi-polar something we call experience. But experience not merely *is*; it points beyond itself to something more. Not only do entities appear, but they appear to *mean* something. Yet they often disappoint us in what they appear to be or appear to mean. And this raises the question of the reality of our experience. Historically this question opens out into at least three. Is reality all experience? Is all experience real? Can there be degrees of reality? At this point we may add another question which has not arisen so far. How do we arrive at, and how can we justify, our belief in the reality of minds or selves other than our own? Then, lastly, we can take up the question which is the root of so many of the doubts as to the validity of our knowledge; that of the status of sensa in the world.

The first of these questions is of importance because of the place it has occupied in the history of philosophy. Metaphysics is essentially an analysis of the nature and implications of experience. We have spoken of structure which is merely inferred, but we had to begin with an examination of the diversities of process found within the unity of experience. All we know immediately is thus of the nature of experience. And though we find in experience certain features which indicate that there are, have been, and will be processes which lie beyond experience, yet we cannot think of any of these as being essentially different

APPEARANCE AND REALITY

in nature from those experienced. On this ground Idealists have based their fundamental contention that all reality consists of experiencers and their experiences.[1] Thus they can (and most of them do) arrive by a short cut at the doctrine of an Absolute[2] whose experience includes all that lies beyond that of finite individuals. And at the same time they find ground for the contention that "the real consists of 'psychical matter of fact.' "[3]

The fallacy in this argument is hidden by the ambiguity of the term "experience" which includes both experiencing and that which is experienced. When, however, the distinction is clearly drawn between the object, which is content of experience, and the subjective act of awareness, which grasps that content, we see that the existence of that which is grasped cannot be regarded as depending upon its being grasped. Admittedly, it is possible that it is transformed and misshapen in the process of being grasped, as Immanuel Kant believed. But, on the other hand, there is no reason to suppose that it *must* be. Since the mind is related to Nature (or developed by Nature) as an organ of *knowledge* it should be presumed that it presents things as they *are*, unless it can be shown that the reverse is the case. And then we should expect (as indeed we find in all cases of illusion) that the distortion is due to some general conditions of knowledge which make it possible to allow for and correct it; and often we find, as in the simplification of physical events in sensation, that the indirect or incom-

[1] The term "Idealism" is often used much more broadly to cover all theories opposed to Naturalism. But in this sense Idealism is not necessarily opposed to Realism. It is, I think, better to confine the term to the school which arose out of Locke's "new way of ideas" and which, from Berkeley to Bradley and its present exponents, maintains that simple reflection shows that the real must needs be experience. The characteristic feature of modern Realism, and perhaps the one point on which Realists are united, is their refusal to accept this proposition.

[2] E.g. F. H. Bradley: *Op. cit.* See especially Chapter xiv.

[3] A. E. Taylor: *Elements of Metaphysics*, p. 23.

plete presentation serves a useful purpose. Cognition is the process wherein the subject grasps the multiplicity of objects within the unity of a single point of view, setting them out in its own peculiar perspective in space, and as occurring in the march of a time order which looks from the past to the future. It is as thus grasped by the cognitive act that these processes become experiences. There is no reason to suppose that their *nature* is transformed by being thus grasped, though it is obvious that the appearance of their relations must change with changes in the point of view or perspective of the subject.

Here again, then, we find the importance of the distinction between the object and the act of awareness which we owe to Professor G. E. Moore. It is the great contribution of the Realist movement in philosophy to have made this distinction clear. Its importance, however, is not so much that it provides a refutation of the short cut to assertions about the nature of the Absolute, which constitutes the weakest and least valuable part of traditional Idealism. For such knowledge of the Absolute as may seem thus to be obtained is so vague as to be worthless. It claims to refute Materialism, but has to deny the possibility of any knowledge of God, any assurance regarding our insight into values, or any confidence in the ultimate worth of the finite individual. For religion, its only indication is to point the way of the *via negativa*—surely the least valuable element (apart from sheer superstitions) in the mystical tradition. Realism has done service in undermining this aspect of Idealism. But it has done still greater service in clearly revealing the basis of our knowledge of the self, an implication of the Realist position which has been worked out most fully by Dr. F. R. Tennant,[1] though in a rather different way from that adopted here. Thus an argument, strange to say, which destroyed the nineteenth century basis for belief in God is

[1] F. R. Tennant: *Philosophical Theology*. 2 Vols.

restoring the twentieth century's belief in the soul. And either in the way adopted by Dr. Tennant or, as we venture to think, with greater directness and more certainty in the way adopted here (by connecting it with the implications of our experience of value) this argument also leads to a clearer perception of the reality of the Deity than Idealism could possibly afford.

From the standpoint of the theory of knowledge, the most important result of this recognition of the distinction between the act of awareness and its object is that it establishes the independent existence of that of which we are immediately aware. It thus removes the question of its reality beyond the reach of any purely logical critique. If the objective world is mere experience it cannot be merely our experience. It must in its ultimate reality be that of the Absolute. But the experience of the Absolute must be very different from that of any finite being. It follows, therefore, that our experience is all to some extent unreal. The criticism of the inadequacy of our processes of perception is thus made to cast doubt upon the immediate data of our experience. And, *a fortiori*, there is no sure ground in immediate awareness for the categories whereby, in processes of judgment and inference, we seek to extend our knowledge beyond the immediate.

The one reliable criterion that Idealism recognizes is the principle of non-contradiction, for any attempt to refute it must be based upon it. This may be put in the form that truth must be self-consistent. But all experience involves, as we have seen, at least a primitive form of thought—an awareness of an object with some element of meaning, or thought of something *about* it. And all reality is said to be experience. The criterion of truth, therefore, in applying to thought is made to apply to reality. So it is claimed that we have a positive criterion of indubitable certainty in the principle that "Reality is self-consistent."

But this very identification of reality with experience, by which the criterion of truth is applied to reality, makes the criterion valueless, for the only experience that we can be sure is real is that of the Absolute. And we do not know what that is. The pathway to real knowledge of any kind at all is therefore closed. Neither sense nor value need really be what they appear to be, nor can we anywhere find a guide to what is ultimately real. Science may help us find our way through the practical difficulties of the day, but neither it nor philosophy can cast any light on the ultimate meaning of life. This is the inevitable result of the identification of reality with experience as worked out by that most consistent of Idealists, Mr. Bradley. It is in vain that he pleads, at the very end of the book, that there is a partially true sense in which "the Absolute *is* its appearances."[1] It still remains much less than a "half-truth" that any single appearance or group of appearances is real. If reality is experience then our experience must needs be so partial that it can constitute no reliable indication of anything that is finally and ultimately real.

The road to reality, however, looks very different when we recognize the significance of the distinction between the act of experiencing and the object experienced. When we cease to call the contents of experience by the ambiguous term "experience," distinguish the agent from its object, the grasp from its content, we see that the thing perceived or otherwise known needs must have an existence independent of its being known. No one suggests that our ordinary acts of awareness entirely make their own objects. Even for the Idealist the object of perception is *given* as a more or less delusive facet of the Absolute experience. But when we give up calling everything an experience and recognize that the act of experiencing is an act of grasping, or gathering within the scope of a mental act, we see that the datum

[1] *Op. cit.*, p. 486.

need be *in no. way* constituted by our act of awareness of it. It presents itself in its own right for what it is and may be accepted as such. The road to reality, therefore, no longer appears as the infinite ascent from the finite to the Absolute Experience but as firm ground at our feet. Whatever is given in experience is, *ipso facto*, real.

But immediately we are faced with the objection: But what about the experiences of dreams, images, hallucinations, illusions, and errors? Are these real? The answer is Yes and No. What is given in experience is real. But what is actually given always suggests interpretations that are not given. The face I seem to see in a dream is a real colour presentation; but it is not a living human face. The heat and the tepid warmth I feel when I place one warm and one cold hand in water are really different sensory data; but I must not interpret them as indicating two different temperatures in the water. The stick that seems to be bent in water presents me with a real visual sensum complicated by the concurrent intuition of real physical existence. The process of complication has been adapted by racial and personal experience to the adjustment of that complication for objects presented by the medium of undeflected light-rays. It therefore suggests the physical interpretation of the colour sensum accurately enough for the part of the stick above water, but inaccurately for the part below.

The facts of illusion, hallucination, etc., therefore, do not affect the recognition of the reality of the datum immediately presented, apart from its interpretation. The sensum simply is what it appears to be. Certainly, if we look at it more closely, or move away, it may change as, for example, the red and blue check looks purple from a distance or blood looks the colour of straw under the microscope. But this is simply the exchange of one sensum for another. Each is equally real as a sensum, though our thought of it as exclusively occupying a certain space is shown to be wrong. So, too, with all illusions of physical perspective. What is actually intuited is really certain minute cerebral processes. But these are lost beyond discovery in the closest introspection. They survive only to complicate sensa, especially visual and tactual and motor sensa, with intuitions of physical shape and movement.

Perhaps the most important of the conclusions which follow from this analysis is that the data of value experience, apart from questions of interpretation, are also equally real. We may be as distinctly aware of the pleasantness of the food as of its taste, of the happiness of a social occasion as of the physical reality of the persons we associate with, of the goodness of an act of kindness or the beauty of a piece of music as of the physical and sensory elements in our awareness of the persons and instruments concerned. The value quality is as objective as any other. It presents itself as a quality to be felt for what it is. As the sensum must be sensed and the physical intuited, so does value wait to be felt. It is as independently real as anything else we experience. It is as distinctive a feature of the objective world. The distinctions between its varying appearances are less decisive than those of most of our sensa. And changes in the values associated with certain objects are more dependent upon changes in the attitude and activity of the subject than are those of sensa. But these facts do not in any way affect its status as an independently real feature of the objective world, of which we may or may not become aware, but which we have no reason to believe is not there for our perceiving, under certain conditions, whether we are conscious of the fact or not.

The difficulties about the reality of objects really begin when the question of interpretation arises. Now much of this interpretation is racial, hereditary, or innately determined; and much more is sheer assumption due to the persistent after-effects of prior personal experience. Only a fraction is due to inferences actually drawn by the individual. It is, however, all open to testing by inference and such tests, in general, abundantly support the assumptions of common sense about the world, making even the common illusions intelligible, and to some extent doing the same even for the uncommon hallucinations. But the question of the reality of the objects thus inferentially known depends upon the validity of the principles upon which the inference is based. So far as the logical and mathematical principles are concerned few will raise a question and, though something will be said later about the criteria of truth, we do not propose to attempt here even an outline of the analysis of the principles of inference or the logical basis of mathematics. Where the question really presses is in the justification of the objective categories of totality, causation, and material substance and, on the side of the subject, the similar categories of personal identity, purposive agency, and spiritual substance.

It is here that our examination of these categories in our analysis of our awareness of structure becomes of great importance. What we there found was that in each case they are grounded in the nature of that which is actually intuited, particularly in the intuition of motion and of purposive effort. It is true that intuition cannot carry us beyond the experience of the present moment. But what we discovered was that the *nature* of that which is intuited in the present moment contained these categories and so presented us with them as principles for the interpretation of experience. We found *cause* in operation in the continuity and the diversity of motion as intuited. Similarly, we found *purposive agency* in operation in the response of conation to sensum and value and its effort at physical control, as intuited. And we saw how the intuition of time and motion gives us the category of *whole and part*, how the intuition of time and purpose gives us the category of *personal identity*.

We saw, too, the origin, in the inter-relation of our data, of the categories of material and spiritual *substance*.

These categories, then, are discovered within immediate experience. They are data of experience as real as any other (as real as the act of awareness and the sensum of which it is aware) so far as they are thus immediate. There they constitute the connecting links which make a structure out of the fluctuating processes even of the present moment. We do not intuit these lines of structure as *extending* beyond the immediate present. But we do intuit them as *pointing* beyond it. To apply them to the interpretation of the past and to the forecasting of the future and to the framing of theories of the distant and unknown is therefore something much less hazardous than a venture of faith. It is simply the acceptation of the principles of structure within what is known and their application in the way indicated by what is known. It is therefore no matter for wonder that these categories are found universally in all human thinking.[1] And it should be no matter for surprise that they justify themselves so abundantly by working so well both in our inquiry into the order of the physical universe and in our efforts to understand, appreciate and forecast the conduct of our fellow men. On these grounds, therefore, we can feel assured of the reality of those things and processes the existence and order of which are attested by well grounded and amply verified processes of categorial thinking. And this, it should be noted, applies in precisely the same way to the structure discoverable on the side of the subject as to that found on the side of the object.

What shall we say, then, of the reality of a perceptual object?—a perceptual object being a complex of process and relations immediately given, together with interpretations of them so habitually assumed that they seem to be

[1] An effective reply to the contrary doctrine of Lévy-Bruhl is to be found in *Primitive Man as a Philosopher*, by Paul Radin.

a part of the given object, the given and the interpretation together constituting what we ordinarily call a perceived thing. Obviously, much in any such perceptual object is not real. On account of the facts of perspective the true spatial relations only occasionally appear. Visual appearance depends on light, upon the fusions due to distance and the limitations of our powers of discrimination, and upon the intervening medium. What can we say then of the reality of these common objects of our world? Are they to be branded as mere appearance because they are to some extent deceptive? Or is there any intelligible sense in which we can speak of their having different degrees of reality? This leads us to define what is meant by "real."

Now there is a tendency to think of "real" as meaning simply "existent." But this is to rob the term of its meaning. All objects have some kind of existence, even dream pictures; but they are usually described as unreal. To distinguish between real entities and unreal ones some have, therefore, adopted the view that the real is the material. This is certainly one of the meanings of the term for the man in the street and a very similar view has been put forward by Professor W. P. Montague in his essay in *The New Realism*: "The real universe consists of the space-time system of existents, together with all that is presupposed by that system."[1] But this seems quite arbitrarily to rule out many conceptions of mind and also does not do justice to the common connotation of the term. For a mirage belongs to the space-time system of existents, but it is ordinarily and rightly described as in some sense unreal. This type of case is met by the definition given by Professor G. E. Moore in Baldwin's *Dictionary of Psychology and Philosophy*, saying that the term "denotes that a thing *exists* and that it is *true* in the sense of being *determined*." Professor Baldwin interprets this as meaning "determined absolutely, that is, in a sphere

[1] Page 255.

or universe, existence in which is the final determination for thought."

If an object to be real must be an absolutely determined existent then, of course, there is no sense in speaking of it as more or less real. But then it must be agreed that none of our common perceptual objects are real in this sense; and it is becoming increasingly doubtful whether the most highly refined and defined objects of scientific thought could measure up to this definition of reality. The term thus defined is therefore becoming meaningless. But common sense does mean something by the notion of reality; and it also means that an object not only exists but is in some sense true. We probably get closest to the common meaning of the term if we say simply that an object is real in so far as it *is* what it appears to be. We can then recognize varying degrees of reality. And the test of the reality of a perceptual object may be said to be its capacity to maintain its appearance upon closer and clearer inspection and fuller knowledge. The irregular, quadrangular appearance of the table top from most angles is thus less real than the solid rectangular object which it is for ordinary thought; and this in turn is less real than the atoms in terms of which the scientist thinks of it. This is, indeed, the common sense use of the term.

We shall interpret reality then as meaning that an object both exists and is true in the sense that it maintains its appearance upon fuller and more immediate knowledge. And as an object may do this with only partial success we shall recognize that in this sense there are degrees of reality. Yet, we must recognize that the term is often used in a sense which does not admit of degrees, the sense of ultimate, final or indubitable reality. This is the limiting case of the appearance which does not change when the object is completely known. When common sense speaks of a thing as "absolutely real" this is what is meant—that it could

APPEARANCE AND REALITY

not possibly appear any different however close our acquaintance and complete our knowledge. Common sense, by absolute reality, certainly does not mean to refer to any hypothetical "Absolute Experience," nor even to a Divine understanding which might be regarded as the standard toward which human knowledge may approximate. When we speak of a thing as absolutely real, in the sense which admits of no question of degrees, we mean that it *is what it appears to be* so that, should any change in point of view or understanding make it appear different, that appearance would be less true than the present.

Thus understood it is obvious that only the most directly known and simplest of objects can be absolutely and finally real as they appear. For all complex objects, all structures (except those immediately given, with their implication of continuity beyond the given) final reality is an ideal limit of thought. By means of scientific investigation we are increasingly coming to know the ultimate reality of physical structure, but we are still far from it. Yet we are very clearly aware, in immediate experience, that there is such a thing as physical structure; and that much, with its immediately given features of four-dimensional space-time, may be regarded as indubitably real. Much the same may be said of structure on the side of the subject. But with simple elements of process, and subjective acts, which appear in their immediacy and can never be more fully known than they are, the case is different. In their ultimate and final reality they are simply given. Yet in that they carry meaning with them, e.g. as presenting physical objects or being of such and such a kind, their reality is not final or absolute. Fuller knowledge may show them up as hallucinations, or closer inspection may reveal them as being of a different kind.

In this sense, then, we must say that all *processes as such*, regarded simply as presentations or data, are initially and finally real. If a change occurs on closer inspection it is a change to a different process. Every sensum is real, every value is real, every mental act is real, just as it appears. But when we pass beyond the actual appearance to its interpretation—a meaning often very difficult to separate introspectively from the pure datum of sense, intuition or feeling—the fact of degrees of reality immediately faces us. Objects as they appear—perceptual objects—are found to maintain their appearance with various degrees of success. The physical objects of enlightened common sense, however, have so maintained their appearance in the face of increasing knowledge that we have reached an almost unshakable conviction of their reality. Almost as much could be claimed for the personally identical, purposive, conscious self, for it is only the bias of our thought toward the objective, and the current tendency to think the physical world in terms incompatible with the common sense notion of the self, that has led to any doubt of its reality. In the details of both common sense conceptions there are, of course, many errors, but the essential nucleus of the common conception has stood well the test of elaborate investigation. Indeed, it is not from investigation of the physical world that doubts of its reality have come, but from investigations of processes of the mind. Neither is it from investigation of the self that doubts as to its reality have arisen,[1] but from investigations of the physical world. When each is examined for itself, without preconceived notions derived from the other, the self and the physical world will appear equally and indubitably real.

In the course of testing the reality of any perceptual object we co-operate with other people, communicating our experience and understanding theirs by means of language

[1] The question, "From what impression do they come?", on which Hume based his attack, was derived from an initial false theory of both matter and mind.

and other forms of gesture and related activities. The object which (as we thus learn) appears the same to other people we conclude has thereby manifested greater reality than that which one person alone can discover, or which looks different to each observer. The former is said to be "objective" or have "objective reality," while the objects which appear different to each observer are called "subjective," or have only the lower order of "subjective reality." Thus an unfortunate confusion is introduced into the use of the terms "subjective" and "objective." It is a distinction, not between that which occurs on the side of the subject and that which occurs on the side of the object, but between objects, some of which, being knowable by only one mind, are called subjective, and others, knowable (or apparently appearing the same) to more than one mind, are called objective. This usage, of course, originates in the philosophical view that all that is observable by one mind only is the product of the subjectivity of that mind, while all that can be observed by more than one mind must exist quite independently of any person's subjective activity. But although probably no philosopher now accepts this account of the matter the distinction between private objects and public objects is still customarily referred to as the distinction between the subjective and objective. In this sense, that which is objective, which maintains its appearance in face of examination by *many* observers, is, in general, rightly regarded as more real than that which is merely subjective.

An important apparent exception, however, to this general rule, is the self and such purely private phenomena as a toothache or our own thoughts. These are subjective in the sense just defined, but are just as real as the body and the tooth and the paper on which the thoughts may be written down, though these are objective, or public. For the test of verification by more than one witness can, in a way appropriate to the peculiar circumstances, be applied even here. One person cannot feel another's toothache, but the fact that many people bear witness to having so suffered, in certain similar circumstances, makes us rank toothaches among objects that are just as real as teeth. Similarly, because every person is aware of his own self and his own thoughts, and communicates this awareness, these purely private or subjective entities are commonly credited with complete reality. The test of objectivity is, in a sense appropriate to the peculiar circumstances, applicable to them; and they are abundantly supported by it.

Now in adding the test of objectivity to our private tests of the reality of a thing, in order to speak of it as having "objective reality," we are dependent upon intelligible communication between individuals, especially in language. The fact that we can make each other *understand* our experiences is the only test we have of their objectivity for we cannot actually *have* each other's experiences. But this test is certainly valid, for it is obvious that if there were no element of sameness about two people's experience they could never begin to understand each other, could never develop a means of intersubjective intercourse. And that sameness must involve some identity of quality (i.e. some degree of likeness) related more or less directly to a numerically identical object. For it is the impossibility of accounting for communicable experience in any other way that has led to the abandonment of Subjectivism[1] in modern philosophy. Communicability therefore implies some degree of objective reality. If a man sees a ship sailing upside down above the horizon at sea the unusualness of such a phenomenon, if he does not know of its possibility through the refraction of light by heat, would probably make him doubt its objective reality. But if his companion says he sees the same thing they must conclude that they are presented with something

[1] The theory that all our immediate objects are private contents of our own minds.

objectively real, although common sense would suggest that the apparent location of the ship is an optical illusion. The same test guarantees the objective reality of the visual datum in the case of rainbows and mirages; and human beings believed in the reality of *something* there, and wondered at its delusiveness, for many generations before they found out the explanation.

The communicability of experience, and agreement as to the existence of an element of sameness in that experience, must therefore be recognized as a valid test of the objective reality of the common object. It is not, of course, a final test of ultimate reality, as the above mentioned cases of visual illusion show. But communicability and agreement are *the* test of *objectivity* and are valid tests of *some* form of reality, thus of *some degree* of "objective reality." This is important in regard to our description of the objective reality of sensa and values. We cannot literally enter into each other's experience of these, but the fact that we can communicate our experiences and agree upon them is a guarantee of their objective reality as such. That which we experience as value, in particular, may involve many disagreements. And we may not be able to communicate it to everybody, for unless others have had the same experience they will not understand us. But the fact that it is experienced at all makes it, as sheer process, indubitably real. And the fact that, in spite of all the blindness and disagreements, human beings do to a large extent understand each other's experience of values—we do communicate with each other about them and to a considerable extent agree upon them—shows that they are "objective" in the sense now under discussion, i.e. publicly observable. With regard to their conditions and relations there may be much disagreement; and experience shows that appearances in these matters are certainly very deceptive. But as contents of experience, along with the sensory and physical, they have an equally indubitable objective reality. They are part of our common world.

This reference to the supporting evidence from other minds raises the question of how we come to know of their existence. We certainly do not perceive them as we perceive physical things. Nor does it seem that we have the same kind of awareness of other minds as we have of our own. Professor C. D. Burns has argued that in social co-operation, such as that of the primitive group, of mother and child, in the use of language for thought and in sympathy and love, there is a wider awareness of mind which is fundamental and primitive, and that "the awareness of 'other' minds is a comparatively late subdistinction, as it were, within the enjoyment (awareness) of mind."[1] This argument supports and develops a similar contention put forward by Professor Alexander, a few years earlier, to the effect that we become aware of other minds directly and immediately in the experience of "sociality"[2] and reciprocal social intercourse.

Most people, I think, will find such a theory exceedingly difficult to believe, even if it can be made intelligible. But the real reason for adopting it is not the positive evidence in its favour but the difficulty of seeing how otherwise such knowledge could develop as early and as unconsciously as it does. It is perfectly easy, of course, to justify by processes of inference, inductions, and arguments from analogy, our belief in the existence of other minds. But it is equally certain that it was not by any such processes that we originally arrived at that belief. We do not begin by becoming aware of the self as an entity to be distinguished from the body, and as the possessor of thoughts and feelings, which are expressed in peculiar forms of behaviour, and then go on to argue that since other bodies behave in the same way

---

[1] C. D. Burns: *The Contact Between Minds*, p. 56.
[2] *Op. cit.*, Vol. II, pp. 32–3.

that behaviour must be an expression of thoughts and feelings similar to ours, and so that body must possess a self similar to our own. But if it is not from such inferences, nor yet from any intuitive direct awareness, then whence do we derive this knowledge?

Alexander and Burns are, I think, indubitably right in arguing that it is in our social experience that this knowledge begins and that it is due to something more primitive than the analogical inferences to which it has usually been attributed. The great difficulty is that, to a mind that had begun by regarding its world as consisting of objects which have no experience and movements which are not purposive, it would require a great leap of constructive imagination to put forward the hypothesis that some of these objects and movements manifested consciousness and purpose. Only after careful discrimination and reflection would such an hypothesis become possible; and yet the assumption of the existence of other purposive, conscious agents is manifested from the beginning of the child's intelligent behaviour.

It is in answer to this aspect of the problem that the view of Professor Stout seems most helpful. He argues that common sense does not begin by regarding its world of objects as inanimate, but that from the beginning "the experiencing individual immediately knows external objects as continuous in existence with his own being, and therefore as fundamentally akin to it, both in its bodily and in its mental aspect."[1] The invention of the hypothesis of other minds is therefore not required. All that is needed is gradually to discriminate degrees of apparent purposiveness in the behaviour of objects. It is a process, not of personalizing various bodily forms, but of depersonalizing some and becoming increasingly aware of the individuality and richness of the personal life of others. This is certainly a process of judgment and inference and is only slowly achieved.

[1] G. F. Stout: *Mind and Matter*, p. 306.

Indeed, the process of depersonalizing inanimate things is slower than the process of development of the understanding of the personality of fellow humans, as is shown by the survival of superstition. Throughout the process it is social intercourse that makes it possible. The child discovers that some things are responsive to its wants and others are not. Inevitably it feels a deeper sense of kinship with the former and alienation from the latter. Even those that actively oppose its wants, that seize the things it wants to seize, it must find more intelligible and kindred in nature than those that make no responses at all. And as it develops the capacity to communicate purposes by means of gesture and speech, and to understand the communication of purpose by similar means from others, the idea of the existence of another self distinct from, but akin to, its own must begin to take definite shape. From then on the development of self-consciousness and the understanding of others make progress together, and each process assists the other. The existence of other selves is thus, at all stages of development, as real to the individual as is his own mind and the physical world.

We are now ready to face the question of the status of sensa—a problem that has harried philosophers through the whole modern period. Sensa seem to naïve common sense to be physical. They seem to critical reflective thought to be mental. They are waifs of the universe: people without a country. But if we give them hospitality in our minds we are rewarded by losing our bodies. And yet if we cast them out into the physical world we are likely to lose our minds. No wonder the poor philosopher sometimes walks with his head in the clouds, since any attempt at a normal existence on earth is made wretched by these pestiferous fellows who will not stay where he puts them and do their job, which is that of holding his experience together.

Try as we will, sensa cannot be made to fit the facts if they are regarded as dependent for their appearance upon physical events and physical events alone. Even when the effort is made to attach them to brain processes, instead of to the objects where they seem to belong, they refuse to fit, as we have seen in our discussion of the theories of Professor Drake and Lord Russell. They must be to some extent affected in their appearance by physical processes, or they could not reveal physical objects. But their appearance must also be affected by something else to account for the erratic nature of their correlation with the physical. This means that, even if they are to be considered as material, their appearance and modification must be regarded as due also in part to the reaction of the subject to physical (i.e. cerebral) processes. But they fit the physical so loosely (the physicist has no use for them at all) and they fit the psychical so loosely (for there is no introspectable difference between the act of awareness of one sensum and another) that it seems reasonable to regard them as not to be classed with either.

This neutral status as regards the physical and psychical is the one which fits best into the rest of the picture of the world structure, as we shall see when we face these problems in the next chapter. And it is the status which best fits the facts as these have been brought out in the long history of epistemological dialectic. Sensa then are differentiations of a "world sensory continuum"[1] which (to borrow a word from the physicist) are "refracted" by the mutual activity, within that continuum, of the processes we call physical motion and subjective or psychical activity. Each sensum is, as it were, a glimpse down the winding corridor of space-time by which the physical processes of the past have at last brought the subject to face and strive to control the present end-process of the physical series in the sensory area of the cortex.

Now let us try to construct an account of the processes

[1] G. F. Stout: *Op. cit.*

that must be involved. The first reaction to the physical impact when it reaches the cortex is the intra-cellular reconstructive response which tends to restore physico-chemical equilibrium. To this there is a further, and probably highly complex, conative response. Some conative responses are merely motor and do not present the sensory object. But, unless we are psychically blind to the stimulus, there is also the conative response we call sensing. Then the sensum appears. It cannot be said to be produced by the act of sensing alone. For the act of sensing is such as only occurs in response to physical stimuli. Without the initial physical processes there could never be any sensa appear. The fact of images does not show that subjective activity alone (i.e. by itself) can produce sensa, for the act of imaging is a response to a brain process stimulated through associative channels; and this associative stimulus is only made possible by the continued after-effects (probably structural) left in the brain by processes due to previous adequate stimulation of the end organ of sense.

An image can thus be understood as the mutual effect of a cerebral process and sensing reaction similar to that which produces a sensum. The only difference is one of intensity of the act. A visual image, for instance, must be projected[1] in the visual field. And if the eyes are open it must compete for visual space with sensa. Normally the sensum is given the greater intensity and the image is presented (by a good visualizer) as a transparent coloured object hanging in space, but not obscuring the sensory field at all. It looks much like the double image of the pen, held a foot from the eyes, when the eyes are focussed on a more distant object. And the explanation would seem to be the same; i.e. that preferential intensity is given to the objects on which the eyes are focussed. The same phenomenon is

[1] Projection is simply the "complication" of an image or sensum with spatial characteristics.

observable in the competition which occurs between the nose, as seen by one eye, and the more distant visual field, as seen by the other, for the clearer place in the visual field. The nose, which, like the poor, is always with us, is a bad loser. But something of it, as filmy as a visual image, most people can see. On the other hand, when, in abnormal cases, there is greater interest in the imagery than in sensation they may blot out the normal sensa and keep the field to themselves. Then we have a case of hallucination.

All the facts, then, point to this kind of co-operation of the physical and psychical processes in the production of sensa, and it is because of this that the sensa reveal physical processes. But we would never know the nature of physical process as spatial (neither one-, two-, nor three-dimensional) if we did not intuit space together with sensa. For the sensa are not extended. They are merely quantitative. It is only because their diversifications of quality and quantity are correlated with spatial intuitions that they come to *mean* space and become a guide to spatial reactions of the body. This "trick of making objects,"[1] as Sir William Mitchell calls it, is certainly an achievement of tremendous importance in the history of animal evolution, but it need only be regarded as a new trick of living creatures so far as the giving of *sensory* characters to their objects is concerned. The recognition of the independent intuition of body (i.e. of space-time) means that, before the presentation of sensa became possible, the creature had an object and, no doubt, vague experience of value. But sensa have made possible an enormous process of complication of the body, without loss of mental control, by simplifying the presentation of the complex physical process into a relatively simple sensory field. Their function is that of symbols which simplify the presentation of processes which would otherwise be too

[1] Sir William Mitchell: *The Place of Minds.*

complex for mental grasp and response. They are counters for the cognitive function which have made possible to animal life the centralized control of a far more complex organism than could have been developed or controlled without them.

To the question, then, as to where sensa are placed there is, in the strict sense, no answer. Strictly speaking the green is neither out there on the grass nor in my head, nor in any other particular location. It is in the world, but it characterizes a certain spatial aspect of the world only from a certain point of view. The sensory continuum is a universal, a world, continuum. But its particularizations of colour, sound, etc., like the particularizations of space, are due to the operation of time. Time, as we shall see, has first differentiated space into space-time (or motion or energy) and set space-time into the relatively stable structures of physical things. Now, working in its two forms of expression—its spatial expression as physical energy and its psychical expression as conation—it refracts the sensory continuum into all the varieties of colour and sound, etc., latent within it. The hammer of mind on the anvil of matter beats out the music of sense, by the cadences of which it the more intelligently seeks its way. The music is not a creature of space; neither is it a prisoner in a finite mind; but its relation to both makes it a guide of the one revealing the forms of the other. But if one insists upon thinking of the notes of the tune, or the colours of light, or the warmth of the fire, or the cold of the air, or the sting of the lash as having location in space then the best location our thought can give them is that which common sense always gives, and which is in accord with their function as guides. We can say that they are just there, at the place on the skin, or on the surface of the rose, or wherever else those physical processes may be to which they call our attention. Or, to descend to technical terms, the spatial location of sensa is a complication due to innately determined and habitual interpretation, and arises from their function as means of directing attention to physical conditions in contact with the end organs of sense or in some place at a distance from the body whence the stimulus issues.

CHAPTER V

THE SELF AND THE WORLD

THE analysis of the preceding chapters has, I think, revealed ample justification for our common-sense belief in the reality of the substantial structure of the physical world and of the purposive agent or self, and in the objectivity of sense and value. But this analysis has more or less isolated certain concepts. We have distinguished the subjective act, the objective entity, time, space, sensa, value, physical structure, form of will. But we must not forget that these are only conceptually isolated. In reality (in the fullest sense of that term) they belong together. In the unity of experience they appear together. They are distinguishable, but not separable. With increasingly close and detailed examination we discover no cracks in their concrete unity which might suggest that any one of them might, after all, be merely an alien intruder or adventitious addition to the whole. Our next task, therefore, is to seek some intelligible view of the way in which these distinguishable entities are related. So far we have only touched on this problem so far as it concerns the status of sensa. We have yet to examine the relation of subject to object, of time to its content, of conation to physical movement and to values; and along with these problems of relation go those of origin, of the roots of temporal process in eternal structure or form.

We shall take the first two together because the second is very significant for the first. We began our analysis of experience by pointing to the distinction of subject and object. And this distinction is fundamental. But we also began, naturally and inevitably, from the standpoint of the finite, individual experience. We had first to analyse the elements that together constitute experience; and as we have

THE SELF AND THE WORLD 125

no access to any experience but our own we began with it. But now, having found the elements which constitute experience, we want to see how they fit together to form a whole. In this whole the experiencing self merely occupies a single point of view, so we have, as it were, in imagination, to stand outside ourselves and see the world as including ourselves and everything else.

Now in our analysis of the various features to be found on the two sides, of subject and object, we found only one feature that is common to both sides. This is time. Suppose now we abstract this common feature and see how the two sides look without it. In abstracting time we destroy all activity on the part of the subject, all cognitions, conations, and feelings (using those terms as *verbs*). We also destroy all movement on the side of the object, all physical process.

On the side of the subject we then have nothing left but structure, a complex, but static, form of will, or fixed purpose. We cannot imagine it as a form of nothing, any more than its acts can be acts of nothing (and we have seen that this concept requires that of some kind of stuff or substance), so we shall think of it as a peculiar differentiation of the universal stuff. It is perhaps dangerous to try to think of it in any more definite terms, since all our concepts are drawn from the physical and transitory; but if we do seek some more definite image of it, then, since the effect of its activity (when it is active) is constructive, we might imagine it as a peculiar form of centripetal tension. It has its own peculiar complexity, but no activity, and there is, of course, nothing more on the side of the subject.

On the side of the object we have space, differentiated into shapes or physical structures. But these are not characterized or correlated with particular sensa or values, for we have seen that such correlation, as it occurs in lived experience, depends on the activity of the subject. Yet the shapes or structures which differentiate space are not shapes or structures of nothing, any more than movement is movement of nothing, or space bare extensity. Once again the notion of stuff or substance helps us; and here both the concept of static structure and that of substantial form put less strain on our imagination than they do on the side of the subject; for we are in the realm whence the terminology of our thinking is derived. We have, too, plenty of experience of *relatively* static structure to guide us and we have the notion of energy, resistance, or inertia which, in its last-named form, helps our imagination with the concept of static, non-sensory, valueless, physical structure, or shape. And, as with static structure on the subjective side, we may think of it as a peculiar differentiation of the universal substance or stuff. If, again, we try to picture this differentiation in distinction from the subjective we may, since its characteristic tendency is the increase of entropy, think of it as a tension or strain that is centrifugal rather than centripetal.

Our difficulty in such a picture of the world is where to place the sensa and values, for they only make their appearance in connection with subjective activity and physical movement. Also they appear somewhat different from every individual subjective point of view. How shall we fit them into a world that is static and viewed, not from any particular standpoint, but as a whole? Now in having spoken of complexities of structure on the side of the subject, and of particular structural shapes on that of the object, we have taken the world at a particular point in history; for all these complexities and particularizations of structure (all particular fixed purposes and shapes) are products of past processes of development. If we think of the world in cross-section at any ideal (non-durational) instant then it certainly must contain a great variety of particular sensa and values. But we cannot find a place for these particularizations of sense and value so long as we are trying to view the world as a whole. We can form some conception of shapes as they

THE SELF AND THE WORLD

are from the standpoint of the whole and not in any particular perspective. Indeed we constantly so think of them. We can do so because they are structures and our thought of them is formulated abstractly by means of the categories. Even its primitive beginnings are categorial. Physical structure is known by thought structure and we can formulate a concept of it from the point of view of the whole. But sensa and values are processes which only appear within particular structures of matter and will, and which are related to these structures differently from different points of view. The polished red table is shiny at one end from here, and at the other end from there; and it is not red, but grey, to the colour-blind person. We are scarcely capable of imagining it to have all these colours together, and many more, from the point of view of the whole. If we are to put sensa and values into our static world, taken at an ideal moment of history, we must give up the attempt to view it as a whole, and peep in through the keyhole of some private, subjective viewpoint and see it in perspective only.

But let us go a step further, and not only eliminate duration and movement as at a certain ideal moment in history, but remove time *and all its effects* from the world, i.e. eliminate all possible complexities of structure, both subjective and objective. Then what have we? On the side of the object there is space, but not matter, for matter is space-time. There are also sense and value. Each is undifferentiated, for their differentiations are processes and therefore require time. But each has its own distinctive nature or texture, for the possibilities of differentiation of them, which time reveals, are distinctive, limited, and orderly. Perhaps undifferentiated sense and value are difficult to conceive, but the analogy of light will help. Colourless white light is refracted by the spectrum into its various colours. So, too, we may regard the undifferentiated continua of sense and value as refracted into all their diversities, the refracting medium being time and the diversities displayed from a particular subjective and spatio-temporal point of view. Thus on the side of the object we find it logically necessary to posit a triple or threefold, non-temporal, world continuum which, to borrow a term from Professor Whitehead, we may call the Eternal Object.[1]

Now need we posit any other eternal character of the world? Is it possible to conceive that the operation of time in space might produce both the order and the difference that we know as the physical world? Certainly we may conceive time as a factor of diversification in space, as well as in sense and value, for such is the part it plays in all our experience. With the impact of time upon the Eternal Object the world as we know it springs into being. It is the vast importance of time, and the need of recognizing a continuity through all levels of development, that seem to have led Professor Alexander to adopt the thesis that "Time is the mind of Space."[2] But, in his theory, sense and value are not regarded as progressively differentiated along with space through the whole process, but only as emerging at a late date. If we decline to accept this unintelligible notion of emergence (a creation *ex nihilo* without even a Creator) then

---

[1] A. N. Whitehead: *Process and Reality.*—The Eternal Object is here conceived, as by Professor Whitehead, as "Pure Potential for the Specific Determination of Fact." But this, I think, does not need to be thought of as a plurality of "Forms of Definiteness." Such straight Platonism seems to me too artificial for anything but metaphor in a philosophy claiming to be Realist. It is appropriate only to Idealism—and that is perhaps a truer description of a metaphysic whose "actual entities" are "drops of experience." A Realism which recognizes the primacy of will, however, needs, not a multiplicity of definite Eternal Forms to be experienced as given, but only an Object with a certain definiteness of nature to impose limitations on active process, and thus explain the emergence of universals, of sameness, of distinctions of kind, amid the flux. Such an object is not a realm of merely subsistent forms, but the concrete nature of Objective Reality. Its potentialities are enormous; but the conditions of their actualization are definite.

[2] *Op. cit.*, Vol. II, p. 38.

the development of sense and value must, all the way through, go hand in hand with the development of physical forms and living organisms. With this alteration, however, we may well adopt, and adapt, Alexander's significant formula, and say Time is the Mind[1] of the universe.

Is time, together with the Object, sufficient then to account for the world, or do we still need another factor that must be recognized as eternal? It seems that we do. Even supposing that time contains a tendency to differentiation (which surely is true) it is still necessary to recognize some factor which imposes order upon its diversification. Now one principle of order is to be found in the given nature of the object. Providing space can be conceived as having a distinctive texture of its own (which is in accordance with recent physical theory), and time is recognized as having a tendency to diversification, both the order and difference within space-time become intelligible. But this is not yet sufficient, for we have as yet only accounted for one kind of order within the physical world; and there are two. There is the tendency to disintegration, called the increase of entropy, which proceeds, apparently, in close accord with mathematically determinable principles; and there is also the constructive tendency of life and mind with its own peculiar type of order, which we distinguish as teleological. To account for this difference we have to posit yet another non-temporal feature, an element of structure which we may call the Eternal Agent, or Eternal Will.

It is not necessary to posit yet another eternal form on the side of the object, for we may recognize the distinctive nature of space as giving definite character to physical processes. Time, operating in space, takes on the form of space-time. But time in its other manifestation, the agency of living

[1] When used in this larger and vaguer sense we spell the word with a capital letter.

beings, is space-free. It is there that we know it primarily as Mind. Yet as manifested there it reveals a distinctive order. It is constructive. It runs counter to the law of entropy which dominates the physical world. We may ask ourselves the reason for this striking contrast of tendency in the two types of temporal process. Is it that, operating in space, time bears in no way the stamp of the form of the Eternal Agent, which it manifests in life and mind? The facts of chemical synthesis, and, still more, the implication of an original order contained in the concept of entropy itself, would indicate that that is not the case. The difference must therefore be due to the intrinsic nature of space. Both in space and in life and mind, therefore, the manifestation of time may be conceived as an expression of the one Eternal Agent. In space, by reason of the medium, it is relatively rigid, tends to expansion without limit, is responsive only to other space-time and not to sense or value. In life or mind it is constructive, non-spatial, but responsive to space-time; above all, it is responsive to sense and value. But over time as a whole, as well as here and there within it, we may discern the influence of the Eternal Form of the Agent.

These then are the eternal entities, and the differentiations of them, which seem to be the logical minimum that must be posited if the addition of time to the picture is to create the world as we know it. When the Eternal Form or Structure (which, since it controls conation, must be regarded as a form of Will) gives expression to itself in temporal process, this process, operating in space, becomes *motion*; expressing itself upon space-time, and responding to the sensa and values, it is *conation*. Thus time transforms the abstract and static Form of Will of our picture into a self and selves. It fills space with all the diversities of structure and process of the physical world. And it diversifies the uniformities of the sensory and value continua into colour and sound, good and evil, beauty and pain, and all their other variations. It

THE SELF AND THE WORLD

is Time, the Mind of the world, that transforms the Eternal into minds and the things they mind.

This, of course, must not be translated into the absurdity that there was once a time when there was no time; nor into the picture, at which the Epicureans used to mock, of God existing for an eternity wrapped up in Himself and then, for no reason that did not exist before, suddenly deciding to make a world. Neither does it mean that time and the world are, in Plato's beautiful figure of speech, "the moving image of Eternity." Nor does it mean, as Augustine suggested in seeking to meet the Epicurean jibe, that God created the world together with time, not in time. It means, rather, that all temporal processes must have their ground in an Eternal Nature, which may or may not be what religion thinks of as God. But, as our discussion of substance showed, this Being must be not only permanent, but the ground of continuity between all the diversities of the world. The Eternal Nature must be the common nature of which intelligence, will, sense, value, space, and time are diversifications. Time itself is therefore an expression of the Eternal. Thus, if we are to speak of the Eternal or Absolute as God and His expression of Himself in time as creation, we must say that God's creation of the world is an "eternal act, an act grounded in the divine nature and, therefore, if we are to use the language of time, coeval with the divine existence."[1]

But the name of God has a much richer content than is justified by the purely logical analysis which we have carried out. We have seen the logical necessity of positing a Substance as the ground of permanence and continuity of the world if the world is to be intelligible. And from the nature of this Absolute must flow all that time reveals. Religion may discover that the Absolute is worthy of trust and name it God. But it is not for philosophy to construct a vision of Eternity.[2]

[1] A. S. Pringle-Pattison: *The Idea of God in Modern Philosophy*, p. 304.
[2] This distinction is strongly urged by Professor John Bailie: *The Interpretation of Religion*.

Our task is the humbler one of defining the concepts in which we must think about our world if we are to make it intelligible and think without contradictions; and that is all we have attempted. In these last few pages we have sought only to define in relation to each other the most ultimate concepts involved in an intelligible view of the world. Incidentally we have sought to present the significance of time in relation to the processes which are its content. And in doing so we have been able also to think of that which is objective from the standpoint of the universal inter-related agency instead of merely from the point of view of a particular subject. This has helped us to understand better the relation of subject and object and, in particular, to place in intelligible relation to each other the agencies of selves and physical things and the medium within which they work.

Conation and motion, then, are diverse forms of time, in the latter united with space and thereby acquiring rigidity,[1] in the former retaining a certain elasticity and its behaviour responsive to sensa and to value. But these are not the only differences. The conational form manifests a growing complexity of structure, but on the side of motion the transition is from complexity to simplicity. This is the familiar fact of increase of entropy—the running down of the universe, the increasingly even distribution of radiant energy, and the tendency towards an eventual complete breaking down of atomic structure, as its most complex forms are now breaking down in radio-active substances. It is only where life is operative in Nature that we observe the process to be steadily reversed. The inevitable question arises as to how the original structure, now breaking down, came to be built up? But this is a question on which science must say much more before any very confident conclusions can be reached by philosophy.

The principle of parsimony, of course, suggests the tempt-

[1] If the Heisenberg theory of indeterminacy is true the rigidity is not complete.

ing hypothesis that, since it is only where life is operative that any constructive material process is going on, it must have been a Universal Life that was responsible for the original structure of the material world. This suggests a theory of the kind put forward by Professor Montague,[1] that the physical universe is the body of which God is the Soul. But any enthusiasm an unwary Theist may have for this kind of proof of the existence of a Deity should be dampened by reflection that the present progressive disintegration of the material body would indicate that God is, if not actually dead, at least suffering from senile decay. Further, even if the body of God could, on such a view, be regarded as eternal, as Montague apparently supposes, the theory also involves the disadvantage that physical evils, like earthquakes and hurricanes, have to be regarded as serious lapses in Divine Self-control. God is relieved of the accusation of being a deliberate fiend by being depicted as a poor weak sinner who cannot keep His body under. His spirit may be willing, but the flesh is weak. It is of little avail that the author of the theory bears Him witness that He has a zeal for good, but not according to knowledge.

Sir James Jeans's theory of the universe as the thought of a Supreme Mathematician,[2] who thinks in us, also suffers from the serious defect that it does not explain why His thoughts should often be, to us, so very evil.

Yet though Theistic solutions of the problem of the origin of the physical order, based on the analogy of the constructive activity of life and mind, are beset by dangers of this sort when people try to arrive at them too hurriedly, and make them too simple, it yet remains true that we have no key to the solution of the problem other than these constructive activities. We have suggested that time is the Mind of the universe, that it operates in space in accordance with an

[1] W. P. Montague: *Belief Unbound*.
[2] Sir James Jeans: *The Mysterious Universe*.

order imposed by the eternal form of will, that this operation produces space-time, and that the peculiar character of space-time (or physical energy) as distinct from pure time (or conation) is due to the nature of space with which it is combined. This would indicate that the original structure of space-time is due to the nature of space and the character given to time by the original form of will. The physical universe is thus depicted as the product of the creative activity of Mind working upon one feature of its Eternal Object and as the expression of a fixed purpose which imposes upon it certain features of order.

But this is not to say that the physical world is the body of which God is the Soul, or that it is the pure thought of God. Both those interpretations transform the physical evil of man into the moral evil of God. From that pitfall of so much Theism the interpretation we are here developing will, I believe, prove to be free. But we have not arrived yet at the point where it is legitimate to speak of God. For a reference to the creative activity of Mind as expressive of an Eternal Will in the formation of the physical world, though it is theological language, does not describe what religion means by God. The Deity, for religion, may be metaphysically something much less, but it is always practically much more. The God of religion is, above all, the source of our highest values and the fountain of spiritual life. Whether the metaphysical principles of Mind and Will we have here elucidated are that also we have not yet seen. So we cannot yet speak of them as divine. There are metaphysical grounds, as we shall shortly see, for regarding this same Will as also the source of all particular personal wills, but the further question of its goodness must wait until we have delved into the problems of value.

There is, however, one very important feature of what theology calls "the problem of evil" which may be discussed here—that of the responsibility of the Creator for those

THE SELF AND THE WORLD

features of the physical world which man finds evil. Rather than use the term "Creator" we should, however, at the present stage of our discussion, speak of "creative principles," for time or Mind, space, and the eternal form of will, which we have distinguished as the factors productive of the physical world, in themselves justify no more honorific title. Here we have two fixed principles which should, therefore, if alone responsible for the course of events, produce nothing but order unless they clash; i.e. the eternal form of will and the given nature of space. If such principles clash, so as to produce confusion, the responsibility must rest with will for seeking to impose on a given nature something incompatible with it. But if they produce order, then the kind of order they produce will be partly due to the given nature of the space and partly to the imposed order of will.

But these principles are not alone. There is a third principle involved in the creative process which is not a principle of order—that of time or Mind. Now time as we know it in space-time has a high degree of order, but not perfect uniformity. Until the discovery of the Heisenberg principle of indeterminacy, and certain other phenomena of the quantum in physics, the uniformity of inorganic processes according to natural law was thought to be complete. To-day, some leading physicists are going so far as to suggest that every quantum has a certain degree of freedom from the causal nexus of the past.[1] But without depending upon these recent experimental results and theories, which may, after all, be upset again within the next few years, it is obvious that if matter is correctly interpreted as space-time then its processes must manifest *some* degree of spontaneity unless time, when operating in space, becomes absolutely its prisoner and slave; and there is no *a priori* reason why it should do so. For time as we know it, space-free, in our own consciousness, has, as we have frequently emphasized, a certain elasticity, and is

[1] E.g. A. S. Eddington: *The Nature of the Physical World*.

responsive to features of the world other than the spatiotemporal, i.e. to sense and value.

We need not assume that the units of space-time are also aware of what we call value, still less of sense. But the *a priori* probabilities in the case, considering the natures of time and space in abstraction from each other so far as we know them, suggest that their union should not result in a process absolutely rigid in its behaviour. To be able to say that it *must* be rigid we should have to know the nature of space, in abstraction from time, so completely as to be able to show that it is such as entirely to overcome the elasticity, responsiveness and experimental character which we definitely know to belong to time in abstraction from space. As a matter of fact we know nothing of space in abstraction from time save its character of being three-dimensional (the attribute of space-time which must needs be due to the nature of space). Thus *a priori* reasoning should lead us to *expect* the physicists to discover some spontaneity in space-time. And if, after a few years, they decide that they, after all, have not yet definitely done so, then we may still expect them eventually to find it. But, so far as present evidence goes, it seems that this has already been achieved.

The operation of time in space is, then, a creative process having a certain indeterminability (i.e. not entirely determinable by the co-operating principles of order) due to the essential nature of time or Mind as elastic, spontaneous and tending to respond to features other than its own expressions and space. Thus the actual arrangement of the physical world is not to be attributed entirely to the order imposed by the eternal form of will and the given nature of space. It is due also to the essential indeterminability of its character as space-*time*. We can see the reason therefore why the universe is not a tidy system. Had a mere mathematician constructed it he would surely have set the stars at regular intervals, the orbits of the planets in perfect circles, the continents in regular array, and the earth's volcanic safety valves safely out of the way at the poles. We should then have a mild and even procession of the weather, no hurricanes and no earthquakes. And when life appeared on earth, if only its free development could also have been confined to forms useful to men, we should have had no physical evil not due to man's inexcusable errors. But instead we have what, from our standpoint, is confusion and evil mingled with the good. And the reason is not that these things are ordered by the eternal form of will, or that they are due to any clash of that will with the material, space, upon which it worked. The reason is instead that the spontaneity or freedom we know in our minds runs in decreasing degree down through all the levels of creation to the ultimate minimal expressions of time of which it is composed.

What then is the contribution to the system made by the eternal form of will? The answer to this question now appears to be: The mathematical character of the system, so far as this is more than conformity to the nature of space. It is a remarkable discovery of recent years that the order of the inorganic world conforms to the creations of pure mathematical thought more closely than to mechanical principles, or any others worked out in a more empirical way. It is this that led Sir James Jeans to the conclusion that we criticized before, that the universe is the thought of a Divine Mathematician. This, as we have already said, is a conception that involves too great difficulties; and further, it is not warranted by the facts, for the conformity appears not to be absolute. The irregularities we have accounted for by the nature of time; but the close approximation to the principles of pure mathematics does imply, as Jeans says, the original imposition of this form on Nature. And as this formal order cannot be attributed to the nature of space, or of time, it has to be explained as due to another original principle or eternal form.

Now it is not merely the principle of Occam's razor, or the economy of hypotheses, that leads us to assume that the eternal principle which stamped its mathematical character upon the physical world is one with that eternal form of will whence our wills are ultimately derived. Vastly different though our wills are in operation from the rigidity of pure mathematics, man has nevertheless discovered those principles within himself rather than derived them from experience. This, too, is emphasized by Jeans in the same book.[1] If, therefore the process of pure thinking (conation with a purely cognitive aim), operating with a minimum of concepts derived from experience and a rich variety discovered as implications of its own principles of operation, has arrived at the principles of order which empirical study of the physical world show to be those which characterize space-time (so far as there is order there and not spontaneity), then the appearance of those principles in these two distinct sets of processes indicates the derivation of those principles from a common source. In brief the order of thought found in our minds[2] and the order of law found in the physical world must both be derived from the one eternal form. Time or Mind, issuing from the Eternal Will, as it operates in space, carries with it the stamp of the same order as it bears in its space-free expressions within the finite wills, or minds, derived from the same eternal Source.

Thus far, therefore, man has no charge to lay against the eternal form whence the physical world derives its order. Our complaint, if any, is against the feature due to its element of spontaneity. But that belongs to the essential nature of time or Mind, to that element in the stuff of the physical world which is common to our own selves and to

[1] *Op. cit.* p. 130.
[2] The fact that this order (the principles of logic and mathematics) is only explicated by the most strenuous thinking of the highest intelligences does not affect the contention that it is always implicitly there.

matter, and brings it in some measure under our control. The bodies which are our means of expression, through contact with which we discover a world of space and sense and value, are only ours to use because of this kinship. They are only the slaves of our wills because, to the rigidity of space, they add the essence that is free. Thus the edge of our complaint is turned by the necessity of the case. And as for the element of law or order in our world, we can only wish that it could have been more complete and strive where we can to complete it. For it is only its order that enables us to understand it, and by foresight shape it to our desires. The spontaneity of the physical world is therefore that which brings it under our control. Its order is that which enables us to control it intelligently. Both are necessary to provide a medium for the life of a mind that possesses the greater freedom in not being itself bound up with space. And the greater freedom is necessary for the discovery of the higher values that human life enjoys.

There is thus a necessary logic that links our happiness and our pain, a logic rooted in the nature of the stuff of which we and the world are made. If we turn our complaint, then, against that Eternal Reality itself, and say that either it is evil or it is impotent and blind, that it cannot itself belong to the nature of an Absolute Being that is omnipotent and loving and wise, then there is only one answer. This is the nature of the Absolute and our charge against His omnipotence is only that He is limited by the conditions of His own nature; and our charge against His love and wisdom is only that it is not in His nature that the least of His creatures should be His slaves. Surely this is not to convict Him of evil. But whether yet His nature is positively good, whether He is indeed what religion means by God, can only be declared after we have sought Him where religion always finds Him— in the experience of the things that are beautiful and true, and of whatsoever is holy and good.

From the problems of time and of the relation of the finite subject to its object we may now turn to that of the relation of conation in the particular, individual mind to physical movement and values. Our consideration of the significance of time has already led us to the view that conation and motion are the diverse temporal expressions of the one eternal form. We have also seen how the temporal expressions, when not in actual operation, seem to maintain their continuity by leaving behind them modifications of structure in the shape of the things of the physical world, on the side of the object, and, on that of the subject, the relatively fixed forms of will. When a stone is thrown up a hill, and lodges in a crevice, the energy put into the throw remains in the form of the new and higher position of the stone. It exerts its influence thence upon other processes as a modification of the gravitational field. So too a decision, or act of will, remains effective when once made. We do not need to be redeciding at every moment of carrying out the decision. We can even forget the original decision in attention to the means, and it still tends to remain directive of conduct towards its goal. It exerts its influence over relevant processes by being a modification of the structure within which they occur. And it continues until some contrary decision or impulsive conation modifies it—just as the stone continues to lie and press upon the same spot until some other movement displaces it.

But the temporal processes (conation and motion), whereby these two structural forms undergo internal change, somehow affect each other, diverse though they seem to be in kind. The question of how they do so is usually spoken of as the problem of the relation of the body and mind. But if the thesis, which we have adopted in a modified form from Professor Alexander, is to be taken seriously, that is a misstatement of the problem. Time is the Mind of the universe, and time is found in motion as well as in conation. The problem is that of the relation between two forms of process and structure, those of matter and those of will. The difference between these two forms is not that one is mental and the other is not. Mind, or time, belongs to both. It is the connecting link which makes their interaction intelligible.

When mind is considered as a complex of thoughts, desires, sensations, and such like "mental contents," and matter is considered as physical events and structures, and time is considered as a mere relation between the beginning and ending of processes, then it is impossible to conceive any interaction between matter and mind, for they have no real stuff in common, only an empty relation. This interpretation of experience is unintelligible. But if we recognize the objective character of space, sense, and value, and the substantial nature of time as the common element in physical and (as we ordinarily call it) mental process the case is different. The problem becomes that of the relation of the expression of time as conation with its operation in space in the complex form of space-time or motion. Somehow the temporal act we call conation seems to affect the transition of space-time between structure and process, i.e. between potential and kinetic. What is conation that it should do this? It is not itself another motion. It is pure time, unspatialized and elastic. It is not limited to a mathematical present, nor a point-instant of space-time; but it gathers a duration inclusive of past, present, and future into the immediacy of a single act. This, as we have seen, is the essence of experience. And it is surely not surprising that in the sphere of space-time where this elasticity of time exerts itself (the cerebral cortex) the procession of space-time should itself be affected. Nor is it surprising that this conative activity should itself be responsive to the procession of spatio-temporal events from outside through the sphere of its operation—the cerebrum. Further than this we cannot go without a great deal more knowledge of physics and bio-chemistry than is possessed at present.

REALITY AND VALUE

For philosophy, however, the important point is that the conception of time as universal Mind, and of conation and motion as diverse forms of its activity, has enabled us to make intelligible the vexed question of the interaction of physical and volitional processes. As we have analysed it, it is not, strictly, the "interaction of matter and Mind," for Mind (i.e. time) is constitutive of both sides. But in the ordinary usage of the term "mind" this phrase may be retained. The ordinary usage of the term is, of course, too well established to be given up, and we have made no attempt to do so. That being the case we had better now define it from the point of view here developed. A "mind" then, in the ordinary sense of my mind and yours, which is practically equivalent to self or ego, is to be understood as a particular, complex form of will, active upon the world through its body, and in that activity aware of the world in a certain perspective. If "consciousness" be regarded as including conation as well as awareness, and the term "point" not reduced to an infinitesimal, then it may be again defined as a point of view from which the universe is self-conscious.

But what now of the origin of minds in this ordinary sense, i.e. of particular forms of will with their inner complexity, their cognitive and volitional activity, their sensing and responsiveness to experience of value? Whence come our finite selves or souls? And how do they ally themselves with their bodies? The picture of the world which natural science alone gives us, without the aid of logical concepts developed in philosophical analysis, leaves these questions hopelessly unintelligible. We learn of a process of increase of entropy whereby some original form of physical structure, exploding into space with enormous temperatures and velocities, is scattering itself without apparent limit and hastening toward an eternal grave in the dead uniformity of thermal mediocrity. But then, suddenly and without apparent cause, on a small planet swinging amid the scattering waste of stars, the process

THE SELF AND THE WORLD

of entropy is reversed. Where all was destruction something constructive has begun. Life rises, phoenix-like, from the ashes of a dying world. A miracle! But, save for the original mysterious structure, the first and the last. And, miracle of miracles, it worked itself! Like Caesar, it came, it saw, it conquered. But, unlike Caesar, it came from nowhere.

From the failure of science to answer our question we turn back therefore to philosophy. The two traditional answers which we find there are those of Traducianism and Creationism, the former asserting that the soul is produced from the souls of its parents as their bodies are from the parents' bodies, the latter affirming the origin of each soul in a new creative act of God who unites it to the body. Professor Tennant, whose *Philosophical Theology* is the most extended and thorough examination of the problems which come under that title published in recent years, adversely criticizes both theories and concludes that the problem lies "beyond the tether of fact-controlled speculation."[1] With his criticisms of Creationism in its traditional forms we would agree, with added emphasis. Like all notions of special interposition of the Deity in natural processes it raises insurmountable moral difficulties, e.g. that He should create souls and doom them to union with bodies tainted with disease, or the seeds of insanity, from birth. The theory reeks with difficulties from the facts of heredity and, as it breaks the principle of continuity, it has no positive philosophical argument in its favour.

Tennant's critique of Traducianism, however, we do not find convincing, as it seems to be based upon an inadequate conception of the soul and of its relation to its ultimate source. His chief objection is "that it involves a quasi-materialistic notion of spirit. The view that souls can be split into parts, can lose some of these parts without being essentially altered, and that such parts of souls can fuse

[1] Page 103.

together into a new one, not only implies that spirit is extended, but is inconsistent with the knowledge that may reasonably be inferred from psychological fact concerning the subject of experience."[1] Such a criticism springs from the view that the soul is primarily cognitive, for the subject, in knowing, does appear as a single, indivisible unity. But the study of conation (and, indeed, of the degrees of consciousness) reveals an enormous complexity underlying this unity of apperception. Thus the fact that the theory of the primacy of cognition (or even the assertion of the *equal* importance of cognition) involves a view of the soul which makes its origin unintelligible recoils against that theory, while the fact that (as we shall see) the recognition of the soul as primarily a form of will makes possible a satisfactory solution of the vexed problem of origin becomes an additional argument for the interpretation we have adopted.

It is a familiar phenomenon of will that purpose begets purpose; the willing of the end leads to the willing of the means; and the multiplication of means is the occasion for the multiplication of purposes. The presentation of a new means, such as a suitable collocation of material, does not *produce* the new act of will; it is only the occasion or opportunity which may call it forth. Will proceeds only from antecedent will, as life from antecedent life. The new act of will is always only a particularization of former will; every new end proposed or striven for is a means to an earlier and more ultimate end of the organism. This is the fundamental law of conation. We trace much of our daily striving back to a few instinctive and appetitive ends, and the rest to certain higher goals we have set before us. The lower types of conation, though now highly differentiated, go back in evolutionary history to the primary aim to maintain self-activity. For even the tendency to multiplication is, in the single-celled organism, a reaction necessitated by its growth beyond

[1] *Philosophical Theology*, p. 103.

a size convenient to the form of life it lives. The higher aims, as I have endeavoured to show in an earlier work, originate in an effort which is essentially the same, but operating on the higher level. "The essential nature of the process of living (from the standpoint of finite consciousness) is to be a finite centre of experience ever enlarging its grasp or penetration of the infinite reality in the midst of which it dwells."[1]

It is also a sufficiently familiar phenomenon of our experience that a definite purpose, or form of will, once fixed, is capable of living an independent life, forgetful of the more ultimate end as a means to which it originated, and even pursuing its own end under conditions which render it out of harmony with the larger purpose that gave it birth. These complexities of will occur within the finite individual self, even though they must needs all operate through the one body. But we have seen that their fixed structure (by which they retain their form or being when not actually operative) cannot be regarded as physical. The form we must postulate as structure of will is not material but a distinctive differentiation of the universal substance. Our wills are therefore complex and internally differentiated structures, but neither spatial nor spatio-temporal. The arguments against Traducianism, to which we have referred, are thus set aside.

Now in an earlier chapter we saw reason to believe that will is present and operative through the whole scale of animal life, even down to the single-celled organism, and including the individual cells of larger organisms. When the single cell divides, therefore, its single ultimate will to maintain its self-activity must develop first the will to change of physical form, an aim induced by discomfort in the existing form, which has grown too large for the skin surface through which it ingests and egests food. No higher consciousness need be involved in such activity than is involved in a vague discomfort and still vaguer expectation of change through its

[1] A. Campbell Garnett: *The Mind in Action*, p. 184.

striving. But with decreasing discomfort the will is formed to maintain and extend the tendency to change which has been found satisfactory. But, unable to maintain a complex form, the will to maintain this form and the will to maintain that, lose their unity and the two forms become oblivious of each other. Thus the single organism becomes two, with two distinct forms of will. In the case of the union of sperm and germ cell the process is reversed. Two complex sets of purposes find themselves at one, striving to order and develop the same physical form with the same physical material. The bringing together of this material constitutes an opportunity for expression for forms of will that lie latent in the wills of sperm and germ. And, as a latent will or fixed purpose always tends to do, they come into operation when the opportunity is presented and so control the growth of the new organism.

Some may be inclined to reject this doctrine because it implies that there is no essential difference in kind between the souls of men and of animals—even that of the amoeba. The difference is only one of form. But this is certainly true of our bodies, so why not of the soul? It is not necessary to suppose a difference in kind to account for man's great intellectual superiority. Difference in form, in complexity of development, is quite sufficient. Nor is it necessary to suppose a difference in kind to account for the moral superiority of men. This also can be explained, as will be shown when we come to the discussion of values, by differences in complexity and in the kind of object discoverable by man's greater intelligence.

Probably the deepest-rooted objection to our theory (apart from materialistic prejudices) is that arising from the belief in human immortality and the disbelief in the immortality of animals. But there is no reason why these conclusions may not follow from our theory. Indeed the weight of evidence is in their favour. The form of will is not a form of matter,

THE SELF AND THE WORLD

and its existence, therefore, in no way depends upon that of the body which is its physical organ. But we must note two further facts. First, the body is its means and opportunity for expression, for seeking and attaining its aims. Secondly, the maintenance and development of bodily function is the ultimate end of much of human purpose, and probably of all animal purpose—for even reproduction we have seen to be merely a development of this fundamental goal of animal effort. With the destruction of the body all opportunity for pursuing this goal is gone. The primary will of the animal, with all the complexities developed by it, is deprived of the conditions which stimulate its activity and present it with its goal. Will, under such conditions, as our experience shows, becomes latent, unconscious, and tends to atrophy. Such we must believe to be the fate of all those forms of will concerned with the material body.

But with man the case is different. In him will has other forms, higher goals. If the human mind has recognized the existence of other selves, or developed within itself aims other than those of physical self-maintenance, it has something yet to live for, yet to aim at, *providing it still has the means and opportunity for seeking those goals*. If it still has means of recognizing the existence of other human souls and of communicating with them, and if there still are possibilities for development of souls and discovery of further values, then we may assume that the life of souls goes on beyond the destruction of the body. Whether these conditions are fulfilled we cannot say with certainty, but the facts brought out by the study of telepathy would indicate that they are.[1]

Telepathy, if it occurs, does not necessarily indicate communication of thought without any physical means. Its

---

[1] Strong experimental evidence definitely supporting belief in telepathy is afforded by an elaborate series of experiments which has been in process at Duke University for some years. Cf. J. B. Rhine: *Extra-Sensory Perception*.

explanation is more likely to be found in some effect of mental activity upon the finer forms of radiant energy which science is disclosing to us—an effect which might be "picked up" by another mind as the receiving instrument picks up wireless waves. The dependence of our thought upon the brain, however, makes it unlikely that a mind suddenly deprived of this organ could immediately and fully express itself in any such way. If there is an ethereal life it would therefore seem that it must involve a period of growth and discovery, with its own problems and need of mutual aid. But as there is no reason to suppose that the form of will does not remain intact, such a life should, morally, begin where this ends, with the additional advantage that the bad habits concerned with the present physical and social environment would have lost their basis and meaning. It is difficult to see how memory, also, could fail to be much impaired. We are here, however, in a realm of speculation where facts to help us are few. The important point is that some form of immortality seems to be rendered probable by the philosophical analysis here developed. Further than that this type of investigation cannot take us. Any deeper conviction must arise as an implication of religious experience.

Finally, it should be said, that though we have called this doctrine Traducianism it yet takes us back to a form of Creationism, or rather, to a loftier notion still. The implication is that of a process of progressive generation of spiritual life, whereby the offspring pass into freedom from the ultimate parent will, and yet never beyond the rediscovery of its meaning for their lives. Will proceeds from antecedent will, even though a form of will may forget its source and lead an independent life. So, through the generations of the past, the will of man must be traced back to its source in the Eternal Will that willed its pursuit of a separate finite life. Such finite lives, though they should forget their source, and few discover it again, are to be seen, therefore, as a means

THE SELF AND THE WORLD

to the attainment of the end of the Eternal Will. This opens up new vistas of thought, but we have not the equipment to venture out upon them until we have completed our analysis of value.

But before our picture of the self and the world is complete and we are thus ready to commence the analysis of value, we have to examine the relation of will, or conation, to the value elements of its experience. Now the inescapable fact is that, in the course of our striving, we are presented with elements of value and disvalue.[1] We may or may not seek them, but they thrust themselves upon us with as much persistence as sensa. We may sometimes be blind to them, as we may be to sensa, but normally we see them, or, as we usually say, feel them. They present themselves as accompaniments of our acts, and on these they make their own peculiar commentary. They vary with the nature of those acts, with their success, and with the way they work together. But this dependence of the appearances of value upon the variations of our activity is the theme of the remaining chapters of this book. Here we shall confine ourselves to the other aspect of the relation—the dependence of variations in our activity upon the changing appearances of value.

Now it is commonly said that we pursue values and seek to avoid disvalues; and, though this is not strictly accurate, we need not always use the cumbersome forms of speech which are often needed to avoid it. The truth is that we pursue *objectives*,[2] i.e. more or less clearly foreseen changes in the situation cognized, sometimes material changes, at other times merely mental, such as a clearer understanding of a

[1] To avoid constantly repeating the double term we shall in general use the single term "value" to cover both positive value and negative, or disvalue.

[2] This term is not here used in the technical sense which Meinong has given it, i.e. anything that may be indicated by the *dass* construction (or "that" clause), but in the ordinary, and narrower, sense of that at which one aims.

subject of discourse. But in our pursuit of these objectives we are aware of experiences of value. And we tend to maintain the pursuit so long as the value experience is positive, and to change our course when its values prove negative. The apparent exceptions, when we persistently pursue a goal in spite of disappointment and pain, are not real, for we only do this under one or more of three conditions. It may be that we anticipate that to give up the difficult and painful pursuit would involve greater experience of disvalue (and values, as we shall see, differ not only in intensity but in preference and scale) than is involved in its continuance. It may be that intensity of concentration upon the objective makes us, at least temporarily, psychologically blind to some or all of the values presented in the course of the pursuit; anticipation of value has set the goal and the effort goes on with its own momentum. Or, thirdly, it may be that the anticipated value of the ultimate goal makes all the intervening troubles appear worth while. In one or more of these three ways anticipations of value carry us through immediate experiences of disvalue.

Thus value, actually experienced or anticipated, determines the choice of our objectives[1] and tends to affect the way in which we pursue them.[2] Thus the *direction of conation, is always determined from the side of the object, not that of the subject.* It is, as we shall see, the *relationship* of our various forms of will, or types of conation, that present the varying shades of value in our experience. But it is the nature of the

[1] "It is inherent in the nature of an end that its content is of value, or at least is so regarded. It is impossible to adopt anything as an end, without seeking in it a thing that is valuable. The valuational material, of course, need not be clearly known as such. But the volitional and purposive consciousness must nevertheless somehow have a sense of its quality as a value, must be held by it and convinced of it."—Nicolai Hartmann, *Ethics*, Vol. I, p. 193.

[2] A fuller discussion of the psychological problems of choice, whereby differences in intensity, quality, and scale of values affect behaviour, will be found in my book, *The Mind in Action*.

THE SELF AND THE WORLD 151

values themselves that tends to determine the dominance of one form of will over another. Our minds are free as against matter within the limits of their control over the movements of the body and of their control, through the body, of its physical environment. But their freedom is a freedom to pursue the values that their experience discloses. Anticipating the values of the future from the experience of the present and the past, man is free to pursue what seems to him good. This he does and he can do no other. His values are the guides of his life. And as he sees them he follows them. His freedom is not a freedom to will that which seems to him entirely evil. But to seek that which seems to him good he is gloriously free.

Does this freedom require effort and involve responsibility? Is it moral freedom? It is the question of effort that is really vital here. In one sense it certainly requires effort, i.e. effort to attain the *objective*, for it is only in such efforts that value is experienced and objectives attained. There is about this interpretation of human freedom no suspicion of the pernicious type of determinism which, either on theological, fatalistic, or materialistic grounds, suggests that human effort is an illusion and makes no real difference to man's behaviour. But the question of moral responsibility arises when our efforts present us with a variety of possible but mutually exclusive objectives, each promising the realization of different values, one of which we recognize as distinctly *higher*, as indicating what we *ought* to do, but another being in certain ways more attractive. It may be nearer, more intense, easier, more familiar and certain. Then is there anything that the subject may do to give the decision to the higher as against the more attractive goal?

Now, of course, in such cases of moral decision the subject may deliberate and seek to concentrate attention on the higher goal and to set aside thoughts of the attractiveness of the lower. He should have learned from experience the foolishness of hastily pursuing the more attractive, and the relative unfruitfulness or bitterness of choosing anything but the best. And such reflections and efforts of concentration and inhibition will certainly tend to give the victory to the higher value. All that is familiar experience. It is the basis of all our efforts to be morally helpful to others and to strengthen and purify our own moral lives. And it is psychologically sound. But it still remains true that there must be a *motive* for this deliberation, reflection, concentration of attention, and inhibition. And the motive can be only another anticipation of value, such, for example, as those associated with one's sense of self-respect, or love of a friend, or thoughts of conscience or religion. Thus it is merely a new, and probably lower but more powerful, sense of value which, under the circumstances, supports the higher. The subject does not escape this way from control from the side of the object. He only brings the fullest and highest resources of the object that are available to bear upon himself. He is still free only to do what seems to him good. But as he can do no other, is he, himself, in any way responsible?

It may seem as though the realm of external values is left in control of the field. But the self will fight to the last ditch for its inner sense of freedom, for the vindication of its power of self-determination. Strange that the self is so loath to part with its burden of responsibility! The fact is that that responsibility is distinctly felt as real, and no sophistication can remove it. The response of will is always to the anticipation of value. But it is will itself (as fixed purpose) that presents the value to consciousness.[1] Will is primary, and

[1] There is a distinction between the will which presents the value and the will which responds to the value presented. This will be more fully discussed in later chapters. For the present, however, we may support our position with a quotation from August Messer: "Our value judgment in general is rooted in a value feeling or in a will that simply and actually exists in us and is acknowledged by us. The ultimate ground of our value judgments lies therefore beyond every purely scientific foundation and proof. We recognize the validity of certain values immediately and upon

without will no value could appear. Yet without the appearance of value there can be no finite act of will. This act, however, is not merely the result of a *vis a fronte* of value. It is a *response* to value. Certainly, the intensity of the response is ordinarily proportionate to the intensity and other attractive features of the anticipated value; and included in these is the loftiness, or otherwise, in the scale, of the value concerned. But now we come to the point of supreme importance. It is a very clear deliverance of consciousness that, when one value is perceived as definitely higher in the scale than another, there is always possible a peculiar change in the complex form of will whereby the rival values are presented as possibilities.

This change is not to be described as an added intensity of the will toward the objective characterized by the higher value. It is rather a surrender of that form of will which presents the lower. This is the ultimate mystery of will. The determination is still from the side of the object. But when the object presents a conflict of the stronger and the higher then something may happen within the self which gives the victory to the higher. It is on the consciousness of this possibility that the persistent human sense of responsibility is based. And there is nothing in all the rest of our experience that need make us doubt its reality. This internal transformation of will is usually felt as the surrender of the lower to the higher self and thus the winning of a larger freedom. But it is the supreme paradox of the moral life that, when the choice concerns the highest value of all, it is felt to be an act of self-surrender—a surrender of the individual will to the Universal. This is the testimony, not merely of orthodox Christians, but of Spinoza, of Gotama, and every other saintly soul. And there is a strange agreement among them that, through the act of surrender, human freedom, whatever it may mean, grows not less, but more real.

the ground of an intuitive feeling."—*Deutsche Wertphilosophie der Gegenwart*, p. 252. (Author's translation.)

CHAPTER VI

VALUE: OBJECTIVE AND SUBJECTIVE

VALUES, as we saw in discussing objective processes, are constituents of our objective world. As to all other such constituents we may be psychically blind to them. And also, like sensa and physical objects, we each perceive them, in their relation to other data, in our own private perspectives. But, as we saw in discussing appearance and reality, this does not mean that they are not objectively real.[1] As immediately given they have that final reality which belongs to everything else with which we have direct acquaintance. Yet as perceived and conceived (grasped together with their meaning) they may deceive us, as do our other data, at times. In brief, as objects of knowledge, values are just as objective and just as subjective as everything else of which we are aware. The really important question at issue when we ask whether they are the one or the other is not epistemological, but ontological; i.e. it is not a question of the status of our objects of knowledge, but of the relationship of appearances of value to other forms of being, in particular the question whether changes in appearance of value are dependent upon changes in the subject or changes in the object.

[1] In similar vein Professor Nicolai Hartmann asserts the "self-existence" of values in spite of "value blindness." "It is as little possible to summon up arbitrarily a sense of value as it is to construct a mathematical truth arbitrarily. In both cases there is an objectively beheld existent, which presents itself, and which the feeling, the intuition, the thought, only follows but cannot dominate. We can experience as valuable only what in itself is so. We may, of course, also be incapable of such an experiencing: but if we are in general capable of it, we can experience the value only as it is in itself, but not as it is not. The sense of value is not less objective than mathematical insight. Its object is only more veiled through the emotional character of the act."—*Ethics* (translation by Stanton Coit), Vol. I, p. 227.

VALUE: OBJECTIVE AND SUBJECTIVE

Now in saying, in the last chapter, that the appearance of varying shades of value is presented by varying relationships between our own forms of will it may seem as though we were asserting that there are no causes of value appearance that are common to a number of different persons. But that, we shall see, is not the case. There are common causes of value relationship because human beings so largely share a common nature; and this statement about sharing a common nature has an even deeper significance than might at first appear—a significance drawn from the common roots of our natures in the eternal form of will. There are also other common causes of value relationship due to the fact that human wills are concerned with a common world of sense and physical objects and other selves. Thus the fact that presentation of values is immediately affected by changes within the individual subject does not mean that the causes of the value experience of one subject are entirely different from and independent of the causes of the value experience of another subject. Thus, we may say that there are objective as well as subjective conditions of value. And it is this fact that accounts for the likeness as well as the dissimilarity of the value experience of different individuals.

But if there is to be any likeness in the value experience of different individuals yet another condition must be fulfilled. It must be a common medium out of which value experience is derived by subjective activity. For the subjective act does not create values *ex nihilo*. Apart from the unintelligibility of any such notion is the fact that values force themselves upon us so insistently, without our seeking them. Though it is through our conative activity that they are presented, they are not simply amenable to our will. Sorrows and pains are persistent, and joys and pleasures are elusive. Our subjective activity strikes them out of an objective world, not by seeking the one and shunning the other directly, but by seeking and shunning a variety of other objects. They present themselves as incidental consequences of our activity, struck out of a medium affected by those acts. So if there is a sameness in the value experience of different persons there must not only be a sameness in their activity, but also of the medium out of which the values are struck. There must be, for all minds, a common value continuum, as there is a common sense continuum. This, of course, does not require a numerical identity of the values experienced by different people, nor a numerical, spatio-temporal identity of the medium. It requires only an identity of kind. Without such identity the value experience of different people could never be the same.

But, it will be asked, since it is admitted that the value experience of different people is not numerically identical, and that very often it is not identical, or even similar, in kind, how do we know that there is ever any identity or similarity at all? The answer is that we know we must be having the same kind of experiences because we can intelligibly communicate those experiences to each other. It is for precisely the same reason that we know we have similar sense and physical experience, that we live in a common world. The proof of it, in every case, is intelligible communication. And there can be no other proof.

So much is made of differences of opinion on questions of value that it is often not realized how largely our experiences are common and intelligible to each other. Differences of opinion arise about the particular occasions of value, the particular perceptual and conceptual objects with which different kinds of value are associated. But on the general analysis of the kinds there is almost universal agreement,[1] a fact proven by the number of different words we

[1] Thus Lord Balfour declares: "The two subjects on which professors of every creed, theological and antitheological, seem least anxious to differ are the general substance of the Moral Law and the general character with which it should be regarded."—A. J. Balfour: *Foundations of Belief*, Chapter I.

VALUE: OBJECTIVE AND SUBJECTIVE 157

have for distinctive kinds of value. Our value experience is sufficiently the same for us all (or nearly all) to give a distinctive content to all these different terms and to understand what the other person means by them. And we do this in spite of the fact that on many particular occasions there may be wide differences as to the value involved. To some extent these differences are due to differences in the content of meaning given to the terms, but more often to differences in affective experience in similar circumstances. There is wide agreement as to the meaning of the term "pleasant" in reference to tastes, but considerable disagreement as to the concrete occasions when it is experienced. In the case of the higher types of value there is probably less agreement as to the meaning of terms, but even so (in spite of difficulties of definition) there seems to be more agreement as to the content of the terms "truth," "beauty," and "goodness" than as to the particular occasions when they are given concrete exemplification. The content we give to the notion of moral goodness, for example, must be derived from our own experience in performance or contemplation of actions so described. If our experience were all the same we would all form the same notion. But even then we would differ as to the application of the term to particular cases because there would often be different understanding of the circumstances. The fact that there is any agreement at all, therefore, shows that the personal experience through which the notion is formed must be very similar. Yet we know that in purely objective respects it has been very different, for different persons pass through a widely different range of situations. Therefore unless there were a high degree of similarity in the purely subjective (private) character of their experiences they could never arrive at any agreement at all on the notion of what is good.

The common nature of value experience is sufficient to secure almost universal agreement on the general analysis of values, although differences arise everywhere as to the particular exemplification of them. In the following analysis, for example, there will be general agreement except for some of the finer shades of distinction and perhaps with regard to the highest forms of value.

Values may be said to possess certain intrinsic differences and also extrinsic differences. The latter, while not part of the intrinsic nature of the value experience itself, are nevertheless characters which affect the response of the will to value. They must be, and are, taken into consideration in any process of evaluation or formation of a judgment of the relative value content of different concrete situations. These extrinsic characters are (1) the duration of the value experience; (2) its permanence, or capacity for repeated enjoyment; (3) its propinquity, the nearer being the more attractive; (4) its purity, or freedom from disvalue, either as preliminary, concomitant, or consequent; (5) its inclusiveness, or tendency to bring other values in its train. The intrinsic differences, or characters, of value are (1) that values differ in kind, e.g. there is a great variety of different pleasures as well as distinctive value experiences of another sort, not usually called pleasures, though perhaps including pleasures, e.g. aesthetic and moral values; (2) that any value experience may have a greater or lesser intensity; (3) that any kind of value experience may be either positive or negative, attractive or repellent; (4) that between certain values there may be differences of scale, i.e. some values, apart from any other differences, seem to be "higher" in their intrinsic nature than others. These nine general distinctions are almost universally recognized. Indeed, it is only the distinctions of kind and of scale that have ever been questioned; and in these cases it has been the exigencies of a philosophical theory attempting to explain value experience that have led to the denial of distinctions which common sense recognizes. This large measure of agreement

VALUE: OBJECTIVE AND SUBJECTIVE 159

in the general analysis of value experience, in itself, therefore, shows that value is in some way objective, i.e. a *common* element in our experience. There are certainly great subjective differences; but our problem must be to explain these without explaining away the objectivity. We must turn, then, to the fuller analysis of the characters about which there exist differences of opinion on the general analysis, i.e. to the problems of differences in kind and in scale.

The different kinds of value experience fall into four broad classes. First, there is the class of sensory values, or pleasures. These, of course, are universally recognized, and, as evidence of the existence of plain distinctions among them, we may point to the fact that many of them have distinctive names. Probably the only question that will be raised upon mention of this class is whether they ought to be regarded as values at all. But that doubt is due to the complication of the broad notion of value with particular moral distinctions. In themselves, and apart from moral issues, everyone recognizes sensory pleasure as a good and its reverse as an evil.

A second group may be differentiated as the biological values. These are experienced in connection with natural impulses which tend, in general, to the maintenance of organic life. Most typical of these are the pleasures of appetite over and above the sensory pleasure involved and quite independent of any recognition of it as a means to an end. But in the same class are the experiences of value and disvalue arising from impulses to the avoidance of pain and danger. All these unconsciously tend to the same end—self-maintenance. Sex is only an apparent exception, for it is a special development of the tendency to self-multiplication which is rooted in the need of the single-celled organism to adapt itself to conditions produced by its ever-increasing size. And all these impulses, if they go far beyond the mere needs of the organism, tend to bring about experiences of negative value.

Next there is a group of values which may be described as psychological. These arise from those natural impulses or instincts which, though in general they tend to the maintenance of the individual or the species, are not so strictly confined to that function. They impel the individual to engage in activities not strictly physiologically necessary and so lead to the enjoyment of a larger life without tending to present negative values unless carried to a very great extreme. These values are still of the type commonly called "pleasures"; but they are the highest type that would be generally recognized as "mere pleasures." They are all pleasures of a kind that the higher animals seem to be able to enjoy as well as man, although man's intelligence has enabled him to find a great many more different ways of enjoying them. In this group are included the pleasures of all forms of play and of activities like hunting, wandering, constructing, the satisfactions of curiosity (as distinct from the higher evaluation of truth) and acquisitiveness, and the pleasures of social and family relationships. In these there is a wide range of value experience which falls below the level of appreciation of aesthetic or moral values and is, therefore, aptly characterized as "mere pleasure." But it arises in activity which, while fundamentally concerned with organic survival, may range far beyond those purposes while still presenting experience of unmixed positive value.

Yet there is a limit to all these pleasures. They have their point, not merely of fatigue, but of satiety, after which they become unpleasant. This seems to be connected with the fact that the activities in which they are enjoyed spring from specific native propensities, interests, or instincts.[1] Something in the objective situation stimulates one of these

---

[1] This term is usually confined nowadays to mere blind reaction tendencies. In *The Mind in Action* I have defended its use to indicate higher types of native propensity and discussed their operation in some detail.

higher animal impulses, such as curiosity, parental care, or self-display. But the objective situation also defines the end as well as the stimulus; and when the process of activity has so modified the situation as to produce this end there is a sense of satisfaction. The impulse to activity dies down and no further pleasure in that kind of activity is obtainable, except through the stimulus of a fresh situation. If the individual is forced, or forces himself, to go on with the activity, it becomes burdensome and distinctly unpleasant, although, until satisfaction had been reached, it was, so far as progressively successful, distinctly pleasant.

Finally, there is another group of values which, without giving any particular metaphysical significance to the term, may be distinguished as "spiritual." It is only here that the description of value experience as "pleasure" is generally recognized as inappropriate. This group includes aesthetic and moral values. Most thinkers also would add a distinctive experience of truth-value over and above the mere pleasure of a satisfied curiosity. Some would also recognize a distinctive religious value, though others either merge the religious with the moral value (some giving it one name, some the other) or regard the religious as merely a composite of moral, aesthetic, intellectual and lower types of value experience.

Pleasures, of course, tend to mingle with these spiritual value experiences; and a certain amount of pleasure or unpleasure is probably a constant accompaniment of them; e.g. positive aesthetic experience probably always includes sensory pleasure, and moral experience often involves psychological pleasures. But the distinction is quite definite; some positive moral and aesthetic experiences actually involve elements of displeasure. Strenuous efforts have been made, in the past history of philosophy, to identify these spiritual values with pleasures; but this theory, Hedonism, has been so riddled with criticism that it is no longer put forward by any thinker of importance. It would be quite possible, of course, to extend the *word* "pleasure," as a technical term, to include these higher values. That term already covers three grades of value experience, as already pointed out. And perhaps there is no greater difference between the spiritual values and the psychological than between the psychological and the sensory. What is important is to recognize that there is a distinction. It would be a great convenience if we had a distinct name for each type; but we have not. We have one term which covers them—"value." We have to keep the distinctions clear by attaching adjectives to that term. So we may speak of sensory, biological, psychological, and spiritual values. But to take the term "pleasure," the connotation of which is derived from the three lower types, and use it also for the fourth would be to blur a distinction which is very important.

The most important difference, apart from indefinable differences of quality, between the spiritual and other values lies in the fact that the former are not subject to the experience of satiety.[1] One can never have too much of them. This does not mean that our capacity for appreciation cannot be temporarily fatigued. An hour in an art gallery or a church service is enough for most people, however good the pictures or the music and the sermon. But there is a difference between this fatigue and satiety. To go on eating beyond a certain point becomes unpleasant. So, too, does the exercise of any of the other native specific impulses beyond its point of satisfaction. There is a point at which all mere pleasures must stop or they become nauseating; i.e. we can have too much of any particular pleasure. But however much beauty there may be in the world, or in a single life, or however long it lasts, it never becomes ugliness. A thing of beauty is a joy forever. And however much truth we win it only whets the appetite for more. While as for good-

[1] This fact is very clearly and beautifully expressed by A. Clutton-Brock: *The Ultimate Belief*.

VALUE: OBJECTIVE AND SUBJECTIVE

ness, though a particular good act may be carried too far, goodness itself can never so increase as to be any less good. These facts are closely associated with the other of the distinctions of value which needs to be discussed in some detail—the distinction of scale.[1] Between the four different classes of value experience we have distinguished—and particularly between the fourth and the others—there is a distinction, not merely of kind, but of level or grade, of higher and lower, a distinction of scale. The unanimity of human opinion on this broad fact is really remarkable. No one who claims to have experience of what we have called the spiritual values, but will recognize that they seem to be in a peculiar way "higher," "better," "worthier" than any of the others. So, too, do the psychological values seem, in a similar way, worthier than the sensory and biological. To over-indulge in the psychological pleasures is a far more venial offence against the community's general sense of value than to over-indulge in the biological—the pleasures of appetite. And where it is merely a question of pleasures (no higher value being involved) a preference for the psychological rather than the biological is generally approved. In comparing purely sensory values with others it is rather difficult to obtain examples of preference not complicated by other considerations of value; but in general it holds good that the sacrifice of a biological, psychological, or spiritual value for a mere sensory pleasure is widely recognized as a choice of the lower.

But *within* each of these four grades the question of higher or lower does not always arise. It is here that the maxim applies, *de gustibus non disputandum est.* Yet these matters of taste are very difficult to separate from questions of scale of value, for many expressions of a preference *within* a

[1] This concept has received in the *Ethics* of Professor Nicolai Hartmann (George Allen & Unwin Ltd.) a treatment which will probably become classic.

certain grade of value also affect matters of higher or lower grade. That is why people, as a matter of fact, do dispute so much on matters of taste. However, in so far as we can isolate a question of preference between two types of psychological pleasure, for example, from any difference of effect upon spiritual values, then it is what the proverb means by a question of mere taste, as distinct from a question of value—by which is meant scale of value. Thus one man's hobby is as good as another's apart from any question of its effect upon aesthetic or intellectual values or any question of his duty to himself or his neighbour. Also, similarly isolated or neutral, one kind of sensory delight is as good as another, while, as between the enjoyments of appetite, it is only a confusion with moral and aesthetic issues (which, of course, commonly *are* involved) that has led to the general view of sex as a low form of pleasure.

Whether this same principle holds good at the level of spiritual values has proved a very difficult question because there is so much confusion of thought on their nature. From the time of the great Greek philosophers it has been customary to recognize the Good, the Beautiful, the True, as a trinity of intrinsic values, distinctly higher than all others, though usually the Good has been regarded as highest of all. At the present stage of our discussion we are not in a position to decide whether this is so. If goodness is necessarily altruistic and beauty and truth are merely egoistic then few, if any, would hesitate to say that goodness is higher. But the meaning of this vague term "good" is the chief of our problems. Some degree of applicability of the principle of equality between these three kinds of spiritual value is suggested by a consideration such as the following. Let us think of a life devoted chiefly to works of practical goodness, but with due consideration for the beautiful and for intellectual values; and think of another life devoted chiefly to aesthetic pursuits, but with due consideration for intellectual pursuits and works of practical goodness; and again, of a life devoted chiefly to the intellectual, but with due consideration for the other two. Is there any sense in which one is worthier than the other? Probably there is not so long as a *due* balance is maintained. The whole problem, however, is really hidden here in the meaning of the word "due." Its very presence indicates the supremacy of moral considerations in deciding the balance; and for the present we may leave the matter there. The significance of the difference in scale, however, immediately becomes apparent if we try to think of a life devoted chiefly to pleasure, but with due consideration of practical goodness, beauty, and truth. We find we have stated a contradiction in terms. If the chief place is given to pleasure there cannot be due consideration for the other three. Being higher in scale it is their *due* to have first consideration.

Now upon the *explanation* of this distinction in scale, as upon the explanation of other facts mentioned in this description of the general characteristics of value experience, there are many differences of opinion. But upon the broad facts of the existence of these distinctions in kind and scale there is, I think, almost universal agreement. They are the general characteristics of value experience which it is the problem of the theory of value to explain. And value experience is so far objective as to obtain for these facts a wide and ready recognition. Differences of opinion arise, however, as to the explanation of them and also as to the concrete cases which may be regarded as examples of them.

It is to this last point that we must next give attention. Why is it that, though we can agree that beauty and truth are higher values than pleasure, we cannot always agree in a concrete case whether a thing is beautiful or not, or between two things as to which is the more beautiful? So long as we were speaking of values in the abstract we were able to accumulate evidence to prove the objectivity of value. As soon as we turn to concrete cases evidence begins to accumulate showing its subjectivity. There is no need to multiply examples, for differences of opinion on questions of value are all too common. Even to the same person at different times there occur changes in the value appearance of perceptual and conceptual data which are otherwise the same. Changes of mood, changes of interest, changes of understanding and of memory affect our appreciations of the value of objects.

But first we should notice that when we pass from the abstract to the concrete we have very definitely changed the topic under discussion. So far we have been discussing the intrinsic characteristics of value as an immediate datum. But when we turn to concrete cases we are discussing the relation of the value datum to other data. It is not value itself, but its relationship to other data that is shown by these concrete cases to be subjective. The test is the same in both cases—that of intelligible communication. In regard to the characteristics of value in the abstract agreement is so great as to convince us that it must be objective. In regard to the relation of value data and other data disagreement is so great as to convince us that the relationship is subjective, i.e. that they are only brought together in the experience of individual subjects, that value does not belong to particular objects except as part of the content of some mind. The recognition of this subjectivity of the *relationship* of values to other data serves as sufficient explanation of such differences of opinion as do exist on the abstract characteristics of value.

This assertion that particular objects only have value for some mind that experiences them and the value together means that we set aside the view often adopted by Realists that objects have a value content quite independently of anyone's experience of them. We must say only that they have *potentialities* of value independently of experience, and

VALUE: OBJECTIVE AND SUBJECTIVE

that in experience those potentialities are realized. Indeed, it is only in the sense of *potentiality* that objects *have* value at all. This is true, not only of the particular objects presented in our experience, but also of the universal value continuum which we have seen the necessity of positing as a feature of the Eternal Object. Except as realized in the experience of specific individuals it is what Professor Whitehead calls "Pure Potential."[1] We have no right, therefore, to consider the possibility of quantities of pleasure existing except as contents of someone's consciousness,[2] nor even of beauty (but only the potentiality of beauty) existing unappreciated.

Professor G. E. Moore,[3] however, has put forward an argument for the existence of value independently of anyone's awareness of it. He asks us to imagine two worlds, one extremely beautiful and the other indescribably ugly and filthy. Surely then, he says, it would be rational to hold that it would be better that the beautiful should exist rather than the other even if it were quite impossible for anyone ever to perceive either. But the answer to this hypothetical case is that we only feel it rational to prefer the existence of the beautiful world because we find more value in *imagining* a beautiful world as real than in imagining an ugly one. The argument, to be valid, requires that we should imagine a world that no one even imagines; which is absurd. Value, therefore, must be regarded as concretely realized only in actual experience. Consciousness alone has value as content. Other things have it only as potentiality.

It is, however, true that values may be presented to our minds without being appreciated. There may be a psychic blindness to values, as there may be to sensa. And, again

---

[1] Cf. Chapter v.
[2] Yet it is with the suggestion of this possibility that Socrates, in the *Philebus*, crushes the contention of Plutarchus that the good is pleasure.
[3] G. E. Moore: *Principia Ethica*, p. 81 ff.

like sensa, they may be more or less clearly present to consciousness. It is when they are most clearly present that they are most effective in bringing about responses or change of conduct. But when only dimly grasped, or when we seem to be quite blind to them, they may, nevertheless, have some effect upon us. It is only from observation of these effects, and from cases where consciousness of what was apparently at the time quite unconscious has been subsequently recovered, that we know of these facts of psychic blindness, either to sensa or values. But these cases of subconscious awareness of values do not affect the thesis that value qualities *actually* exist only as content of experience, for the subconscious is, after all, only an unusually disconnected part of the content of experience.

A more important objection arises from another misunderstanding against which we must guard. It may be said: If there is no value unless a person is conscious of it then the same must apply to disvalue; so if a man commits a crime but does not see that it is wrong then there is no disvalue in his act; we cannot say that he ought not to have done it. But there are two sources of error here. The reference to what he "ought" to have done confuses a judgment about the objective right and wrong of an act with one about the moral goodness of a motive—a distinction to be discussed more fully later. And the statement that there is no disvalue in the act overlooks what has already been said about potentiality of value experience. (For it must be remembered that we are here speaking of felt value qualities, not validities.)[1] The fact that a man does not feel the moral disvalue which other people who contemplate his act find in it only shows that he is blind to its value potentialities.

Actions or motives, then, possess that value quality, of which the moral consciousness becomes aware, only in the

[1] For this distinction, cf. below, Chapter VII.

VALUE: OBJECTIVE AND SUBJECTIVE

same sense as pictures possess beauty, i.e. as potentiality. This does not render this possession any less important. Potentialities are *powers*. A beautiful picture is a picture that has power to contribute to the experience of beauty. A morally good action is an action that has power to contribute to the moral experience of a personality. It is by their power to affect the moral consciousness that we judge of actions as to whether they ought or ought not to be. It is not the sense of moral evil itself that ought not to be, or the sense of moral good itself that ought to be. These are contents of experience, which necessarily must be, according to the nature of our activity, for they are the guides to that activity. Experience of positive value quality in itself is not the end that we ought to pursue; nor is the reverse experience the end that we ought to avoid.[1] The end, whatever kind of value is involved, is always some concrete achievement of mental or practical life—to paint this picture, to cure this disease, to find out how this works, and so forth. It is the function of qualitative value experience to *define the end* for us, to inform us when we do well and ill.

Value and disvalue, in this qualitative sense, are characters or qualities which the world reveals to us, by the light of which we find the way we *ought* to go. A crime is defined for a person as morally wrong when he experiences a sense of guilt upon contemplation of committing it or having com-

[1] This is well stated by Professor H. O. Eaton in his work on *The Austrian Philosophy of Values*, p. 369. "The paradox (of values) consists of the fact that it is impossible, in the world of values, to secure what one wants by directly seeking it out. This has long been recognized in popular adage in such sayings as warn against the direct search for pleasure. The New Testament recognizes this paradox when it warns that he that findeth his life shall lose it, but he that loseth his life shall find it. The text adds the condition that the life shall be lost for the sake of an ultimate goal—for 'My sake.' " It nevertheless remains true that morality itself can be made an objective of the moral life. The manner and extent to which this can be done receives clear treatment by Professor N. Hartmann, *Ethics*, Vol. II, Chapter II.

mitted it, or of moral reprobation at the thought of anyone else committing it. Only if he feels the evil of it himself does he really see it as wrong; anything less than this is a mere judgment of utility, custom, or some other non-moral question. It may be, of course, that he sees no *reason* why it should be wrong, but merely accepts, with sympathetically developed value experience, the beliefs of others. Or he may have reflected upon the nature and consequences of the act and, with or without suggestions from others, have experienced its negative value potentiality. Or he may have committed it and suffered remorse. But it is moral value experience that, in one way or another, defines the act as evil, or another act as morally good.

The potentiality of the act for positive or negative value in the moral experience of the person who commits it is, however, something that has an independent reality of its own. So, too, a picture's potentiality for beauty in the aesthetic experience of the person who contemplates it has a reality of its own. This remains true although there are people who cannot appreciate the value potentialities of either. The value character of a person's experience depends on the nature of the subject and his acts and attitudes; but it also depends upon that of the things and thoughts he contemplates. It is this that gives to the value potentiality of things, thoughts and acts a certain objectivity. It is precisely the same kind of objectivity as is possessed by the sensory potentiality of physical things. A certain pigment has the potentiality of redness for normal conditions of vision; but for the colour-blind person it is grey; in the dark it is black. Common sense says it *is* red. Only when we need to maintain a special kind of accuracy need we say: It has the potentiality for red under conditions of normal vision. So, too, of an act which the general moral conscience condemns, or of a picture which the general aesthetic conscience praises, common sense says the one is wrong and the other is beautiful. Ordinarily the philosopher can adopt the same form of speech. It is only for certain purposes of discussion[1] that accuracy need compel us to say instead that normally, the one is potentially distressing to the moral conscience and the other potentially beautiful. It is, however, very important to remember that the *only* sense in which things, thoughts, or acts *have* qualities of value is as potentialities.

Even when this is recognized there is a further important distinction to remember. The value potentialities of things, thoughts and acts may be immediate or mediate. When they are immediate we say the object has intrinsic[2] value. It is such as by its own nature tends to produce experiences of value in those who have experience of it. Thus food, friendly social intercourse, a picture, or a kindly act have intrinsic value. But the oven that cooks the food, the words required for intercourse, the painter's brush, or the money which was the instrument of kindness, have value only as means. And in both cases, whether intrinsic or as means, these things have value only potentially. We should not say that they *are* values, but only that they *have* value. And even those things that have intrinsic value are not themselves intrinsic values. Intrinsic values, considered in their character as immediately experienced qualities, are pleasure, beauty, truth and goodness in all its forms. It is, as we shall see, from the relation and comparison of certain characteristics of these value qualities to each other that we become aware also of distinctions of obligation and validity.

The intrinsic value of anything, then, is its capacity to contribute elements of value to human (or animal) experience and to make this contribution immediately—not

[1] This necessity arises only when value qualities are being considered in abstraction from questions of validity. For this distinction see next chapter.
[2] Cf. W. D. Ross: *The Right and the Good*, p. 115, and G. E. Moore: *Philosophical Studies*, p. 273-5.

merely as a means to something else, but as it enters into immediate experience when acted upon in an appropriate way. Bread has intrinsic value because of its capacity to satisfy appetite when eaten. A cinema show has intrinsic value because of its capacity to amuse when watched. A work of art has intrinsic value because of its capacity to produce aesthetic experience when contemplated. A noble action or a crime has intrinsic value because of its capacity to contribute positively or negatively to the moral experience of an individual when performed and contemplated. Perhaps in this last case many will feel that the ground stated for regarding the act as right or wrong (having intrinsic moral value) is inadequate. Is a murder only wrong, it will be asked, because it is apt to trouble the murderer's conscience? And if he has no conscience, is it then not wrong? The second question we have already answered: the value potentialities of an object have their being quite independently of the question whether they are realized or not in a particular case. But the former question requires some further elucidation.

We have to do here with a confusion between the explanation of three different questions. One question is as to the reason why value qualities, which have concrete reality only as content of experience, are regarded as in some sense attributes of entities which have an existence independent of our experience of them. The answer is: Because those entities have a certain capacity for affecting our value experience. The other question is: On what features of these entities does their capacity to affect our value experience depend? The answer to this will consist in a description of the technical characteristics of a picture which determine its potentialities as an object of aesthetic experience, on the consequences or aims of an action which determine its potentialities as an object of moral experience, and so forth. Unfortunately, when we simply ask: Why does this picture appear beautiful? or Why does this act seem wrong? the question is ambiguous. It might mean either of the questions above and will for most people mean both. So the answer to one only does not satisfy.

But there is still a third problem that may make us feel that we are giving the wrong reason for the attribution of moral value to action when we say it depends ultimately upon the capacity of action to affect moral experience. It will be said that moral good and evil are matters of the conformity of the motives or the consequences of actions (there are two schools of thought here) with certain objective standards and not primarily a matter of conscience; i.e. that the experience of moral value (conscience) is simply a more or less accurate awareness of a character which is intrinsic in the nature of conduct. Now the reason for this stand is the feeling that any theory that regards moral value as primarily depending on the moral conscience must make moral standards ultimately subjective, which is to subvert the essential notion of value, especially moral value. But while we would very definitely affirm that standards of value must be ultimately objective we deny that this involves a setting aside of the validity of the moral conscience and its primacy in all questions of moral value. This, however, is the principal theme of later chapters. Here we may simply state the general grounds for the position that the moral value of actions depends primarily on their capacity to present moral experience, i.e. upon their effect upon conscience.

The fundamental reason is that it is only because we have moral experience that anything at all is describable as morally good or bad. Apart from conscience the moral issue does not arise. We recognize this in describing the animals as non-moral. The killing of a child is an evil to the child and to the mother and to society. But if it is done by a tiger it is not a moral evil. If it is done by a man, however, it may be a moral evil and is one if he is sane and if it is done deliberately or in passion, or if any higher moral conduct could have avoided it; i.e. the action can only be regarded as "wrong" if it is such as may affect a moral conscience. And whether it *should* be regarded as wrong can only be decided in the light of such objective standards as may be discovered by the moral conscience. For only in the light of the moral conscience can either an individual or society discover objective standards.

The fact that these standards are *discovered* rather than *established* by the moral conscience (which, as we shall try to show, is true of both private and public standards) does not mean that conformity or non-conformity with the standard *ipso facto* makes an action right or wrong. If so, then the tiger's actions must also be right or wrong. The existence of a standard which is independent of conscience means rather that according as actions conform to that standard they have the capacity for affecting the moral experience of the person who is rightly sensitive to moral values. It may be argued against this that in speaking of a person who is "rightly" sensitive to moral values we have admitted that it is the standard that makes the conscience itself right. This is so, but it does not mean that anything could be in any sense either right or wrong except it in some way might affect a moral conscience. However good or however evil may be the effects of an action, or whatever its motive, it cannot be described as either right or wrong except according to its potentiality for moral experience.

All value qualities then, even the moral, only have concrete reality as contents of consciousness; and other objects (with one exception) have value quality only as potentials for the presentation of value to consciousness. Those which have immediate or intrinsic potentialities of value are the particular objects the obtaining or maintaining of which we make our objectives or ends. In a subsidiary sense, the

VALUE: OBJECTIVE AND SUBJECTIVE

means which is needed to achieve the objective, but is not immediately available, also becomes an objective or end and has value as such, but not intrinsic value. In all these senses persons have value. They have intrinsic value for us as potentials for many of our value experiences and they have value as means to many other objects of intrinsic value. But (this is the exception mentioned above) there is a unique sense in which persons have value. They have it not merely as potentials for other people's value experience, but as content of their own. They are the very vehicles of intrinsic values. Thus if our objective is a world in which the utmost possible value shall be realized it can only be achieved through the continuity and development of personalities. And the same must be true if that is the objective of a Supreme Being. This is a part of what is undoubtedly the most important argument for immortality. It is also the foundation on which every plan of social betterment must build and the ultimate justification of all such plans.

In summing up this discussion of the subjectivity and objectivity of values, then, we may say that the status of values in the world is closely analogous to that of space and sensa. Space, sense, and value are the three qualities which the time process differentiates for us into their various kinds or forms. They are potentials for particularization or concrete realization in time. Apart from time space would be mere potential. It is concretely real as space-time. In persons time is not entirely absorbed in space but is, in mental activity, space-free. And in this more complex form of the operation of time not only is space concretely realized[1] or experienced, but also sensa and values are experienced. Sensa function as guides in our dealing with space-time, and together with space-time constitute objects which function in the presentation of values. And in perception

---

[1] At this level concrete realization means experience, but whether it does so at the lowest levels we do not know.

and thought, just as a sensum, by the psychological process of "complication," appears as a quality of a particular space which conditions its presentation, so a value, by a similar process of complication, appears as a quality of the sensory-physical object which conditions it. Thus we come to speak of space as the primary quality, sensa as secondary qualities, and values as tertiary qualities.

This usage, I think, may be retained so long as it is clearly recognized that the secondary and tertiary qualities do not simply inhere in the primary, or, together with the primary, constitute independent particular things. The three qualities together, in their particular differentiations and combinations, constitute our perceptual data and the whole world of our experience. But the world of our experience is always a perspective, a selective arrangement of existence, the appearance of it from a particular point of view. Thus sensa are not, strictly, qualities of the particular space the perception of which they complicate. They are qualities of the world from a particular point of view; i.e. the sensory continuum of my present experience is the sensory quality of the world from my present point of view, or the sensory quality of my present perspective of the world. And it is, as such, immediately and finally real. A different point in space, or colour-blind eyes, or a change of light would constitute a change of point of view, a difference of perspective; and it would have an appropriately different sensory character. So, too, the spacial differentiations, or shapes, which I perceive, are the spatial character of this particular perspective of the world, and as such entirely real. It is only when I assume that the same shapes would hold good in another perspective, or bring experience gained in other perspectives to bear in my interpretation of this one, that I am deceived.

So, too, our value experience is a quality of the world from our own particular point of view and as such entirely

VALUE: OBJECTIVE AND SUBJECTIVE

real. Our point of view is constituted by all the factors that enter into the conditioning of that experience. This includes the external physical world and our own body, our own mind and other minds, all facts of the present and of the past that condition present experience. Personal and racial history is, of course, particularly important in the constitution of our point of view, or perspective, of the world, for the determination of the value character which it shall bear. And this value character of the perspective, because it is immediately given, is absolutely and finally real. It is as real as the spatial and sensory character of the perspective. But we are even more likely to misinterpret it. We are apt to forget it is only a perspective, that the values which "complicate" the appearance of objects are apt to look different in a different perspective. Just as we tend to think the sensa belong inherently to the physical thing, and so must appear the same to everyone and must be the same under all conditions, so we are inclined to think that the beauty belongs inherently to the picture and the moral evil to a particular kind of crime; then we think that everyone should see these things the same as we do, and we forget that different circumstances alter the value of cases. And just as the child, in trying to depict a spatial perspective, is apt to introduce into its picture interpretations derived from other perspectives, and so gets its picture "all out of perspective," so too do we, in drawing a conceptual picture of the moral character of a perspective, introduce interpretations derived from other perspectives and so get our moral view "all out of perspective." But neither in the one case nor the other do these mistaken interpretations affect the reality of what is immediately given.

Only if we accept the reality of what is immediately given in a perspective can our knowledge of it be of use in our dealing with the real world. But every perspective requires interpretation if it is to guide to actions required to change the perspective (by changing objects in it or changing our point of view) in a desired way. And the interpretation of a perspective requires an understanding of its conditions. Some understanding is required if we are to direct our own way among the objects it contains. Still more understanding is required if we are to draw a map, or a picture, or write a description, which may be of use to others. These statements apply equally to the spatial and to the valuational character of perspectives. And in all cases there is required a knowledge of the general principles, or universal conditions, of the kind of perspective in question (moral, aesthetic, visual, etc.), and also of the details of the factors conditioning the particular perspective in question. In the case of visual perspectives the general principles are those of optics, physiology, mathematics, the theory of light, and the chemistry of colour. In the case of pleasure they are the principles of the psychology of sensation and motivation. In the case of truth we need the principles of logic and epistemology, for beauty those of aesthetics, for morality those of ethics and the psychology of motivation. In the general theory of value we are concerned to elucidate the broad principles involved in the interpretation of every value perspective, the general conditions of value experience.

If there were no such general conditions or principles of interpretation value experience would be irrational, meaningless. Yet we do find meaning there and, with a very imperfect understanding, yet direct our way from value to value. There must, therefore, be general principles underlying our value experience; and to some extent we must understand them. Further, if some general principles were not common to the value experience of all people we would not be able to communicate them intelligibly to each other or find any practical help in applying principles that we have learned from others. Yet undoubtedly we do. In the matter of pleasure the understanding of the principles of its production is the basis of the whole commercialization of the provision of it. In truth-seeking the existence of general principles is very obvious. In aesthetics it is also plain, for training not only improves technique of artistic production, but also the capacity of artistic appreciation. In morals and religion, some such principles must be understood, though very difficult to define, or else all our attempts at moral and religious instruction could have had no effect upon moral progress; and if one generation cannot profit from the lessons of another could there be any progress at all? Further, only by some agreement on moral principles could human beings have developed a moral tradition and system of law; and this agreement could never have been reached except on the basis of common elements in moral experience. Finally, we may appeal to introspection and the fixed tradition of value discussion. There is an element of content in the notion of value which is stubbornly objective, and we simply cannot believe that the conditions of our value experience rest in our individual selves alone and are not somehow common to the race.

Throughout the whole realm of value there must therefore be objective standards, i.e. principles of interpretation of perspectives which, if applied with full knowledge of the conditions of the particular perspective, would give a true interpretation in every case. Such general principles, indeed, are widely recognized and applied. We know that when we look at a case through spectacles of personal interest or affection for the person concerned it distorts our value perspective in one way. And when we look at another case where jealousy or envy enter into our perspective it is distorted in another way. We know a great deal about how values are hidden from our eyes in some cases and specious values introduced in others. We know that, in normal circumstances, certain kinds of acts have this value and certain other acts another value. We know a great deal about the general principles, even of moral value, which is (after, or together with, religion) the most difficult of all the value sciences. The objectivity of standards of value must, therefore, be admitted. No interpretation of the conditions of value, therefore, which fails to account for its objectivity can be satisfactory. And yet this interpretation must give sufficient validity to our immediate experience of value to show how, through our personal, private, subjective experience we can, tentatively and erringly, find our way to standards that are valid for all. Our problem is to find a general theory of value which fills these conditions.

Our attempt to solve this problem will be chiefly concerned with an analysis of the subjective conditions of value experience, and we shall find that the presentation of this experience depends on relations in operation of our complex forms of will. But it must be remembered that this analysis of the conditions of presentations of value is not an explanation of the values themselves. Values are objective. They are differentiated by our conative activity from an objective value continuum. There could be no common ground in our value experience if that continuum was not common to all of us and if its potentialities were not definite. Like the spatial and sensory continua it reveals a definiteness of structure manifesting to us its variations of quality, scale, kind, and intensity according to the nature of our activity. The value scale, therefore, is integral to the nature of the Eternal Object. Our volitional activity discovers values that are *there*; it does not create them. The activity of the subject can do no more than disclose the potentialities definitely resident in the object. This is the conclusion of our epistemological inquiry; and in the psychological investigation which follows it must not be forgotten.

CHAPTER VII

VALUE AND WILL

IN the last chapter we were concerned with *awareness* of values and we saw that we are aware of them as qualities characterizing a particular perspective of the world, qualities of the world from a certain point of view defined by present and past conditions, physical, physiological, psychological, and social. The changes in value experience we saw could be attributed to changes in perspective, so that, if we are to learn, from the values of our differing perspectives, what will be the values of certain other perspectives, we need to understand the general conditions affecting the values of perspectives, as well as the particular conditions of the perspectives concerned. With this understanding of the epistemological status of value experience we are ready to turn to the explanation of its most general conditions. And this takes us back to the relations of value and will.

In chapter five we saw that there is a reciprocal relation between value and will in that the appearance or presentation of value seems to depend in some way upon will, and also that will is responsive to value. It is because of this second point that it is so important to be able to interpret correctly our value perspectives, so that, for example, when the prospective punishment of a person who has injured us appears to us as a good, we may be able to discern how far this appearance is due to our anger, how far to traditional notions of justice, and how far to a desire for the reform of the offender and the protection of others. It is this that is meant by the interpretation of a value perspective; and it is obvious how important for that interpretation is an understanding of the dependence of value appearances on will or conation. It is with the fundamental

182   REALITY AND VALUE

character of this dependence that we are chiefly concerned in this chapter. But first it is necessary to clear up a certain ambiguity arising from the other relationship—that will is responsive to value.

This responsiveness of will to value effects a peculiar complication of the meaning of a value judgment, a complication that is the source of untold confusion in our thinking.[1] For it follows from this that every value judgment is more than merely a statement that a certain object, in a certain perspective (or in all perspectives) has a certain value quality. It means also that the will acknowledges a certain demand in regard to that object. We may say The food is delicious, The picture will be beautiful, This act was mean, That act would be noble. These are value judgments and they not only mean that something is, or was, or would be, or will be the case, but that certain things *ought* or *ought not* to be the case.[2] When we ascribe value to a thing we not merely affirm that it possesses certain potentialities of quality, we also acknowledge a certain *obligation* toward it—that it should be appreciated, preserved, produced, etc., or, in the case of negative values, that it should be destroyed, or changed in some way. This may be summed up by saying that every value judgment expresses awareness of *quality* and acknowledgment of *validity*.[3]

[1] This fundamental ambiguity of the term "value" is well brought out by Professor J. Laird in his discussion of the three different types of value theory.—*The Idea of Value*, especially Chapter IX.

[2] The phrase "ought to be" applied to things does not, of course, imply an obligation upon the thing, but a general obligation upon all who can affect its being to give it being or maintain it in being. And this general obligation, applied to a particular individual, is relative to his other obligations. He ought to fulfil this obligation so far as he can without neglecting greater obligations. Thus understood the phrase is not open to the criticisms urged against Professor Urban's use of it by Dr. Ross in *The Right and the Good*, p. 105.

See also discussion of Hartmann later in this chapter.

[3] The thought of values in the sense of validities and obligations has been conveniently distinguished by Professor Urban as "the axiological

But in this it is the awareness of the quality that is primary. The acknowledgment of validity or obligation is an explication of the meaning involved in the nature of the quality. For it is according to the character of the quality as positive or negative, higher or lower, more or less intense, and so forth, that the will tends to respond. The process of *evaluation* of an object is the process of attentively observing and summing up the various differentiations of value characterizing it. The *valuing* of it is the consequent response of will seeking to maintain, increase, change or abolish it according to the result of the evaluation. It is true that when we speak of the "value" of an object, and especially of the "comparative value" of several objects, we often mean value appearance in the light of this process of evaluation; i.e. on our theory, value appearance in the light of a perfect understanding of all the conditions in the given perspective. Further, we even speak of the value of an object as though a perfect evaluation could define its value independently of any particular perspective—which is a misunderstanding. In all these cases the interest is not so much in the qualitative character of the value appearance as such, but in the nature of the demand it makes upon the will after "evaluation." The term "value" is being used with the emphasis upon its implication of validity, of obligation, of containing an "ought." But this is the ultimate rather than the primary meaning of value. It is philosophically suicidal to neglect it. But it is very confusing, and adds to the difficulties of exposition, if we attempt to confine the term to this use. It is much better to recognize that a value *is* a quality and *implies* an obligation[1] or validity.

point of view" and, following his lead, the philosophical problems concerned in the study of our consciousness of validities and obligations, particularly of questions regarding their subjectivity and objectivity, have come to be known as Axiology. Cf. W. M. Urban: *Valuation; Its Nature and Laws*, pp. 16 ff. (George Allen & Unwin Ltd.)

[1] Professor Münsterberg, in *The Eternal Values*, objects to the treatment

Philosophy is deeply indebted to Professor W. M. Urban for his emphasis upon the fact that value means validity and objective validity. But in his thorough-going rejection of every attempt to treat value as a quality or relation he has felt it necessary to describe value as "a wholly unique and irreducible form of objectivity, lying between being and non-being, but not itself a form of being."[1] In a later work,[2] acknowledging that this language is highly sophisticated even for philosophers and such that the plain man cannot learn to talk, he seeks to guard against the danger of making value appear unreal. Value and validity are not existences, he still maintains, but "they have never, except by processes of abstraction, been separate from existence. The perceptual object, the aesthetic object, the historical happening, the moral act—what are these objects when the value element is abstracted? . . . Value has meaning only in connection with things. The meaning and value of things is the very essence of their reality."

Keeping in mind our earlier definition of reality we can agree with these statements. But, even in the sense in which the value of a thing is its validity, its being an objective, or being as it ought to be, does not that value or validity rest upon those characters of existence which we have designated their value quality?[3] Can we imagine any sense of values as obligations on the ground that the term is purely negative and, in so far as it seems to have positive reference to an open choice between what we ought and ought not to do, misleading. This seems to me an over-statement, but calls attention to the necessity of emphasizing the important point that value as a validity has no necessary reference to any counter-tendency. It is simply a positive demand upon the will. To it the will naturally and inevitably responds. Conflicts of value qualities mean conflicts of will, but when once one value is recognized as "higher" its obligatory nature admits of no exception. The "ought" is clear even though the appeal of the lower value *quale* proves stronger.

[1] W. M. Urban: "Value and Existence," in *Journal of Philosophy, Psychology, and Scientific Method*, April 1916.
[2] *The Intelligible World*, pp. 155-7 (George Allen & Unwin Ltd.).
[3] Cf. W. D. Ross: *The Right and the Good*, p. 105.

in which the terms "ought" or "valid" can be used which does not ultimately derive its significance from some person's qualitative experience of beauty, conscience, truth, pleasure, or satisfaction of desire? Apart from these aspects of experience value, in any sense, is inconceivable. And until we can relate the "ought" to these aspects of experience it remains unintelligible. The requirements of intelligibility, which it is Urban's merit to have so clearly stated, demand that we shall interpret the validities of our value experience with reference to their quality.

In this connection it will be profitable to refer to Professor Hartmann's distinction between the Ought-to-Be and the Ought-to-Do. It is his thesis that value is a Platonic "essence" which has "ideal self-existence." When the course of reality is contrary to this "it fixes the contradiction as a relation of opposition and strain, and denies the real which contradicts it, however well-founded this may be ontologically; it stamps it as contrary to value and sets against it the Idea of its own proper structure. The moral consciousness feels this opposition in the form of an 'Ought-to-Be.' "[1] "In this sense value and the ideal Ought-to-Be are indissolubly bound together. They are not on that account identical. The ought signifies direction toward something, the value signifies the something itself to which the direction points."[2] "Ought in this sense is not Ought-to-Do, which refers to a volitional subject. It is only an ideal or pure Ought-to-Be. Because something is in itself a value, it does not follow that someone ought to do it; it does mean, however, that it Ought to 'Be,' and unconditionally—irrespectively of its actuality or even of its possibility. Accordingly, there is sense in saying that universal peace among nations ought to 'be.' That has a meaning, not in so far as peace is actual or possible, but in so far as it is in itself valuable. Yet it would be senseless

[1] Nicolai Hartmann: *Ethics*, Vol. I, p. 233.
[2] *Op. cit.*, p. 247.

to say that a single individual ought to bring peace about."[1] This exposition closely fits the view we have adopted. The "ideal Ought-to-be" is a character manifested by the objective "essence" by reason of its relation to the reality which enters into experience. Whether the value itself is better described as an "essence" or as a qualitative potentiality of the Eternal Object depends on epistemological or metaphysical considerations which we need not again raise. The important point is that it is the nature of the objective value that determines the nature of the "ideal Ought to be." And, whether the reality of affairs conforms to the Ideal or not, it remains true that so-and-so ought to be. There does not need to be a conflict between the ideal and the actual in order for there to be an "ought." But when there is a conflict Hartmann speaks of this as a "positive Ought-to-be" to distinguish it from the ideal.

It must be clearly understood, however, that the notion of ought-to-be derives its meaning from that of ought-to-do.[2] It is true that in many cases where we recognize an ought-to-be we do not feel an ought-to-do, simply because it is beyond our power to affect the situation. But nevertheless we always recognize, as Hartmann himself says, that "I ought to do what ought to be, in so far as it 'is' not, and in so far as to make it actual is in my power."[3] And it is this that gives the Ideal its meaning as an "ought." When we say that universal peace ought to be we mean that it is a collective obligation upon all people to seek to maintain and pursue it. Even when we speak of a condition of affairs entirely beyond human control as one which "ought not to be," or say that it would be "better" if it

[1] *Ethics*, Vol. I, p. 247.
[2] On this point Hartmann does not seem to me to be sufficiently clear, although in a later chapter he seems to recognize it explicitly in speaking of the "ethics of Ought—whereby is always meant primarily Ought to Do."—*Op. cit.*, Vol. II, p. 33.
[3] *Op. cit.*, Vol. I, p. 248.

VALUE AND WILL

were not so, the ground of such an assertion is that the condition tends to arouse the *will* that it should be different—a will that can only take the form of an idle wish because so powerless. Even here, therefore, the element of validity or obligation in the notion of value is derived from its appeal to the will. When we say of an object of art that it is "just as it ought to be" we mean either that it is just as we would wish to make it or as the artist ought to make it; or else we are implicitly personifying the object and perhaps the whole system of things of which it is a part and implying that they are under obligation to be beautiful.

Thus everywhere the notion of validity or obligation derives its meaning—not from its actually being an object of will or desire—but from the fact that it does make a claim upon the will, a claim to which the will tends to respond. At the same time the important fact must always be kept in mind that, as between two or more values, the validity of the claim of each depends, not on the intensity or any other such power of appeal, but solely on the relative *scale* of the values concerned. Where there is conflict of values the question of obligation or validity is determined by the one claim or appeal being *higher* than the other. Where there is no conflict the element of validity in a value experience rests upon the fact that its claim or appeal is unopposed. Were it not for the fact that values do make such an appeal they would not possess the character of validity.

But, as we have already shown, value cannot be regarded as an inherent (only as a potential) quality of particular objects. Values are only inherent qualities of perspectives; and it is very easy to be mistaken as to what features of that perspective (physical and psychological) contribute its different value qualities. Thus understood we avoid the mistakes commonly implied in describing values as qualities, i.e. the making their existence purely psychical and subjective or treating them as constituent elements in the nature of particulars independent of the perspective in which they are presented, and so making it impossible to account for their variability. Values, then, are primarily qualities, but in that they carry with them a demand upon the will they also imply an "ought," and every value judgment implies the *acknowledgment*[1] of an obligation or validity.

The validity or "ought" implied in the value judgment is thus the one-way relation of the value quality to the will. But this is not merely a relation to the particular will of the person who is aware of the value. The value is seen as having this relation to *any* will that could possibly respond to it in the way that it demands. Thus when I perceive beauty in a building, in recognizing that it is beautiful I acknowledge that I ought to appreciate it; but my recognition also means that I think others ought to appreciate it. Thus in every value judgment there is implied, not merely a private experience of value and a belief that, in the same circumstances, others may have that experience, but also a recognition of an obligation which is not merely personal, but general. Here we have the full significance of the objectivity of our value experience. It carries with it the implication of an objective standard of conduct, an implication which we cannot escape and which is the presupposition of all our discussion of values, validities, and obligations of all kinds.

Yet the value that comes to us with this broad claim upon the general will is a value that appears to us in a purely private perspective. As soon as we recognize this privacy of perspective the claim of its value appearances upon the general will is modified. Perceiving that a particular value experience is relevant only to a personal perspective (or, in popular language, to "individual experience") we see that its validities and obligations must have a similar rela-

[1] Cf. W. M. Urban: *The Intelligible World*, p. 145.

tivity. If, then, we should conclude that experience of values is in no way objective we would also be driven to admit that there are no common validities and obligations. But the inescapability of the recognition of these, together with the communicability of value experience, forces the recognition of common elements in value experience and therefore of common obligations and validities. But these we have to recognize as modified by the degree in which our perspectives differ.

Obviously there is much in common in the value perspectives of all human beings, and especially of those who have grown up in the same cultural tradition and the same community. Nevertheless, it is obvious that there must always be some differences, for not only every person, but every situation, differs somewhat. There must, therefore, always be a certain latitude in the statement of objective standards, a latitude that must widen with wider differences of perspective. These conditions of objective value judgment are, of course, generally recognized. But it is important to see that these generally recognized conditions, and the generally recognized ways of meeting them, follow necessarily from the general theory of value here being developed. It is also important to recognize that in this way we can approach toward the statement of standards that are ultimately real. If we could not do so our value experience would have to be declared intrinsically illusory, for every value presents itself with a claim to be finally and generally valid.

The problem of explaining values without explaining them away is therefore that of vindicating this claim for each and every apparently conflicting value. We must be able to show that the apparent contradictions are due to the inadequacy of our apprehension of the values in a given perspective, or misapprehension of their relevance to the conditions of the perspective, i.e. to the complexities of our own will and to the objects (sensory, physical, and social) concerned in their presentation. We must be able to show reason for believing that the value quality of every momentary perspective, if fully and correctly apprehended together with the other factors in the perspective, would present a demand upon the will which would be finally valid. This demand, which we shall endeavour to show is always there if only we could see clearly enough to acknowledge it, is what is meant by the Absolute Standard of value. It is the Ought, with a capital O, that is present in every situation. It is an objective standard, in that it would hold good for every individual *in that situation*. It is not objective, in the sense of holding good for every situation. The attempt to assert rigid objective standards in that sense must necessarily fail. We can state broad principles in the fields of morality, aesthetics, and other forms of value. But they can never be more than useful guides for the interpretation and apprehension of the values in a given situation. We make a sad mistake if ever we begin to think that goodness or beauty actually consists in the adherence to any such principles.

The objective standard of value, then is one that is valid for every person in a given situation; and it is presented to any person in that situation if only he has insight enough to appreciate its values, and knowledge and understanding to see what they mean for practical conduct. This is the claim of value and this claim we must uphold if we are not to dismiss value as illusory. But we must distinguish this objective standard from the subjective standard, which is the meaning of the values in a situation as an individual actually does apprehend them. However the values of the present situation are comprehended or misunderstood by an individual, as they are seen they present to him an "ought"—more or less clearly defined. This present "ought," this subjective standard, claims to be absolute; and yet experience shows that it is not final, that it may be misapprehended, that if we follow it we may find we were mistaken, that if we examine it more closely we may find its meaning transformed. This is the paradox of value experience; and it has only two possible explanations. Either value is an illusion and life has no meaning at all; we cannot even be sure that it is best to say "Let us eat, drink and be merry, for to-morrow we die." Or else the subjective standard is an approximation to an objective standard which has absolute validity.

If we adopt this latter view then two principles become clear which, since value imposes obligations upon us, we must speak of as duties. They are the duty to be faithful and the duty to be intelligent. By the former I mean the duty to respond to the appeal of value as we see it, to do what it *seems* to us we ought to do, for not to do this is to deny the essential meaning of value, and only if we do it can we find out whether we are mistaken or not, and so learn by experience to understand values better. The duty to be intelligent is the vitally important complement of this. It means the obligation to seek to discern and fully appreciate all the elements of value in a situation and correctly to interpret their relation to the subject and to objects concerned in their presentation, and also to discover and correctly use the means that will best achieve the objectives that are thus presented. This duty to be intelligent arises, not merely from the value of truth, but from the nature of value experience itself, in particular that values are not maintained or attained unless their conditions are fulfilled (they require more than good intentions), and secondly, that the obligation which value experience imposes is an obligation to the *realization*[1] of values and that this obligation is not fulfilled by unintelligent action which fails to realize them or even destroys them.

If we ask for proof that life has meaning, that value

[1] "An act . . . is right because it is itself *the production of a certain state of affairs*" (italics ours).—W. D. Ross: *op. cit.*, p. 46.

experience is real if only we understand it properly, there can be none given *a priori*. The only answer is the appeal to experience. If by fulfilling the two duties which the reality of value implies we find that we do discover values that are fuller, higher, and more durable then our philosophy of value receives empirical justification. But there is no other way of justifying it save by trying it out. We can find only too many people in the world to-day who say that they have tried it and proved it false. They should conclude, if they were consistent, that life has no meaning at all. But one wonders whether they have really tried it and whether they understand what they say. For even in this age of spiritual confusion they are vastly outnumbered by the host who, though they may never have applied these principles very consistently or well, are yet convinced, from such experience of them as they have had, that they are sound.

Assuming then that the element of validity or obligation in our value experience is not entirely illusory, any explanation of the conditions of that experience, i.e. any general theory of value, must do justice to both the subjective and objective standards implied in it. This is the crux of the whole problem of value. By reason of this problem theories of value tend to fall into two main groups, the subjective and objective. Professor Laird aptly describes the latter as the "Timological,"[1] from the fact that they find the ultimate determinant of value in some reality independent of the subject, a view which found its most typical early expression in Plato's *Timaeus*. It is this type of view which we have here adopted in describing value as an objective character of reality which makes its own peculiar appeal to the will. The former, the subjective, Laird divides into two (a) the "elective," which attributes value to the natural tendency of everything to persist in its own being and behave in its

[1] J. Laird: *The Idea of Value*.

own way, (*b*) the "appreciative," which attributes value to psychological interests.

On the elective theory value is present in the relations even of inanimate things. It has not necessarily anything to do with experiences of pleasure or other goods. Such things are only values because of the tendency of the will to respond to them. "Whatever *matters* to a thing, or concerns it, is a value or disvalue to it." Value is here interpreted exclusively in terms of what we have called "validity," though it would be unduly stretching that term to apply it to inorganic tendencies. If our own value experience could be so interpreted, i.e. if what we have called value qualities were quite irrelevant to our value experience, then it might be possible that our experience of validity or obligation is only our awareness of a phenomenon that is universal in Nature. But, since the element of validity is unintelligible apart from value qualities, it is quite an illegitimate use of the term "value" to extend it to relations or tendencies where these qualities are absent. It may be the case, of course, that inorganic things have experience of value qualities and that the "natural election" they manifest is their response to this experience. But if so then the form of Timological theory we have advanced covers such cases. The "elective" form of value theory, therefore, need not concern us further. We are left with the appreciative or subjective, and the Timological or objective.

The great difficulty of all forms of the Timological theory is to do justice to our subjective experiences of value. It is the element of objective validity in value experience that is the ground for this interpretation. But if value is interpreted exclusively as validity it means that there is no true good save the best. It becomes necessary to maintain a single ideal end as the goal of all valuation in each of its forms, e.g. as in Plato, an Ideal Goodness, Beauty, and Truth. All our imperfect, subjective experience of value has then to be regarded as a partial and mistaken view. The difficulty is to explain the values we have without making them appear unreal. If we deny their claim to be real and objective *as they appear* then they are blind guides that lead the blind.

We escape these difficulties, however, when we regard values as objective qualities appearing, like sensa, in particular perspectives and having their character of validity, or obligation, by reason of their relation to Will.[1] Concerning value as quality it is sufficient to say, with Laird: "We may appreciate much that is not *excellent*; but it is begging the question to say that value and excellence must be the same."[2] But in that values claim to be *valid*, to present us with distinctions of positive and negative, higher and lower, their claim must be recognized. If there is any mistake it can only be our blindness to some higher value presented by the situation, or our misapprehension of the particular acts and objects to which the values relate. Error in the realm of value must not be in the presentation of values which do not in any way belong to the situation; it must not come from the side of the Object. For if it did the claim of value on the will would be invalid. It would be inherently deceptive, an illusion. Error, therefore, if value is not an illusion, must come from the side of the subject and be remediable by faithfulness and intelligence, as we have suggested. No explanation of the conditions of value can be true (unless value itself is illusory) unless it is consistent with these requirements.

It is such an explanation as this that we must set out to give. But it may be asserted at once that it is quite inadequate simply to state some theory of the ideal end.

---

[1] I use the capital W because, as we shall see, these validities or obligations are ultimately intelligible only in the light of their relation to a complex elaboration of Will of which the finite individual, and the particular volitional tendency which they directly affect, are but a small part.

[2] *Op. cit.*, p. 322.

To formulate some such ultimate standard in the realm of moral value has been the chief goal of inquiry in Ethics. Many and various have been the statements of it. For Plato it was the harmony of the soul. For Aristotle it was the fulfilment of man's chief end, considered as the exercise of the intellect in philosophic contemplation. For Epicurus it was pleasure. For the Stoics it was the life according to reason. For Augustine it was peace. For Aquinas it was to know God and enjoy Him forever. For Spinoza it was the intellectual love of God. For Butler it was the good conscience, and for Kant the good will. For most modern philosophers it is either self-realization, or some form of harmony, or the enjoyment of beauty, friendship, and other goods according to an empirically established scale.

In all these ideal ends, when their meaning and implications are fully expressed, there is much more agreement than at first sight appears. But, even supposing complete agreement were reached, we need some assurance that this agreement has a sound basis and some indication of how to attain the end. For both of these we have to go to our everyday experience of values. And if these are pronounced as illusory because they do not seem to agree with the ideal end then it is robbed of both direction and assurance. It is, unfortunately, the case that most discussions of Ethics have begun at the wrong end. They have regarded their fundamental problem so that of the definition of the highest good instead of inquiring first by what method we are to find what is good. They have compared and classified value experience instead of analysing its conditions. They have studied the objective standard by the method of dialectic, whereas what was first required was to study the subjective standard by the method of analysis.[1]

It is the merit of the subjectivist or "appreciative" theories

[1] "The first task of a general theory of value is psychological analysis." —W. M. Urban: *Valuation: Its Nature and Laws*, p. 9.

of value that they have at least begun at the right end. In spite of their inadequacy, and often their inconsistency, they have, historically, been the most stimulating and fruitful theories. The Hedonism and Utilitarianism of Bentham and Mill, postulating that the good is pleasure, in spite of the inadequacy of the notion and the impossibility of deriving any consistent altruism from it, provided the philosophical stimulus of the great reform movements of the nineteenth century in England. And in the cases of Butler and Kant, though both were firmly convinced of the reality of an objective standard of value, yet the distinctive and stimulating feature of their teaching is their emphasis upon a subjective factor, in the one case "conscience," and in the other "good will."[1] The important modern movement in value theory, also, began with an interest in the subjective factors and a tendency to adopt subjectivist theories. This is true of its originators in the Austrian school of Brentano, Meinong, and Ehrenfels; of Croce, in Italy, who is chiefly responsible for arousing the modern interest in Aesthetics; and of the three American writers who have done so much in this field, Urban (in his early work[2]—the first important book on the general theory of value in English), R. B. Perry and De Witt Parker. Professor Urban, however, is now one of the stoutest champions of Objectivism, so we shall turn for a defence of the Subjectivist viewpoint to Perry and Parker.

As already stated, the great difficulty of any Subjectivist theory is to do justice to the notion of objectivity which is implicit in all our thought on questions of value; and this

[1] Yet, as indicating the inadequacy and inconsistency of their positions, we may note the statement of Professor Hastings Rashdall: "The ethical system of Kant (assisted in England by the influence of Butler and his followers) has produced a hopeless confusion between the question whether Morality consists in promoting an end and the question what that end is."—*Theory of Good*, Vol. I, p. 216.
[2] *Op. cit.*

requirement is clearly recognized by both writers. Professor Perry[1] speaks of value as a character of objects, but not an intrinsic character. It is simply a character they have in virtue of their relation to one or more subjects. It is the attitude of the subject that gives the object its value. It is not the case that certain objective qualities intrinsically *are* values and appeal to the will, or conative tendency, or interest of the subject. These tendencies are reactions of the subject to various kinds of object, due to the innate and acquired character of the organism. Broadly, such tendencies are spoken of as "interests," whether positive or negative, cognitive or merely conative, and value is merely a name for the fact that some subject has an interest in a certain object. Value is defined as "any object of any interest." Value is simply the character ascribed to the object in virtue of its being an object of interest to a subject, so that, if it is the object of many interests on the part of many subjects, it may be said to have very much of this character —very much value.

Upon this basis Perry tries to justify our well-established convictions regarding the comparative worth of our varying objects of interests and, in particular, to justify an objective standard of values. He distinguishes four notions which may legitimately be employed for the critical comparison of values. These are correctness, intensity, preference, and inclusiveness. Correctness, however, is simply concerned with the question whether the person concerned really *is* interested in the object or not and whether it really *is* an object which would satisfy that interest. It is, of course, an objective test that works by reference to objective facts and by communication of experience; but it is not a test of how much interest there is in a given thing and therefore, on Perry's definition, not a test of how much value it has. "To judge an interest to be correct or incorrect does not in any

[1] R. B. Perry: *The General Theory of Value.*

sense predicate more or less of the interest, and thus does not in any sense predicate better or worse of its object."[1] The other three notions, however, intensity, preference, and inclusiveness, do yield measures of greater or lesser interest; and that would mean greater or lesser value. "Intensity" has to do with the strength or vigour of the interest,"preference" with the fact that any particular interest may be more completely satisfied with one object than another, "inclusiveness" with the fact that some objects satisfy many interests and are therefore said to be "better" providing the intensities and preferences are equal.

Now since we have maintained that every value appeals to the will we must recognize that the interests or responses of the subject do indicate some measure of the value for it on that occasion, so far as the subject has correctly interpreted his value experience. We must also recognize that these interests do vary in intensity, preference, and inclusiveness. These distinctions of interest do operate in the determination of our subjective standards of value. But it is *only* with the subjective standard that they are concerned. At least, this is certainly the case with the standards of intensity and preference. A statement of an objective standard of value must be able to assert that all men ought to value A above B because the nature of A is such that it is intrinsically more valuable. But if X *prefers* B to A, or is more *intensely* interested in B than A, then these standards, in themselves, offer no ground for a decision of the question whether in this he manifests good value judgement or not. X's interests (on this theory) confer more value on B than on A and, so far as the principles of intensity and preference are concerned, that is the end of the matter.

In the notion of inclusiveness, however, Perry finds a standard which can be used to decide certain questions left undecided by intensity and preference, and which must be

[1] R. B. Perry: *op. cit.*, p. 612.

given a certain priority to the other standards if the seeking of the greatest value is not to defeat itself. And this standard, he believes, even gives us an objective criterion whereby we can often say that A, independently of my preference or intensity of interest, or yours (though not independently of everybody's), is better or worse than B. So far as inclusiveness is used as a purely subjective standard there is, of course, no doubt of its applicability to problems of comparative value. Other things being equal, and providing that the interests concerned are wholesome, we may admit that there is more value in an object that satisfies both my interests, A and B, than in one that satisfies one only. So, too, if two or more interests which, taken severally, are mutually conflicting, can be synthesized or integrated in one composite resultant interest, then there is more value in the more inclusive satisfaction which may be thus obtained than in the satisfaction of either interest, as existing separately, at the expense of the other. Perry points out that such a fine integration of interests is obtained in the "all-benevolent will" and shows, on this basis, that the greatest value is possible only to the harmoniously developed personality. But he also applies the standard objectively to argue that a harmonious society is superior to a state of conflict between persons, and to support the humanitarian plea for "the greatest good of the greatest number." It is assumed that the principle of inclusiveness does not require that the two interests should be interests of the same subject, but "the object which James and John both like is better than the object which either or both dislike."[1]

But this transition from the subjective standard is only achieved through the ambiguity of words. If X is positively interested in A, i.e. if X values A, then we may say that A has value in the eyes of X. And if A is similarly valued

[1] R. B. Perry: *op. cit.*, p. 646.

by a million people then it has value for the million. Further, since, on this form of the "appreciative" theory of value, the value of an object is its character of being the object of interest, A then has much of this character, much value. In this sense a broadcast concert should be said to have much value because it can be so widely enjoyed. But here the phrase "has much value" merely means "is much valued." Yet it may easily be interpreted to mean "is greatly to be valued," "ought to be valued," or "is very valuable." And the same reason for this fuller meaning might be given, i.e. "because it can be so widely enjoyed." But in this second meaning we have passed from the mere factual notion that the concert is widely valued (is the object of favourable interest by many) to the ethical notion that that which is widely enjoyed ought to be valued, i.e. sustained and promoted. A surreptitious transition has been made from value as a quality to value as a validity, and thus from a statement about something subjective—a private perspective —to its objective implication.

The term "valuable" (and its comparative "more valuable" and the synonym "better") never mean merely that, as a matter of fact, a thing is valued. They mean rather that it is worthy to be valued whether it is valued or not. This significance is revealed, if, for example, I say "Millions of people like to smoke opium in China, so in China opium-smoking is very valuable." No. In China opium-smoking is *widely valued*; but that does not make it *very valuable*. Because Foo and Lee both like opium-smoking that does not make it any "better" than if Foo alone liked it, while Lee and all the rest of the world detested it. And it is just as misleading to say that "The object which James and John both like is better than the object which either or both dislike."[1] Again, it is similarly misusing terms to argue "If to James' interest in pushpin there is added John's

[1] R. B. Perry: *op. cit.*, p. 646.

interest in poetry, there is more value in the world than there was before; pushpin *and* poetry are more valuable than pushpin *or* poetry."[1] Only if the two interests are interests of the same subject can we say that it is more *valuable* to have both. If not then we can say that there is more valu*ing* in the world than there was before, and that pushpin *and* poetry together are more valu*ed* than either pushpin *or* poetry severally.

Most of us would agree that probably a world in which there is more positive valuing, and thus more positive value experience, is a world more to be valued, a better or more valuable world, a world rather to be maintained and developed, than a world in which there is less. But it would be a mistake to assert that it necessarily must be so. On the other hand most people would assert that the little world of classical Attica was intrinsically better than the vast barbarian world of Scythia and Ethiopia—and this conviction is not based on any calculus of relative quantities of positive and negative interests. It is a sheer affirmation of a distinction of scale of values and involves a refusal to believe that the mere fact that a thing is "more valued" necessarily renders it "more valuable." In short, the character of "being valued," or "being an object of interest," does not, *ipso facto*, constitute the "value" of an object, or mean that it is "valuable" for any individual other than one who actually feels a positive interest in that object. The attempt to treat value as an objective character of things, which is simply given to them by the interest attitude adopted toward them by individuals, thus breaks down as soon as we analyse the ambiguities on which its plausibility depends. Professor Perry's elaborate and brilliant thesis does not, after all, yield an objective standard of value, and consequently cannot be regarded as an adequate explanation of our value experience. If a subjective theory of value is

[1] R. B. Perry: *op. cit.*, p. 648.

to find any validities at all it must seek them within the nature of the interested subject itself. How far this type of approach can succeed we shall see as we proceed. An excellent example of it is given us in the theory of Professor Dewitt Parker.

CHAPTER VIII

VALUE AND WILL (*continued*)

As a scholar who has approached the problem of value from the side of Aesthetics rather than Ethics we have a fresh and interesting treatment of these questions from Professor Parker. His theory is more consistently subjectivist than that of Professor Perry except for one feature forced upon him by his studies in Aesthetics—the influence of "form" in value. He clearly recognizes the need of explaining our experiences of obligation and validity, but seeks to derive them from the inner structure of the self rather than from any feature of the objective world. Interests, for him, do not, in any save a metaphorical sense, confer value on objects; the value belongs directly to the interest itself. It includes pleasure, yet is something much more than pleasure. It is defined as "the complex experience of satisfying desire,"[1] and, owing to the imaginative factor, it "pertains not only to the terminus of satisfaction but to the entire process of desire-seeking-fulfilment."[2] The Spinozistic doctrine is upheld that "in no case do we strive for, wish for, long for, or desire anything because we deem it to be good, but, on the other hand, we deem it to be good because we strive for it, wish for it, long for it, or desire it."[3] Yet our values are not a mere welter of satisfactions and dissatisfactions without any system or order. We must therefore recognize certain "dominant systems of interests more inclusive and complex than what are usually called instinct, sentiment, complex, or *Gestalt*, for they include several of these. These systems contain values qualitatively alike."[4] Such are self-

---

[1] D. H. Parker, *Human Values*, p. 26.   [2] *Op. cit.*, p. 410.
[3] Spinoza, *Ethics*, Pt. III, Prop. IX.
[4] D. H. Parker, *Human Values*, p. 45.

preservation of health, comfort, ambition, workmanship, love in its various forms, knowledge, play, art, religion. Motives like hunger and sex are not included in this list "because they lack the normative character peculiar to the major interests or because they are provided for by interests which include them in their scope."[1] And moral values are excluded because all values are moral in the larger sense in so far as they create standards and release imperatives, while "moral values in the limited sense are special values of love and ambition."[2]

But the recognition of about eight "dominant interests" among the multiplicity of our motives is still far from explaining the ordered hierarchy of values in a normal and well-developed personality—and still further from explaining why the ill-balanced personality should often be so acutely conscious of the lack of balance; i.e. the "normative character" of these dominant interests has still to be explained. Part of this explanation is given in the recognition that value experience is affected by certain facts of its structure or form. We are not given the reason why this should be so, but it is stated as an empirical fact and these "principles of form" are carefully enumerated.[3] The principle of "unity in variety" or "organic unity" is that "wherever value exists there is an organization of experience of such a kind that it contains a number of discriminable elements arranged in a pattern, and that these elements, each and all, contribute to the realization of the desire that is the root of the value, and that, finally, if the desire is fully realized, there are no superfluous elements." Second, the principle of "identity in difference . . . asserts that while value usually attaches to a definite object, that object appears in multiple guises"; the theme and its variations in music and the varieties of play within the rules of a game

[1] D. H. Parker: *op. cit.*, p. 47. [2] *Op. cit.*, p. 47.
[3] *Op. cit.* Quotations are all from Ch. IV.

are typical examples. Obviously these first two principles are closely related. Third, the principle of "balance," "a certain equality of opposites," and "since there is always an identity underlying every relation of equality balance may be regarded as a species of 'identity in difference.'" Fourth, "evolution," "the unity of experience which is created in the process of the working out to a conclusion, to fulfilment, of an interest or purpose. The value achieved belongs to the whole process of development," yet in the process the value accumulates, grows, so that it is complete only at the end." Fifth, the principle of "hierarchy." "In any experience of value, not all the distinguishable elements are on the same level; some are focal, others in the fringe, some are accented, others belong to the background; some are more, others less significant; some dominant, others subordinate; and frequently the elements are arranged in an order of relative importance."

Why values should exhibit these characteristics of form does not appear from Professor Parker's theory; and he rightly and emphatically asserts that value is not *merely* a matter of form—that "without desire these forms are empty and valueless." But any theory of value which emphasizes the primacy of interest (or will or conation) in the presentation of value must give a reason for the importance of matters of form. And it should be perfectly clear that no place for the influence of form or structure can be found in any theory which adopts the Spinozistic formula that we deem a thing good *simply* "because we strive for it, wish for it, long for it, or desire it." This theory is too simple to account for the complicated nature of the facts. If that were so then the highest and greatest values would only be matters of simple, straightforward satisfaction—the simpler and more straightforward the better. The glories of the "tragic harmony" of the life that integrates and overcomes and yet accepts the inevitable—the life which

Professor Parker himself extols as the highest good—would be simply inexplicable. Why should value be enhanced by a balance of contrasts, by variations on the theme, by a process of evolution before attaining the goal, by position among other values (hierarchy) if the satisfaction of desire were all that mattered?

Now if value experience is rooted in desire, or will, and yet is not merely a matter of the simple satisfaction of a desire but depends upon, or is enhanced by, certain complexities of structure, we must look for the roots of those complexities of structure in the structure of desire or will itself. These facts of form or structure in value experience are too well established to be simply set aside as too vague to be of importance. Parker has done no more than clearly state facts recognized since the time of Plato. It is, indeed, only in modern times that there has been any strong tendency to regard value as arising from anything else but form. Can we, then, synthesize these two points of view by finding that the form or structure involved is integral to the interests themselves? I think we can. Reflection seems to show that wherever there is value experience there is not merely a single desire involved, but at least two, one primary and more remote and the other subsidiary but more immediate.

Our thesis is this—that *value experience arises as the mutual effect of the operation of a primary and a subsidiary will*, the pursuit of a nearer and a remoter end.[1] It is positive when

[1] This view is also adopted, with certain important differences in interpretation on the part of each, by Professor L. T. Hobhouse in *The Rational Good* and by Professor H. J. Paton in *The Good Will*. Professor Hugo Münsterberg's theory, in his *Philosophie der Werte* (and in the English *Eternal Values*), is also similar, though for him validity is determined by a super-individual will immanent in the self, and value quality is a satisfaction obtained in harmony of action with that will. It should be remembered also that, on our theory, the nature of the values presented in experience depends as much upon the determinate potentialities of the Eternal Object as upon the complexities of will which selectively realize those potentialities in experience.

there is harmony of these two aims, negative when they conflict. There is positive value felt in the satisfaction—or the progressively successful prosecution—of every desire, not merely because it is a satisfaction of that desire, but because every such satisfaction is a contribution to some remoter end (not necessarily actually envisaged), or rather, because the conation involved is, or has been up to the point of satisfaction, working in harmony with a more primary or fundamental form of will. The various kinds and grades of will involved in our different types of value experience we must study in the pages that follow; but first the nature and function of this relationship between the nearer and remoter aim must be made clear.

In the first place we should note that an act of will does not have to be retained in consciousness in order to remain generally directive of activity. Normally, when we set ourselves to any but the briefest and simplest tasks it does not. We temporarily forget the end in attention to the means, and we can pass from stage to stage of a process—especially where the varying stages are familiar—without pausing to think of the ultimate end; yet each subsidiary aim and effort are dominated by that end. In such cases there is satisfaction in the progressive activity, in attaining the end of each subsidiary aim, and in reaching the final goal. And this will be the case even when the final goal is not clearly envisaged from the outset but only defines itself gradually as the activity proceeds—as is often the case in artistic production and play, and as is the case in the naïve sex interest of an uninstructed young person (if there still are such unfortunates), and as must be the case in such instinctive activities as the nest-building of birds.

In the second place we must note the tendency, in any long and complex process, for the subsidiary aims to become independent of the ultimate goal.[1] The very fact that the ultimate goal is either ill-defined in the first place, or forgotten in attention to the means, gives this independence to the subsidiary aims. Further, since the subsidiary aims may themselves involve a number of operations, each successful operation is itself a source of satisfaction (because of the harmony of an immediate and somewhat remoter end), and so the pursuit of a subsidiary aim may be carried beyond what is requisite for its primary purpose, even to the detriment of that more ultimate purpose. But when this is discovered there is a sense of disvalue which tends to supercede the sense of value attached to the further pursuit of the subsidiary aim, and so tends to bring activity into line with the main purpose again. Even where the further aim is ill-defined this tends to be the case, as in artistic construction; we feel our way to what we want by experimentally doing a little of this and a little of that until we find we have the object at its best; the activities of creation and appreciation have not foreseen their end from the beginning, but they have found their way toward it by means of the values experienced at different stages. So, too, in developing our social relationships, our hobbies and many other interests, actual experience of value is our guide to the realization of ends vaguely present, but not explicitly formulated, from the beginning.

Here we see the function of value experience in life. The self is a hierarchy of forms of will which cannot possibly be explicitly defined in idea, but which make their presence felt in experience of value. The impulsive responses to objectives toned with prospective value have their temporary satisfactions, but over and above these temporary satisfactions are larger satisfactions and dissatisfactions which tend to make their appearance whenever the imme-

[1] "Good and evil arise in so far as the one will can be divided against itself."—H. J. Paton: *The Good Will*, p. 122.

VALUE AND WILL

diate efforts (gratifying though they may be in themselves) tend to run counter to the larger aims or forms of will. Neither satisfaction nor dissatisfaction, of course, appears without *some* consciousness of the more ultimate end, of the apparent harmony or disharmony of the immediate effort with it. But the value experience tends to encourage the immediate effort when in harmony and to discourage it when out of harmony; and in both cases it tends to draw attention to the nature of the more ultimate goal. In cases where the ultimate goal is determined by facts in the psychophysical structure that are purely innate it, of course, must at first be quite unconscious, only coming to consciousness as acts are performed (from some other motive) which tend toward its realization. Such acts would be coloured by a distinctive positive value tone which encourages their further pursuit and so leads on to complete realization of the goal. This is certainly the way in which the sex instinct draws the individual on to its consummation. It probably accounts for all the complex instinctive activity of animals. And, though the pursuit of the higher values is not properly described as instinctive (a term which should be confined to interests at the animal level) it is in a very similar way that the ultimate aims here involved gradually define themselves. In those cases, however, where both the nearer and more ultimate end are clearly defined in consciousness the operation of value and disvalue is much plainer. Any act, however pleasant immediately, that is seen to be in conflict with the ultimate goal is recognized as having disvalue; and any act, however disagreeable, that is seen to contribute to the ultimate goal is recognized as valuable.

We can now see the reason for those characteristics of form, that attach to value experience, which Professor Parker has enumerated. They are due to the fact that value always involves this complexity in the operation of will. A subsidiary activity pursues its end with freedom from the constraint of the larger purpose; but as it *apparently* contributes to that purpose or otherwise it *tends* accordingly to bring about experiences of value and disvalue. Value experience therefore involves the existence of a larger purpose and the free movement of a subsidiary purpose or purposes. Here is the secret of all the *formal* characteristics of value—unity in diversity, identity in difference, balance or equality of opposites with its underlying identity, evolution or the working to a fulfilment, hierarchy or orderly distinctions of position and importance. All of these become explicable in the light of the doctrine that for there to be an experience of value there must be an activity which is free to pursue its own end but which only discovers values if, and as, it contributes to some larger end. Value experience then becomes intelligible as Nature's means of directing the free activity of the creature to larger and more ultimate goals which either cannot, at that level, be consciously presented at all in terms of specific meanings or cannot be always kept in mind. As sensa function as a guide to the relations of the external physical object so values function as a guide to the internal forms of will.

It is important, however, to recognize the significance of the two words italicized at the beginning of the last paragraph. Values only *tend* to appear. It is quite possible to be psychically blind to them even though they are genuinely presented to consciousness; the whole psychology of the abnormal abundantly proves this. Secondly, it is the fact that the activity directed by the one end apparently contributes to the more ultimate aim that tends to present the experience of value. The function of value experience is not to direct the subsidiary activity as to *how* to attain its goal. That is the function of intelligence. The function of value is simply to keep the goals of the subsidiary forms of will in harmony with the ultimate or primary.[1] The moral conscience, for example, implies the operation of a certain higher form of will. When, in pursuit of some other goal, we perform actions which are not in harmony with what *appears*, in the present state of our knowledge, to be in line with the fulfilment of the higher goal we *tend* to experience a bad conscience. So, too, having set for ourselves the goal of health, if we do something which we think militates against health it seems to be an act of disvalue, while those actions we *think* are healthy thereby appear to have value.

The *appearance* of value and disvalue is thus a function of the *real* harmony of the forms of will concerned in the activity. Value is experienced when primary and subsidiary will work together, disvalue when they are at cross-purposes. This holds true even when the means willed is *mistakenly* viewed as contributory to the remoter end willed. The meaning of value, as stated above, is not to inform us *how* to achieve our ends, but to inform us when our subsidiary, superficial, and immediate aims are in harmony with the primary, fundamental, and more ultimate aims—aims that often are too deep and broad for specific formulation. This is the sole meaning of values and in this they never deceive us. Every value experience, when thus rightly understood, is absolutely real. Our errors lie in failure to discern higher (or deeper) values which are sometimes present in a situation—psychological blindness—and in misunderstanding of ways and means to the achievement of the more ultimate aims and of the specific conditions that would constitute their realization. In brief, errors in value judgment are due to value blindness, and to misunderstanding of the relation of the value element in experience to other data. But these

[1] As our analysis proceeds it will be shown that in the hierarchy of will the more fundamental or primary forms of will are also the more ultimate or higher. The higher goals are only later in explicit, conscious formulation by the individual; they are determined by the deepest strata of will, basic to the nature of the self.

sources of error cast no doubt on the reality and validity of values in their intrinsic nature.

It is not, however, the mere fact of harmony or conflict of motives, or will, that produces the experience of value. If the motives or interests are on the same level then their conflict does not attach a sense of disvalue to either. If a man wants both to read a book and to play tennis there is a conflict of interests; but neither interest is subsidiary to the other, so neither takes on an appearance of disvalue, though disvalue attaches to the idea of failing to satisfy either. We have not yet examined the question of the nature of the more ultimate aim that gives to such activities as these that value character we call pleasure, but we can take the fact of the pleasure for granted. If the man considers nothing else but the pleasure of the situation he will simply balance his preferences. But he may extend his consideration to other matters. Presently he remembers that on account of the absence of some club members to-day he will be needed to make a four. Tennis now becomes a social obligation, while to stay home and read appears as rather inconsiderate to his friends. The new elements of value and disvalue that thus enter into the situation are due to the fact that the two lines of conduct now appear, the one as in harmony with a certain end recognized as primary or higher, the other as out of harmony with it. Obviously, it is not mere harmony or disharmony in itself that affects value experience—except so far as that involves frustration —but the relation between two different orders or levels of purpose. Value experience reveals some kind of hierarchy among the ends or forms of will within the self. It is to the nature of this hierarchy that we must now give our attention.

Here we again face the "normative" character of value, its character as "validity" and its claim to "objectivity." It is because of this feature of value experience that Professor

Parker restricts his list of the major interests and values in the way above mentioned. These, he says, "give a relative validity to the ordinary rules of good conduct. Moreover, each of the major interests claims the whole of life for its sphere."[1] Thus arise our conflicts of value. "Man has no single morality, no simple conscience." But yet we bring these major conflicts of value under the criticism of a certain higher principle, a value arising from the fact that "the mind is in some sense a whole and not a mere collection of elements." "Personality is therefore no mere fiction, but a fact. It is, moreover, the kind of fact we know of as an interest." "It follows that criticism exists at every level of the stratification of the mind. Each interest is subject to the criticism of the system of which it is a member; even the major interests, as members of the self as a whole, are not exempt. Only the supreme interest is exempt, because there is no further point of view from which criticism of it could proceed." This supreme interest can be no other than "the interest of the self as a whole," and it must judge other interests according to their contribution to it.

Here we have a recognition, then, that there is a hierarchy of interests within the self; and we also have a transition from value considered as the mere process of satisfaction of a desire to an explanation of the "normative" character of value experience as a criticism which the more inclusive, higher-level interests pass upon the lower. The consequent scale of values is ultimately egoistic, for altruism only enters into the system through the fact that one of the eight major interests is love, in its various forms. And this has to be made subservient to the interest of the self as a whole. We shall raise the question later whether this can be a sufficient account of our highest moral experience. For the present we wish to stress two other objections to this exposition.

[1] D. H. Parker: *op. cit.*, Chapter v. The other quotations following are from the same chapter.

In the first place it simply cannot do justice to the objective character of our value experience. On this view the conviction we have about every question of validity, that others ought to share our view, is sheer illusion. Normative questions are merely questions of the interest of the individual self as a whole. There can be no question as to whether one object of art is really more beautiful than another. Its value for each of us simply depends upon the satisfactions our particular kind of personality can obtain from it. The only principles for criticism of a work of art are those "of success, of co-operation of elements within a whole, of adequacy to the total self."[1] On this theory there could be no grounds for any effort to raise the standard of artistic appreciation of the population. Indeed, it would be better, it would seem, to cultivate a common level of taste which could be universally satisfied to the full by the cinema and popular radio music! Such a conclusion the author of the theory and every other lover of the beautiful would, I am sure, hasten to repudiate. Yet how can it be logically escaped if there is *no standard of the beautiful outside the private individual self, no higher standard for anything than the interest of the self as a whole?*

Our second criticism of this view-point is that its view of the hierarchy of interests, or of will, is altogether inadequate in that it assumes that the more inclusive interests may be built up on the basis of the less inclusive. This is a fallacy all too common among psychologists and philosophers, and is due to thinking of mind on the analogy of a material structure. In material structures the larger units are made up of the smaller. One begins with the less inclusive and by a process of composition passes to the more inclusive. But in thought and volition the process is reversed. One begins with the general and passes by a process of analysis to the particular. Memory is, of course, a process of accu-

---

[1] D. H. Parker: *op. cit.*, p. 338.

mulation of particulars. Therein it reveals its dependence upon the physical. But thinking is not. Even the passage from observation of numerous particulars to thought of them as a class is fundamentally a process of analysis which, from the individual wholes, derives their common characters and defines them accordingly; and the formation of a general law is similar in the movement of the mind involved. So, too, with will. Every new volition is a specification of, or a means to, a pre-existing purpose or conative tendency. We never dream of looking for the explanation of any specific effort in any other way—unless we are thinking of its physical occasion.

How, then, can "dominant systems of interests" be "compounded out of simpler responses," as Psychology is alleged to have shown?[1] We may agree that there are certain native interests of an appetitive or instinctive nature, such as control the desires for food and drink, for the avoidance of pain and danger, for constructive and social activity, for play, etc. But the desire for health is not a mere combination of these. It is consciously formed out of recognition that it is necessary to a great variety of purposes—indeed to most of our other purposes. But that means that instead of being a dominant interest it is a means to many interests; and when we make one particular satisfaction subservient to health we really only apply the principle of inclusiveness; we prefer not to sacrifice a large number of permanent interests to this temporary satisfaction. The other major interests in Parker's list are motives recognized as native by Professor McDougall and many other psychologists either as instinctive or as native propensities of a very general kind. The only exceptions are art and religion, with which we shall deal later. And native propensities, or instincts, of this type must be recognized as specializations of the fundamental conative tendency of the living organism, the effort

[1] D. H. Parker: *op. cit.*, p. 45.

to maintain its own organic activity. They have been developed as specific tendencies toward specific types of end through the long history of racial evolution; and the value experience of pleasure is presented in their successful operation because such activity is in harmony with the still more fundamental, primary, or inclusive form of will from which they are derived. Value is thus plainly due, here, to the harmonious operation of primary and subsidiary forms of will rooted in the psycho-physical structure of the organism.

What then of the supreme interest—"the interest of the self as a whole"? Is this merely a composite of the eight or more major interests? Each of these interests tends to absorb the whole activity of the personality if no check is put upon it by the others or by something higher. Is the interest of the whole simply a systematic balance of interests? Is there not a positive interest in personal self-development, not merely a system of frustrations? Yet the mere putting together of a number of more or less conflicting interests could only produce frustrations. There could be no positive value experience arise from making the pursuit of one of these ends conform to conditions which did not conflict with the other interests for there would be no satisfaction gained, only one satisfaction partly lost and others saved from subsequent loss. The fact that there is a sense of positive value in such self-control shows that there is a positive interest of the self as a whole which is more than a mere negative balance of contending forces. Is this, then, something derived consciously from other interests as is the interest in health? Is it merely that we *see* that a certain order and balance of motives within the personality is best calculated to the greatest fulfilment of all our desires and so seek to maintain it; i.e. is the interest of the self as a whole a mere formulation of a hedonic calculus? If so then it is not a higher or dominant interest, but merely a means that serves many interests, like health.

But there are two decisive objections to such an explanation of this higher (I do not say "supreme") interest. One is that it is certainly not so egoistic as it would be if arrived at in that way, love being only one of a number of interests to be integrated and universal love an extremely mild one at that! The other objection is that long before such a notion could be formulated by explicit thought processes the values due to the presence of this interest are felt. We feel our way to a formulation of the notion of what constitutes the good of the self as a whole by reason of a value experience that is felt as integration is achieved and as the capacities for freer and wider self-expression are developed. The "interest" in cultivation of self-harmonious powers of expression and in the use of those powers in ways that call forth the spontaneous, but controlled, expression of native tendencies is something that is there from the beginning, that merely has to become explicitly recognized and defined. It does not have to be created or formulated as a deduction, i.e. as a means observed to be necessary to other ends. Still less does it just grow as a kind of cumulative effect of conflicting impulses.

From this fundamental and primary interest of the self as a whole—the earliest and most general of all interests of the individual—all less general interests (specific conative tendencies, or forms of will) may be regarded as derived. Their specific formulation is either innately determined or derived more or less consciously during the life history of the individual, either directly from the primary will or mediately through the subsidiary interests. The primary principle of conation may be expressed by saying that "every living organism, so long as it is conscious, constantly seeks to express itself in ever changing activity,"[1] or again, that "the essential nature of the process of living (from the standpoint of the finite consciousness) is to be a finite centre

[1] A. C. Garnett: *The Mind in Action*.

of experience ever enlarging its grasp or penetration of the infinite reality in the midst of which it dwells."[1] It is from an apparent harmony and disharmony with this ultimate individual interest, or form of will, that all our higher value experiences (all save the very highest) are derived, as our remaining chapters will show. And it is this ultimate form of the individual will that gives its character of validity or invalidity, directly or indirectly, to all our value experience, even in the lower ranges of the scale, though it itself, as we shall see, becomes subsidiary to a form of will that, at the loftiest level, transcends the values of the individual.

This primal, non-specific volitional tendency is readily recognized by popular thought, for it is felt in all our restlessness and in our enjoyment of play and hatred of enforced inactivity. Man is never content to do nothing. The mind is perpetually active and life cannot long stay still. Nor can this urge be attributed to any specific impulse of appetite or instinct, for it is precisely when there is no stimulus to activity that we go out to seek a stimulus—to find something to do, some means of personal self-expression. Many philosophers have recognized the importance of this fact, although, owing to pre-occupation with either cognition or material and mechanical processes, its significance has escaped the majority. The psycho-analysts found in it the key to the understanding of neurosis, although they have tended to give it very one-sided interpretations. More recently Professor Hocking has made it, under the name of the "will to power," the key to his interpretation of human nature, though, unfortunately, not recognizing that it cannot be regarded as supreme.[2]

Psychologists, while one cannot say they have not recognized the fact, have, however, been slow to see its importance. The reason for this, however, is not far to seek. In itself it is the vaguest and apparently least important of

[1] A. C. Garnett: *op. cit.*   [2] W. E. Hocking: *Human Nature and Its Remaking.*

VALUE AND WILL 219

tendencies. It is significant for the understanding of play, but of little else until we come to the higher forms of value experience; and these Psychology has been inclined to leave to the study of philosophers. Further, Psychology, being a young science, has not ventured as yet to assert its right to, and need of, certain categories of its own, such as those which many biologists have recently insisted must be recognized in their own field, and such as all biologists employ, whether explicitly recognizing the fact or not. Psychology has simply taken over its categories from biology and has endeavoured to interpret behaviour in physico-chemical terms *plus* such non-chemical concepts as those of the "organism" and the "struggle for existence" which were already in use in the biological sciences. In particular the affective-volitional life has always been interpreted as tending merely toward the maintenance of the individual and the species. The organism is conceived as initially uninterested so long as nothing occurs to disturb its organic equilibrium, and its interests are all conceived as originally directed solely towards those adjustments which tend to ensure the survival of individual and species. The fact that our principle has received so little attention from psychologists is therefore not surprising and constitutes no reason why we should hesitate to give it recognition.

This fundamental will to activity is not, however, entirely vague and devoid of character. Its demand is for any activity rather than none; it is quite impossible for the mind to be conscious and yet entirely inactive. But its demand is also for an activity having two specific characteristics; (*a*) it must be constantly directed upon some new object; (*b*) it must be self-harmonious. The first characteristic reveals itself, in particular, in two well-recognized facts. First, that attention requires a constant change of object. Spontaneous attention wanders naturally from one object to another, or from one feature of its object to another, constantly eliciting something fresh. Voluntary attention can only be held to a single object in so far as it can constantly elicit new items or relations within or about that object. Secondly, that there is no satisfaction in the mere monotonous repetition of a single act. It is not merely activity we want, but something new to do. A rhythmical repetition of an act may create a satisfying sense of harmony providing there is variety within the rhythmical series, but the same rhythmical series soon fails to satisfy unless we can introduce variations upon the theme; indeed, once a series has become familiar as a whole, so that the part means the whole, it becomes unsatisfactory and monotonous to go on repeating it without variations. The demand for something new in the object is *constant* through all activity.

The second requirement for satisfying activity is not quite so obvious but of very great importance. Most of our activity is, of course, directed to the attainment of specific ends and, if not self-harmonious, tends, therefore, to be ineffective and self-defeating. This, in itself, seems sufficient explanation of the unsatisfying character of such activity. But even where no particular aim is in view, as in pure play, non-practical thinking and aesthetic activity, the same principle is evident. We find no satisfaction in activity that is not self-harmonious. We want variety. But we must have an internal harmony of our activity through it all. This demand of the finite self for internal harmony, we shall see, provides the principal key to the understanding of the value character of the theoretical, also to aesthetic, and most of our moral, values. These higher forms of value become intelligible as qualities of experience presented when the will to achievement of a particular objective is in apparent harmony with this most general ultimate or primary will of the finite self—its will to activity that shall be ever new and always self-harmonious. And the demands of the values presented through harmony and disharmony with this higher will, we shall see, account for most, but not quite all, of the validities or obligations in our value experience.

If it be objected that many people, having reached maturity, seem to settle contentedly into a routine that contains little or nothing new the answer is that, having reached the limit of their capacities, they are now fully occupied with the mere problem of self-maintenance. The finite self is not capable of limitless expansion. The task of maintaining life at the limit of a finite capacity is sufficiently absorbing. A routine is never quite the same and the constant recovery of what is constantly being lost is at this stage equivalent to the discovery of the new. Further, if the personality is well integrated and the environment suitable, activity becomes very self-harmonious, so that the most satisfying value experiences of life often come after maturity.

Before further pursuing this investigation of the higher values, however, we must show that our formula applies to the lower. Even at the level of sensory pleasure the explanation appears to hold good. There are, of course, many exceptions to the general rule that pleasant sensations are wholesome and unpleasant ones injurious; but so far as the immediate vital activity of the organ affected by the stimulus is concerned the principle is sound.[1] Now we cannot, of course, introspectively discover any form of will directed to the maintenance of efficient functioning of the end organs of sense. But if our earlier interpretation of the nature of life and of organic processes is accepted then some such feature of vital structure must be recognized. The processes involved are neither conative, nor mechanical, but may be described as hormic.[2] Sensory pleasure may then be understood as arising from a harmonious operation of primary

---

[1] G. F. Stout: *Manual of Psychology* (Fourth Edition), pp. 388–9.
[2] A term introduced by Professor T. P. Nunn and used by Professor McDougall and others for organic processes which are teleological in character but not necessarily conscious.

and subsidiary hormic tendencies in the activity of a sense organ consequent upon stimulation. This then brings our interpretation of hedonic tone in sensation into line with the explanation of pleasure and other forms of value experience at higher levels. It does not constitute a proof of such an explanation of sensory pleasure, but it shows that it need not be regarded as an exception to the general explanation of value experience which would cast doubt on the wider principle.

At the level of the simple physical pleasures of appetite the co-operation of the will-to-the-end and the will-to-the-means (primary and subsidiary forms of will) is clear. The stimulus creates a vague want and each particular purposive act that appears to tend to fulfilment of the want tends to present an experience of pleasure; in so far as it appears to be frustrated or to fail the experience is not pleasant. The pleasure is not found in the final condition of satisfaction, except so far as the further activity of contemplating the past activity may be pleasant, or in that there may be sensory pleasure in sheer rest after a period of intense activity. The pleasure is found chiefly in the process of pursuit, i.e. during the time when the dual process of will or conation is in harmonious operation. This generally recognized and yet paradoxical feature of our pleasure experience is thus made intelligible by our formula for the explanation of value.

At the somewhat higher levels of desire the same principles are found to apply. Even the pursuit of a goal such as escape from danger or the pugnacious destruction of an opponent's power, though fear and anger are in themselves unpleasant emotional experiences, takes on a pleasurable tone when the activities involved in the successive means to the end are being successfully pursued. Still greater, of course, are the unalloyed pleasures of pursuit where the emotional tone itself is pleasant as in successful pursuit of the goals of social and family life. An instructive case in this connection is that of competitive play. There is a certain amount of displeasure in playing a losing game because the goal set is not being progressively attained. Yet the normal sportsman finds that there is still a balance of pleasure. This is often, certainly, no sensory pleasure for there may be considerable fatigue and painful strain. It is a pleasure of pursuit; but in what does the satisfaction lie? Here our recognition of the general will to activity enables us to find an explanation. So long as the various conative processes involved are in harmony with this primary implicit aim the experience is pleasant; i.e. it is still a pleasant game if activity is being directed toward constantly fresh objectives with abundant variety in the situations and so long as the player can maintain a self-harmonious set of activities. It is monotonous and discordant activities that spoil a game. It is the smooth working of systematic efforts through an abundance of novel situations that give it zest. A game like that is worth while whether we win or lose.[1]

In our *reflective reconsideration* of a value experience, also, it can readily be shown that the question at issue is always

[1] Though the value experience of play depends directly on this ultimate form of the individual will it is not felt as higher than the values dependent on subsidiary biological interests. This exception to the general rule (see below), that the values presented by the more ultimate forms in the hierarchy of will are felt as higher, is intelligible in view of the fact that pure play (activity for activity's sake) lacks the purposive character of complete conative activity. Aimless activity is better than none, but it is not practical self-expression in the full sense. That requires purpose. For this reason we invent forms of play which stimulate natural interests and so introduce purpose into it, e.g. hunting and competitive games and exhibitions of skill. The pleasure is then derived from a double source. Pure, aimless play is weak in pleasure and low in the scale of value simply because it is aimless, and so only incomplete self-expression. Of the higher forms of play it is not felt that their value is *lower* than that of the biologically useful activities, only that, because the latter, in their effects, are inclusive of so many other values, they usually are more important. When play becomes imaginative, and therefore aesthetic, it belongs distinctly to the higher values. Cf. Chapter x.

that of whether the nearer and remoter ends concerned were really in harmony or only apparently so, and whether the remoter end, with which the nearer was in apparent harmony, was itself in harmony with other more important ends, so that there should be no disharmony, even to the most ultimate end concerned. Under such re-examination the appearance of value which an experience had at first worn may be entirely changed, or value may be seen to reside in an experience where it was not at first recognized. We then regard the later and more reflective estimate, in which account is taken of the more ultimate ends, as the true one. At each stage of such a consideration of value it is the *apparent* harmony of nearer and remoter ends that gives to the acts or objects concerned their apparent character of value. But at each stage it is because this apparent harmony is believed to be real and ultimate that the existence of the value is asserted as a fact.

In all our practical evaluations, therefore, and in all our experiences of pleasure, we see that what is involved is the harmonious operation of primary and subsidiary forms of will. We make this the test of the implications of validity or obligation in our qualitative experiences of value. And we find that it is the existence of such harmony that tends to present the positive qualitative character of value in all the lower forms of value experience. The study of these value qualities, as well as such questions of validity as arise on the lower level, has shown that value is always concerned with the harmony of the more immediate with the more ultimate volitions, aims, or efforts. Sometimes the more ultimate aim is one set by one of the major biological tendencies, interests, or instincts (if that use of the term be allowed); sometimes it is some higher, more reflectively developed aim such as health, or personal efficiency, or self-development, or some sentiment of love or ambition. Sometimes it is that most general and fundamental of all the forms of our will, the will to continuous active life, self-harmonious and ever-varied.

As already suggested it is to this fundamental form of the will of the finite individual that most of our higher value experience, both as quality and validity, is due—as quality because its implicit presence in all our activity tends to give a peculiar value tone to that experience, and as validity because the presentation of this higher value always constitutes a demand upon the subsidiary volition also concerned. Thus every act tends to have its higher value, as good or bad, beautiful or ugly, true or false—a character we tend to project upon the object or the specific deed with which the will is concerned.

Every such value character presents its demand upon the will, requiring acknowledgment that this is as it ought to be or as it ought not to be. The validity or obligation is thus the demand of the higher, primary, more ultimate form of will upon the immediate and subsidiary—a demand made in accord with the appearances that enter into the situation. But though relevant only to the appearances its claim is felt as absolute. It would be a repudiation of the most characteristic feature of our value experience to deny that claim. Yet we must either deny it or show that this subjective standard of good and evil thus presented, though tentative and erring so far as its reference to specific deeds and objects is concerned, is yet a guide, and our only guide, to the realization of the highest good; i.e. that it is by faithful following of the subjective standard, in the light of a careful and critical examination of its apparent implications, that we find our way to standards of value that are objective or valid for all—and to our own highest good. If we can show this we shall not only have explained our value experience, but also vindicated its validity.

Now the ultimate will of the finite individual—the will to an activity that is self-harmonious and constantly new—

is both cognitive and practical in its operation. It is fulfilled through activity in the seeking of knowledge, through exercise of the imagination, and through the practical activity of the individual in moulding the malleable processes of the world around him. It thus affects our intellectual, aesthetic, and moral values. It cannot explain our highest moral experience but it nevertheless, as we shall see, carries us far. We shall find that it is the root of most, but not all, of our fixed beliefs about values and, when understood, provides us with a standard for criticizing them. If it were our ultimate standard then we should never have risen beyond a fundamental egoism. Professor Dewey speaks as though it were the ultimate criterion of value when he mentions "the one value of the worth of discovering the possibilities of the actual and striving to realize them."[1] It is a welcome surprise to receive this much confirmation of what we also regard as the source of most of our validities, coming, as it does, from one who is accustomed to repudiate all absolute standards. The greatness of great men is not seldom shown in their inconsistencies! It is this standard, so clearly recognized in an unexpected quarter, that we shall see emerge from our study of truth, beauty, and the lower form of the moral conscience.

But already the place and function of value in the world is becoming clear, and the analogy between it and sense is helpful. The sensory continuum reveals its potentialities in our experience as it is refracted by those processes which begin in the physical world and end in the complex response of mental activity; and they serve as a guide to the subject in its reaction to the physical world, simplifying and revealing complexities of that world beyond any possibility of the subject's immediate grasp. So, too, value is refracted in the mutual interaction of the complex forms of will within the

[1] John Dewey: *The Quest for Certainty*, p. 304 (George Allen & Unwin Ltd.).

structure of the self and serves as a guide to that conative process in pursuit of an immediate end. Attention tends to be confined to this immediate end; but the value experience, making its demand upon the conative tendency thus dominating immediate activity, tends to direct it in harmony with the more ultimate end. Because of the complexity of the object and so of possible lines of action, and because the self contains a hierarchy of forms of will, the values presented are sometimes conflicting in their demands. But where this occurs those values due to the effective presence of the higher forms of will are recognized as higher values; it is to them that the sense of higher obligation attaches.

This sense of obligation to the value highest in the scale is, as we saw in an earlier chapter, not an all-powerful influence on the will; the appeal of lower values (which, if it were not for the presence of the higher, would also appear as valid, validity attaching to the highest) may be stronger on account of their intensity, etc. Further, reflection may show that there are greater, and higher or equally high, values involved in the present pursuit of objectives immediately characterized only by lower values. For these objectives may be means to the higher. This is the case with the attention we must necessarily give to many economic concerns at the cost of devotion to intellectual or artistic pursuits. The whole process is very intricate, but the general principles are clear. Value experience, as mere unreflectively experienced quality, functions as a guide and restraint tending to keep the immediate and lower forms of volition in harmony with the more ultimate and higher, which tend to be forgotten even if they have ever been more than vaguely implicit. At the higher level of *contemplation* of value experience its demand upon the will is explicitly acknowledged; and its distinctions of degree and scale and implication are the ground of our recognition of obligation and validity.

CHAPTER IX

TRUTH

IN attempting to define the conditions of the value experience arising in our cognitive activity—the value we describe as truth—it will not be necessary to engage in a dialectical discussion of the various theories of truth. Our problem is to give an account of the facts that will do justice to the experience studied; and the great problem here, as in the whole realm of values, is to vindicate the claim of the subjective appearance of value to be faithfully and intelligently followed as guide to values that are objectively real. In our general study of values, and particularly of the lower values or pleasures, we found that value experience arises in the harmonious operation of primary and subsidiary forms of will, the harmonious pursuit of nearer and remoter ends; and the most ultimate or fundamental of these, we have suggested, is the will to an impact of the self upon the world in self-harmonious activity, continuously extending its cognitive grasp of reality and purposive moulding of its malleable features. This is a limitless objective, but none the less tangible. We must ask ourselves (1) does the cognitive aspect of such a goal really define the ultimate end of our intellectual activity, and (2) does the harmony of cognitive activity with this end provide an adequate account of the value character of the theoretical? It is merely incidental to this inquiry that we shall be led to give a definition of the criteria of truth. An answer to the first question, however, will involve a brief analysis of the cognitive process.

Now cognition involves, in the first place, the apprehension of objects. But the mere presence of one or more of these objects to the knowing subject does not constitute the complete cognitive act. No cognitive object is ever merely present to the subject. As Professor Stout says, "Our transient experiences as they come and go can never be complete objects of thought. In thinking of them we think something about them, 'that they exist,' or are felt or are of such a nature."[1] In brief, every complete act of cognition involves a judgment. But even a judgment does not stand alone as an isolated cognitive act. The cognitive process is a continuous activity and every judgment is a part of a continuous accretion of knowledge; i.e. the new judgment needs to be accepted with belief as an addition to a growing whole of knowledge. Thus the complete act of cognition involves three distinguishable phases: (a) the simple experience of the object, (b) the formation of a judgment in which this object is a term, (c) the acceptance of this judgment (or its rejection) as a constituent element of a whole of knowledge, i.e. its acceptance as true.

Not every judgment, of course, can be accepted as an addition to the growing whole of knowledge. Two judgments that are seen to be contradictory cannot, while the contradiction is recognized, both be accepted as elements in a single whole of knowledge. To do so is simply a psychological impossibility; and in this sense the logical principle of non-contradiction must be accepted as a "law of thought," that is, as a regulative principle expressive of the relations necessarily holding between events. It is a requirement rooted in the ultimate form of will that activity shall be self-harmonious. If, then, the new judgment is observed to be contradicted by a judgment already held, then one of the two must be rejected. If the new judgment is not accepted, then its contradictory is accepted; and perhaps also some reformulated variant of the new judgment, which is not seen to contradict any judgment already held, is also accepted.

This cognitive activity, more or less complete, is con-

[1] G. F. Stout: *Manual of Psychology* (Fourth Edition), p. 101.

tinuous with the waking consciousness. It may be variously directed by different conative factors, such as the stimulation of a special curiosity; but it is not dependent upon any specific urge. It is a general and permanent feature of consciousness that the subject should be cognitively related to its object in this active way, eliciting explicit awareness of one new element after another in its world of objects, formulating and accepting or rejecting new judgments, and thus continuously expanding its cognitive grasp of that objective world with which it, the subject, finds itself confronted.

The span of its explicit consciousness being relatively small the subject endeavours (with more or less success) to keep past experience available to explicit recognition in the form of acquired meaning and memory. The future, lying beyond the span of present consciousness, it seeks to bring within that content in the form of expectations or anticipations of its own, or other people's, or some hypothetical being's experience. The past that has never entered its own consciousness it seeks to reconstruct hypothetically as an imagined scheme of experiences that some other subjects have had, or that it might itself have had in certain conditions, had it been then present. Even that which lies beyond all possibility of experience by any such subject as itself (such as the inner structure of the atom, or the process of formation of the solar system) it seeks to bring within its cognitive content in a form interpretable (because only thus intelligible) in terms of an imaginary subject under certain imaginary conditions. Thus does the cognitive activity of the human subject seek to gather within its cognitive grasp or content all the present, past and future actualities, and even all the mere possibilities and potentialities of its objective world. It builds up and fills out continuously its body of judgments, which we call knowledge, going far beyond all that might minister to any ulterior end, so that one is driven to the conclusion that, for the human subject, the increase of knowledge is an end in itself. And, though this end is not so strongly manifest in some human beings as in others, and in many is pursued much less than are the practical ends, yet it may be said with some confidence to be manifested in some degree by all. At least it is so widely manifest as to justify us in finding in it the basis of the equally widespread valuation of truth.

This, then, is the remote, the ultimate, form of will operative in our cognitive activity. It is the operation of this will that gives to the acquisition or maintenance of any item of apparent knowledge or truth its character of value experience. The more clearly and intensely this ultimate end of cognition is present to consciousness, or has been effective in the shaping of habitual mental attitudes, and the more important appears to be the bearing of the particular item of knowledge concerned upon this ultimate understanding of reality, the more vividly is the value of truth appreciated. The immediate or primary end in any cognitive act is confined to the elucidation of the particular object or problem before the mind. Some judgment about it must be formed and accepted, and for this a certain analysis and synthesis is required. There is a certain pleasure and satisfaction in all such intellectual activity; and if the judgments serve some practical end, as they usually do, there is a further sense of value (practical value) due to this harmony of ends. But whether there is any practical value in the judgment or not, by reason of its harmony with other judgments, it can be accepted as a contribution to knowledge, there is attached to it that further sense of value which we call truth. The immediate will to the formation of a particular judgment, the elucidation of a particular fact, has operated in harmony with the remote end (probably not explicitly thought of in connection with it) of the further cognitive grasp of the real world. And this harmony of primary and subsidiary forms of will gives its peculiar value *quale* to the experience.

Now the value experience we call enjoyment of truth does not necessarily indicate that the judgment thus believed to be true really is true, i.e. constitutes a genuine cognitive grasp of reality. The value is a quality that is experienced because certain of the ends operative in mental activity have co-operated in a certain way. Because of this quality the judgment concerned is felt as true. And men have laid down their lives for the value they experienced in believing errors which they felt as true. What the individual then has is a private view of "truth-value."[1] But this private view is seen through the perspective of a set of judgments accepted after insufficient testing, some of which are not a genuine cognitive grasp of reality.

The private view of "truth-value" may be called the *subjective criterion* of truth—the criterion of immediate personal experience being always subjective. But when we speak to each other of the truth of certain propositions we mean, not merely that we have a certain private value-experience in contemplating those propositions, but that they express a genuine cognitive grasp of reality. This we may call the *objective standard* of truth. As this objective standard is the only standard that can be in dispute, or be communicated, between two different persons, it is always this standard that we refer to when we say a proposition is true. The relation between the objective standard and the actual experience of "truth-value" is this: that when we have experience of "truth-value" we always believe the proposition concerned is in accord with the objective standard; and a proposition that is in accord with the objective standard of truth is, we always believe, one which, properly

[1] The quotation marks are used in referring to the subjective value experience because the simple term *truth* always implies objective validity.

understood, must possess the character of "truth-value" for every mind in which sufficient relevant judgments are present and are also in accord with the objective standard; and we believe that this must continue to be the case however the volume of relevant, objectively valid knowledge grows.

Truth, then, may be provisionally defined as that character of judgment which constitutes it, when accepted, a contribution to our cognitive grasp of our world. The *experience of "truth-value"* occurs when the will to the immediate end of cognitive activity, the acceptance of a particular judgment, works in harmony with the ultimate aim of all cognition, the cognitive grasp of our world. This is our *criterion* of truth. It is immediately experienced. But it is a subjective criterion in the sense that it is describable only in terms of the way in which objects appear to a particular subject. The *ultimate aim of truth-seeking* is the cognitive grasp of our world. This is the *standard* of truth—that which truth must measure up to to be true. It is an ideal standard, not something immediately experienced, and so cannot act as a criterion.[1] But it is objective, in the sense that it is describable in terms of relations between real events, open, under certain conditions, to the experience of all.

Now let us proceed with the analysis. As stated, the ultimate end of the cognitive effort is to build up a larger and larger body of judgments about terms given in the objective world, tending to gather the whole of that world, including all its implications and potentialities, in some form, into the cognitive content. But this end is pursued under the guidance of two checks, one positive and one negative. The negative check we have already mentioned. It is that of the impossibility of the subject's accepting two contradictory judgments while the contradiction between

[1] By "criterion" I mean a means of testing whether anything is in accord with a "standard." A "standard" may be conceptually definable but not empirically available as a "criterion," e.g. the straight line.

them is explicitly known. It is true that we can think two contradictory judgments at the same time and know the contradiction; but we cannot *accept* them both. It is also true that we can accept them without observing the contradiction, though the more often they are thought of together the more likely is the contradiction to be noticed and thus one of them rejected. And it is true that we can accept one at one time and another at another time, although they are known to be contradictory. But the more systematically we compare one judgment with another and think our judgments together the more likely are we to reject permanently one or the other. This check therefore operates to exclude certain judgments from our structure of knowledge, and the more industrious we are in gathering new judgments into our structure and forming judgments of critical comparison between our judgments the more effectively does the check operate.

The other and positive check lies in the fact that the terms of our present awareness are largely thrust upon us and we cannot escape from them, while, at the same time, past experience, for the most part, determines the meaning given to present experience. Thus a large proportion of the judgments we make is forced upon us by experience. Our making and our accepting them and our inability (often) to reject them are due to force of circumstances and to the psychological laws of our nature. Even a psychopath cannot entirely ignore all facts in building up his fanciful world. Much less can a normal mind. Here, then, we have a positive factor guiding and acting as a check upon the process of our building up of that body of judgments we call our knowledge. Many of those judgments we are forced to make and we cannot reject. If, therefore, they are found to conflict with any previously formed judgment, or if any later judgment is found to conflict with them, then, so long as these forced judgments are thought of and their opposition to the other judgments is noticed, those other judgments cannot be accepted. It is in these judgments forced upon us by experience, therefore, that a rigid foundation is laid for the structure we call knowledge. Any judgment which is not seen to be contradicted by any judgment in the structure may be accepted. But when two judgments are found to be in conflict, then, if the decision is left to processes of thought, the implications of all the judgments concerned are worked out until one is found to imply the rejection of one of our inescapable judgments arising from experience. It is then rejected. And if no such result can be reached then each judgment is held in abeyance, perhaps tentatively applied, but not confidently accepted. In brief, no two judgments can both be accepted as satisfying the ultimate end of cognition, the cognitive grasp of reality, the end which dominates the experience of truth-value, if those two judgments are seen to be contradictory.

It is, of course, only a very small part of our world that can be actually experienced at any one time, or, indeed, in any human lifetime. But it is the function of thought to transcend these limits. This it does in the formation of expectations of experience, and these expectations are always more or less conditional. The judgment "It moves," for example, may be a simple formulation in thought of an actual experience. It may, however, refer to an object or a movement which is not now experienced, but which will, in due course, necessarily be experienced. Or it may refer to a movement which may be experienced only under certain conditions. Or it may refer to a movement which cannot be actually experienced at all. In the first instance it is not immediately obvious that any element of expectation is necessarily involved, and we must return shortly to the discussion of this case. In the second instance the judgment expresses an expectation of actual experience under the sole condition of the continued existence of the individual and the world order in which he finds himself. In the third instance there may be no expectations of any actual experience of movement on the part of the individual making the judgment; yet the judgment does express an expectation that *under certain conditions* a movement may be experienced. In the last instance we are still further from any expectation of *actual* experience of movement, as when a physicist speaks of movements within the atom. But the assertion of movement is still only intelligible as expressing the expectation that under certain unrealizable, hypothetical conditions, movement *would* be experienced.

In the last three cases, therefore, the form in which the cognitive act grasps its object is, quite evidently, that of an expectation of experience. In these cases, to say that the proposition is true is to say that, under the stated or implied conditions, the expectations expressed by the judgment would be realized. Truth is the agreement of the expectation of experience expressed or implied in the judgment with the actual or possible realization of such experience under the conditions expressed or implied in the judgment.

But what of the truth of judgments of the first type? Here the judgment does not seem, at first sight, to express an expectation of experience, but simply to perform upon the lived experience certain acts of analysis and synthesis. It formulates in thought an experience actually present. But closer inspection of this process will show that all formulation of experience in thought includes the formulation of expectations regarding that experience. It is this that is involved in the fact that we never simply think an object, but always think something about it. Every meaning involves expectations. This will become clear if, instead of the judgment "It moves," we take the judgment "It falls," and suppose that the judgment refers to a heavy column overhead. That this simple formulation in thought of an experience actually present is fraught with expectations becomes immediately apparent in the behaviour which follows upon this mental grasp of the situation. So, too, with the judgment "It moves." It has no meaning at all apart from the expectations of continuation and variation of experience involved in it. And the judgment thus formulated can be accepted with belief, i.e. accepted as an addition to the stock of knowledge, only so long as it is not found to conflict with other accepted judgments. And this means that the expectations involved in, or necessarily aroused by, the formation of the judgment must be in agreement with all judgments imposed upon the mind by experience. So here again the truth of the judgment consists in the agreement of the expectations of experience expressed or implied in the judgment with the actual or possible realization of such experience under the conditions expressed or implied in the judgment.

In all types of judgment about matters of present fact, then, truth consists in this sort of agreement between expectation and realization. The same will readily enough be seen to be the case with judgments about the future. With regard to judgments about the past, however, the position is not quite so clear. But the difficulty here is only parallel with that regarding statements about matters which it is impossible to experience. The expectations involved in such statements are hypothetical and conditional. When I say that William the Conqueror won the Battle of Hastings in 1066, I express the belief or expectation that a person present at a certain place near Hastings on a certain day in 1066 would have been able to observe certain events. The statement is true if, under the implied conditions, the implied experience would have been realized. Thus, here too, truth means the same kind of agreement of expectation with realization, and the cognitive aim is seen in every case to be the gathering within its content, in the form of experience and expectation, of ever more and more of its objective world. The objective standard of truth may therefore be more closely defined as the agreement of the actual and conditional expectations of experience implied in a judgment with the realization of that experience under the conditions implied.

Now if this be what is meant when we say that a judgment is true, then we are able to point to a certain positive basis for that body of judgments we call our knowledge. The truth of a judgment can be known when its expectations are actually realized in experience. We actually do have the experience of knowing truths when and as our judgments are demonstrated, our expectations realized. This is not to say that the judgment is self-evidently true. It is not. It is proved by experience. Though the judgment always involves an expectation, and though its fulfilment must always lie temporarily beyond it, yet, because we live in a "specious present," a duration, and not in an infinitesimal instant, expectation and realization can be experienced in the one living moment. We actually have experience of the realization of present expectations. Indeed, most of our experience is of this character. It does not come as a surprise, but as expected. The judgment and its proof can thus be cognized together. And in so cognizing them we may have an experience of indubitable truth. Where this proof by experience is possible we have an *objective criterion* of truth in the sense that it is describable in terms of objective, or real, events, open, under certain conditions, to the experience of all. But this type of truth-experience is a very fleeting one. It cannot last for more than a part of one pulse of experience, one specious present. It lasts only while the judgment passes from "not now, but still present" to "not present, but past." No such judgment can be taken and made the basis (while still retaining its certainty) of a further series of judgments of any considerable extent. For while the further series based upon it is being formulated it fades into the past, and as it becomes past it loses its certainty. Even though the demonstration may be repeated we can never be *quite* sure that the judgment and the demonstration we have in experience now are *quite* the same as those we had before and on which this series of inferences was based. Certainty, therefore, in matters of concrete fact, can be obtained only for particular judgments of the living present.

What, then, of the vaunted certainty of such abstract general principles as we find in Logic and Mathematics? Are they, too, proved by experience? And is their certainty also limited to the present? Our answer is that objects of pure thought are none the less objects of experience for being abstract. As abstractions, however, time and change form no part of their meaning. They are known as unparticularized, independent of time, as universals. So the certainty of any proposition made about them is not limited to the present. But the meaning of such propositions still consists in the expectations they arouse. Such propositions, apart from expectations about concrete objects, also arouse expectations about abstract objects of thought. The proposition, $2 + 2 = 4$ arouses the expectation that the mental operation of addition performed with the integers 2 and 2 will bring me to cognition of the integer 4; and this expectation being realized in experience I find the proposition true. And as the objects of experience in this case are nontemporal abstractions, the judgment is not bound to any particular case or event. It is a universal. All judgments about pure objects of thought are of this type. It includes judgments about adequately defined hypothetical entities, for these, too, may express expectation of consequences for thought which may be experienced by realization in thought. And even such judgments as these are added to our stock of truths, for, since even hypothetical entities are composed of elements abstracted from experience, judgments about entities so constructed have a bearing upon knowledge of the potentialities of the real world.

Judgments of this class, then, are proved by experience, as are judgments regarding concrete particular facts. They are self-evident only because, to prove them by experience, we need examine no other experiences than those involved in contemplating the judgments themselves. But the fact that these judgments may concern universals gives them a distinctive importance. For when we take the cases of concrete fact as instances of the universals dealt with in our abstract judgments we are able to carry our conclusions as to concrete matters of fact far beyond the range of experience. Yet such reasoning is always obsessed by three sources of uncertainty: (*a*) that the concrete cases reasoned about may not be fully and accurately defined in the abstract concepts which are employed; (*b*) that a failure of thought may have resulted in an assumption of self-evident connection at some point in the argument where none such existed; (*c*) the point mentioned above, that a train of argument always involves reliance upon the uncertain factor of memory. The reliability of the conclusion of such a train of reasoning is, of course, enormously strengthened when we can work back again from the judgment about universals to a judgment expressing some particular expectation and that expectation can be simultaneously realized in experience, as is done when we test an hypothesis by experiment. But even then absolute certainty is confined to the judgments of the present moment verified in present experience.

But though the objective criterion of truth (realization in experience) can only give certainty to this very limited range of judgments, yet it does give us the assurance that there is objective truth, even though it be only the moment-to-moment truth of our realized expectations. Man's search for truth, however, as we have seen, goes much further than this. It assumes that there is truth to be found far beyond the range of present experience, truth about the past and future, and about the present which is beyond experience, and even truths which can never be brought in any way to the test of the objective criterion of present realization. And we certainly have the experience of "truth-value" arising from such judgments. The demonstrable truth of present (i.e. "speciously" present) judgments is an important contribution to our search for truth, but it is a bare beginning. If we had no other criterion for our "truth-value" than this the search for truth would play a part of little importance in human life. But the search for truth goes on beyond anything that this standard can guarantee. And it is a search for objective truth—the agreement of expectation with a certain form of reality. The search is carried on in the faith that objective reality makes our judgments either true or false, and that truth according to this objective standard can be found. This faith is implicit in the structure of the form of will which determines the working of the ultimate end of cognition. But the criterion of this search for truth beyond present experience is neither the self-evidence of the judgments nor their present realization. These truths are sought and such judgments are believed, but they are not, in the strict sense of the term, known to be true. They are only known to have the appearance of "truth-value." This appearance is determined by subjective criteria. Yet these subjective criteria are believed to lead to objective truth. To see how this comes about we must return to an examination of the processes whereby judgments are accepted and rejected in the building of that structure we call knowledge.

When a judgment is formed and accepted (and thus valued as true) what is there about it that makes it appear to be an element in our cognitive grasp of our world; i.e. what is the subjective criterion of truth? Even though we are able to formulate the objective standard of truth as the cognitive grasp of our world that does not help us, for our very problem is to know when (apart from present experience) we have cognitively grasped our world and when our cognitions are mistaken. Yet in this dilemma the essential drive of our natures to cognitive activity compels us to go on forming judgments about the objects presented in experience. But, as has been said before, we cannot hold two contradictory judgments if we see the contradiction between them, a limitation which we have traced to the value requirement that activity shall be self-harmonious. No judgment, therefore, can be added to our stock if it be seen to be inconsistent with other judgments that are allowed to remain in that stock. Each new judgment we are able to form we gladly accept if we can, for if it can be accepted it has value. It is a new mental act with a fresh object; it bears the appearance of an addition to our cognitive grasp of our world. Sometimes, therefore, we accept new judgments with but little comparison of them with other judgments, especially if such judgments have a value in addition to their mere "truth value," i.e. are the sort of thing we want, on other grounds, to believe. But always it is the consistency of the new judgment with other judgments already held, whereby it is accepted or knitted into the growing structure, that gives it its appearance of "truth-value." i.e. of being an item in our cognitive grasp of our world; for none but judgments which appear consistent can be added to our stock of judgments about the world. The law of noncontradiction, or the internal interconsistency of our judgments, becomes therefore our subjective criterion of "truth value." The act of judgment which is consistent with our other judgments appears to be true, to have value, because it appears to be consistent with the ultimate end of cognitive activity, the cognitive grasp of our world. Other acts of judgment appear not to be true, to have the disvalue of falsehood.

This subjective criterion then (the interconsistency of our judgments) is our only criterion of truth beyond that of the truth realized in the specious present. Yet its objective validity depends upon the interconsistency of the knowable world. Unless the principle that a thing cannot both be and not be, both have a property and not have it, holds good in the world of knowable objects, the Law of Non-contradiction can be no criterion of truth in our thoughts of those objects. But as we *can* only think according to the Law of Non-contradiction, we must assume that this law holds good in the world of our objects if we are to *think* about them at all. We may recognize that it is just a vast assumption to believe that Reality conforms to the nature of our thought. But without that assumption, though the purely practical and empirical grounds for cognitive activity would still remain, thought, in so far as it transcends the judgment that is verified in the specious present, would lose its "truth-value"; it would not appear as an activity wherein we extend our cognitive grasp of our world. But this further pursuit of the "truth-value" (the effort to engage in cognitive activity of a kind that continually extends our cognitive grasp of our world) is an essential characteristic of the human mind. So in all our thinking we assume the Law of Non-contradiction to hold among the objects of our knowledge, and we adopt it as the criterion of the truth of our judgments. And, long before the individual has explicitly thought of the nature of his criterion, he experiences and recognizes the "truth-value" and the "error-disvalue" of his various judgments.

But the interconsistency of our judgments is a purely subjective criterion. As we only too often discover, from the objective criterion of realization in experience, a judgment may be perfectly consistent with all our previous judgments and yet be false. The fact that a new judgment is quite consistent with all our present knowledge, therefore, is not a guarantee that it is a further item in our cognitive grasp of our world; and if it is not then its appearance of "truth-value" is illusory. But though false, the individual, in such cases, has no means of knowing it is false. It is inconsistent with the ultimate end of his cognitive activity; but for him it has the appearance of being in harmony with that end because it is consistent with his existing body of judgments. Consequently, to him it appears to be true. But suppose later experience, e.g. further experiments, force him to form judgments which are inconsistent with this judgment or with some deductions from it. Then, if he cannot doubt the judgments formed on the basis of this new experience, the earlier, contradictory judgment begins to appear false and is rejected. Further, he has formed a mass of judgments with regard to other selves. He believes in the essential similarity of their experiences to his, and in the trustworthiness of certain of their reports of their experience. Consequently one of the mass of judgments, with which a judgment of his own must be in harmony if it is to appear true, is this—that the facts set forth in the judgment must be consistent with other people's experience. So when he learns that someone else has performed an experiment and found results inconsistent with his judgment he is led by that, too, to doubt his former judgment.

But in all this critical examination of his judgment the man's criterion is still the purely subjective one of the interconsistency of his own judgments for, once his thought passes beyond present experience, he has no other criterion. But he has learned from experience that what is consistent with this criterion to-day may not remain consistent with future judgments based on a larger experience. Yet these judgments, being inconsistent now, all seem to be true. If he were satisfied to cling to these judgments, and not enlarge his experience in any way that might force the acceptance of inconsistent judgments which would force the rejection of some now held, then we would have to say that "truth-value," for him, consisted in the possession of a body of consistent judgments, and that the only criterion of truth, for him, is the interconsistency of his judgments. But the only occasions on which human beings do this are when they value something dependent on the acceptance of certain judgments more than they value truth itself. In so far as truth is sought the effort is made to test the interconsistency of judgments and to discover the grounds for new judgments with which to test the old. In this is revealed, once again, the nature of the "truth-value." It is found, not in the mere building up of a body of interconsistent judgments, but in the building up of a body of judgments so marked by interconsistency that they appear to be a cognitive grasp of the objective world—an appearance that they have on account of the implicit assumption that the mind's incapacity to accept two contradictory judgments (if it sees the contradiction) implies that there are no contradictions among the world of its objects—i.e. that the Law of Non-contradiction holds among them.

Thus we see that the subjective criterion of truth accepted in our thought, though the only criterion that can take us beyond present experience, is not necessarily the ultimate standard, but that, used in conjunction with the objective criterion of momentary realization in present experience, it is accepted as indicating harmony with another standard —that the judgment in question should be an item in the subject's progressive cognitive grasp of its world. And this standard (on the view that it is the same world that is grasped by different individuals—a view which we must hold if we are to believe in the intercommunication of selves) we must describe as objective. Thus it is that, passing out beyond the transitory assurances of the objective criterion, the individual strives, by means of his subjective criterion, to obtain a wider truth that shall yet be objective i.e. valid for all. And this he does in faith for, not only has he no grounds for the assumption that his objective world contains no inconsistencies, but, even granting this, his subjective criterion of consistency only assures him that of two contradictory judgments he must reject one. It never tells him which one to reject. He decides that (if he decides at all, and in cases where he cannot put it to the test of present experience) by choosing the lesser evil and holding to that judgment which is most persistent or which is linked with the greater body of his judgments. And this criterion never completely assures him that even the most thoroughly consistent body of judgments is ultimately or objectively true. It merely appears true because it appears consistent; and the more points of consistency to be found in his body of judgments the more certainly true do they appear.

This consistent body of judgments has its roots in terms given in experience. Some of its constituent judgments, so far as memory can assure the individual, have been actually verified in experience. One or two of them may be held with the absolute certainty of that which is in present process of verification. As I sit here, e.g. I continuously hold, in my specious present, the judgments that I exist and that I see black and white objects before me; and these judgments are in a continuous process of verification. But, apart from such small range of certainty, the individual's convictions must rest on the consistency of his judgments with each other; and his pursuit of truth must base itself on the assumption that the objective world is as consistent a whole as his subjective criterion of truth demands that his body of knowledge should be. Only thus can man, in the midst of ignorance and error, and with a merely subjective criterion, carry on his search for truth beyond the narrow limits of his present grasp. That this effort does sometimes yield truth we continuously discover as our expectations are verified in experience. In the faith that, rigorously pursued, it will continue to yield much more truth we go on with it. For the "truth-value" we thus obtain and enjoy is among the most precious experiences that life offers.

So great is the value of truth to many of the finest human minds that its pursuit tends, in those devoted to it, to become the ultimate end that gives meaning to all the rest of life. It is the "religion" of modern science and tends in scientific circles to be regarded as the *summum bonum* to which all other goods must defer. For Aristotle it was the highest good and at least one modern philosopher has gone so far as to say that "The problem of living is the problem of knowing and the desire to live is the desire to know."[1] Yet it is no mere accumulation of knowledge of particular facts that satisfies this desire to know. A catalogue of unrelated facts in which no meaning can be discerned whereby they point beyond themselves is the dullest thing with which the human mind can be occupied. All truth is of value, but, as Professor Taylor remarks, "it would be a paradox to say that all truths, because equally true, are equally valuable."[2] Truths vary in value according to their significance, which means according to the degree in which they help us to extend our knowledge and gather up its scattered fragments into a unified whole. Truth-seeking thus culminates in philosophy. Intellectual value is determined by the cognitive part of the goal of the ultimate will of the finite individual as such—the will to expand continuously its grasp or penetration of the reality in the midst of which it dwells.

Summing up, then, our conclusion is that the standard of truth is objective, that its criterion is also objective as to its foundation in the demonstrations of immediate present experience but subjective in so far as the search for truth

---
[1] Warner Fite: *Moral Philosophy*, p. 283.
[2] A. E. Taylor: *The Faith of a Moralist*, p. 46.

goes beyond present experience. Yet in spite of this tremendous element of subjectivity in our criteria of truth, we find that, the more we use those criteria, objective and subjective, the larger grows the body of knowledge which we can mutually accept as true. And this fact, surely, indicates not only a certain common constitution of the human mind and a common objective spatio-temporal-sensory world with which we are dealing, but also that we are dealing with a common objective world in the realm of values. In particular the validity of this feature of our value experience has been indicated by showing that the subjective criterion, faithfully and intelligently followed, is a genuine guide, and our only guide, to an objective standard of value.

CHAPTER X

BEAUTY

It is only in recent years, concomitantly with the growing recognition of the importance of the general theory of value, that Aesthetics has begun to receive from philosophers the attention it deserves. Consequently it is still in a more chaotic condition than any other branch of philosophical inquiry. Nevertheless, a few fairly general points of agreement seem to have emerged. One of these is that, although experience of the beautiful always includes pleasure it is not merely pleasure, but includes something else that is distinctive in itself—or at least that it is a unique kind of pleasure.[1] Secondly, that standards of beauty are, in some sense and in some degree, objectively valid. Thus even a writer whose theory is so far subjective that he can say "that all beauty is the expression of what may be generally called emotion and that all such expression is beautiful" nevertheless emphatically affirms that "judgments of (aesthetic) taste claim to be valid for all men."[2] Thirdly, that in the perception of the beautiful we are far from being mere passive receivers of an impression, i.e. that aesthetic appreciation is an active process which itself contributes to the nature of the experience, thus accounting for the great differences in appreciation of the beauty of an object by the same person at different times and by different persons at the same time. Fourthly, that this activity is some form of contemplation. Fifth, that the interest involved is divorced from all questions of the utility or truth of what is con-

[1] Professor Alexander defines the aesthetic experience as a pleasure arising from "satisfaction of the aesthetic impulse," which, in turn, is described as "the constructive impulse diverted from practice and become contemplative."—S. Alexander: *Beauty and Other Forms of Value*.
[2] G. F. Carritt: *The Theory of Beauty*, pp. 296 and 299.

templated. Even Ruskin, who strove to link art and morality, recognized this, while Oscar Wilde says bluntly "All art is quite useless,"[1] and Kant, in the *Critique of Judgment*, lays it down that "The satisfaction which occasions the judgment of taste is disinterested."

When we inquire more specifically as to the distinctive nature of the contemplative act thus disinterestedly (not uninterestedly) occupied with its object we find less agreement. There is a fairly wide consensus, however, that it at least involves, if it does not actually consist in, an activity of the imagination. This seems to be what Professor Alexander has in mind in ascribing it to the constructive instinct "diverted from practice and become contemplative."[2] It is certainly the chief characteristic of the notion of *Einfühlung* developed by Lipps and his school in Germany —a word specially used to denote the imaginative fellow-feeling with others and the reading of a spirit into things. For Kant, what he called the "judgment of taste" consisted essentially in a harmonious interaction of the imagination and the understanding. And Croce, though his Idealistic philosophy leads him to confuse the issue by identifying "expression" (his term for the essential aesthetic activity) with "intuition," is quite definite that expression means imagination. Perhaps the most definite on this point is Professor R. G. Collingwood, who says, "The mere act of imagination, by being itself, by being this act and not a

[1] Oscar Wilde: *The Picture of Dorian Gray*.
[2] Alexander, however, rightly points out that the activity often does not reach the level of explicit imagination. "Rather it is ideal supplementation, 'tied ideas,' as when we see the ice cold. Or it may not reach the conscious level at all." If by conscious is here meant "explicit," this statement should, I think, be accepted. But as we have no single word that covers both explicit imagination and this imaginal supplementation at the perceptual level it seems to be necessary for purposes of Aesthetics to extend the meaning of the term to include these lower level processes. We shall use it in that sense.

different act, generates in its object that unity which is beauty."[1]

But while the importance of imagination in aesthetic activity is generally admitted there is, by no means, agreement that this is the whole of the matter. In many of our aesthetic experiences we can hardly detect any activity of the imagination. We seem to be simply drinking in the beauty that is there. Particularly is this the case where the sensuous element is predominant, as in listening to music or watching the slowly changing colours of a sunset. We may explicitly indulge the imagination, but we may also remain spellbound, without articulate thought, enraptured with sheer sensuous delight. Yet Croce voices what is practically the unanimous opinion of thinkers on the subject when he says that "nature is only beautiful for the man who sees it *with the eyes of an artist*. . . . Without the aid of imagination nothing in nature is beautiful."[2] And Professor Prall, who lays more stress on the sensuous and less on the imaginative, than do most authorities, nevertheless says "Aesthetic experience, full and complete, not only requires tremendous training beforehand, but intense activity at the time."[3] Thus any suggestion that, where sensuous appreciation predominates over constructive imagination, we are merely passively allowing ourselves to be affected by the sensa is set aside.

This activity is, for Prall, an intuition of form and quality which stops short of the full practical perception of things with their meanings in significant relation to other things, but which, he thinks, in its own peculiar intensity, probably involves processes in the body extending further than anything required for mere perceptual activity. "Discriminating perception focussed upon an object as it appears directly to sense, without ulterior interest to direct that perception

[1] R. G. Collingwood: *Outlines of a Philosophy of Art.*
[2] B. Croce: *Aesthetics.*   [3] D. W. Prall: *Aesthetic Judgment.*

inward to an understanding of the actual forces or underlying structure giving rise to this appearance, or forward to the purposes to which the object may be turned or the events its presence and movement may presage, or outward to its relations in the general structure and the moving flux—such free attentive activity may fairly be said to mark the situation in which beauty is felt."[1] Setting aside the purely hypothetical suggestion regarding corporeal processes we can, I think, agree that this is an accurate description of our activity in very many of our aesthetic experiences, especially in those which seem to approximate most closely to sheer sensuous enjoyment.

This suggestion from Prall we can then take together with one from Collingwood, who emphasizes the fact that imagination is an *incomplete* cognitive process. It stops short of the complete cognitive act involved in thinking proper, simply because it is not interested in the truth of the ideas it entertains. The complete cognitive act not only formulates a thought but accepts or rejects it, as we have seen in our discussion of truth. But in imagination thoughts are formulated for their own sake, without reference to their consistency with the already accepted body of judgments. Imagination is thinking divested of any practical or theoretical objective, thinking which has no aim beyond the process of thinking itself. It is this that divorces art from all questions of utility and truth, giving it a world of its own.

Now reflection on those cases of aesthetic appreciation where the sensuous effect of the object is enjoyed for itself and imagination is either absent, or so inarticulate that it scarcely seems to occur at all, shows that here a similarly restricted activity of contemplation is occurring at the perceptual level. We have already referred to the fact that true perception always involves more than the mere awareness of a datum, that it goes on to think something *about* the

[1] D. W. Prall: *op. cit.*, p. 57.

datum. In particular the datum is normally observed as a sign of the existence of something. It is apprehended by thought as revealing a reality. Thus every sensum tends to mean for us a physical thing; and our thought is of the thing it means rather than of the sensum itself. But in aesthetic activity we divest ourselves of practical interest. The sensory datum is apprehended for its own sake without reference to the reality that it means. All attention is given to sheer sensory quality and relations—to quality and form —as they are in themselves apart from their meaning. Such apprehension naturally becomes far more vivid, accurate, and full than it can be when the chief interest is in the meaning of things. It is the artist's own peculiar way of looking at things; and his powers of abstraction from reality and customary interpretation enable him to perform those analyses upon which his technique is based, such as the analysis of spatial relations required for drawing in perspective and of colour for its reproduction on canvas—feats of isolation from reality and practical significance quite beyond the ordinary person.

The peculiar kind of contemplation involved in aesthetic activity appears, then, to be one in which the apprehension of quality and form is divorced from practical meaning and reality, and where the articulate formulation of thought is divested of its normal relevance to utility and truth. Unfortunately we have no single word for these partial mental processes which underly percept and concept respectively, but we may speak of them as aesthetic appreciation and aesthetic imagination, or simply as appreciation and imagination. The former is concerned with perceptual beauty and the latter with conceptual beauty. Of course, in most of our aesthetic activity both are combined; especially is this the case in the enjoyment of plastic art. In music and contemplation of natural beauty, however, the factor we have called appreciation often predominates almost to the exclusion of imagination. But in poetry, drama, and literature generally, imagination is always the more important by far.

It is significant that Professor Prall finds it impossible to bring the beauty of literature adequately within the scope of his Aesthetic, while those writers who emphasize the imaginative factor usually fail to appreciate fully the importance of what Prall calls the "aesthetic surface." Both factors need to be taken into account to explain the full sweep of aesthetic experience, but the difficulty is to see what they have in common that makes them both factors in the presentation of the beautiful. Part of the solution to the problem may be found, as we have suggested, in their common character of incompleteness and in their consequent freedom to occupy themselves more intensively with the strictly limited object to which they attend—the immediacy of sense and imagery abstracted from the practical interest in reality. It is this distinctive type of contemplation, more restricted than truth seeking, yet freer and capable of greater intensity, scope and accuracy within its own sphere, that is essential to aesthetic experience. It is through this kind of activity, and this alone, that there is presented within our perspective that peculiar *quale* which we call beauty—or its antithesis ugliness.

Not all persons are capable of this activity or capable of it in the same degree, nor is any one person capable of it at any time, nor equally capable of it in his attitude toward all objects. One must have the aesthetic capacity or he cannot have the aesthetic experience, just as he must have the sensory capacity or he will lack the sensory experience. And, with beauty as with sense, it is possible for one who possesses the capacity to let it fall into abeyance —to be temporarily psychically blind. Yet the analogy here is not quite complete, for the sensum is probably presented whenever the physiological process in the cortex is complete, but we only become aware of it in the act of sensing; and psychical blindness is due to the omission of this act. Aesthetic blindness, however, is due to the failure to adopt the aesthetic attitude, to engage in the distinctive type of contemplation which is aesthetic, so that the aesthetic *quale* is not even presented. It is more analogous to a failure of the physiological organ to function. But as aesthetic sensibility depends upon the adoption of a special attitude, distinct from the ordinary practical one, aesthetic blindness is much commoner than sensory.

Whenever the aesthetic attitude is adopted, however, i.e. whenever we engage ourselves in "imagination" and "appreciation" (in the senses defined above), aesthetic values are presented. Yet even here it seems possible for a further psychic blindness, definitely analogous to that at the sensory level, to occur. The beauties seen in a picture, for example, vary greatly with our mood. Most often this must be due to differences in the activity of imagination and appreciation, resulting in differences in the *quale* presented. But there may be distinct awareness of sense data and images without awareness of their beauty—and then suddenly the beauty of them flashes upon us in a way which does not seem to be due to any addition of sensory discrimination or imagination. So psychic blindness, even in this narrower sense, does seem to occur in regard to aesthetic values and is probably due, here as in other cases, to the negative effect of an emotional interest tending, as emotional interests always do, to divert attention from whatever is contrary to its aim.

But though we have aesthetic experience whenever we adopt the aesthetic attitude that experience is not always positive. Ugliness as well as beauty makes its appearance— and we never see it, any more than we do beauty, unless we are engaged in genuinely aesthetic activity. That is why society can be blind to the ugliness of so many things that bring "profits" or grosser satisfactions; it is simply because attention only dwells upon these things with practical intent, never in aesthetic contemplation, with the artist's eye. But, apart from this homily, there is a theoretical importance attached to this fact that our activities of aesthetic appreciation and imagination sometimes present to us the ugly instead of the beautiful—and that we never see ugliness anywhere until we do adopt the aesthetic attitude toward things. It shows that there are other conditions of the beautiful besides the mere engaging in the activities we have called appreciation and imagination. It is these other conditions that are the crux of the aesthetic problem and the difficulty becomes most acute when we ask for the explanation of ugliness. And it is here that we shall find help from our general theory of value. We shall take first the type of beauty that depends upon imagination.

The fact of ugliness shows that it is insufficient to say merely that aesthetic experience is a product of the activity of the imagination. The mere absence of imagination does not present us with ugliness; it simply fails to present any aesthetic experience at all, positive or negative. Consequently, it cannot be the mere presence of imagination that presents us with beauty. There must be some other condition. What, then, is the condition which imagination and appreciation must fulfil (or which must also be present) in order that there may be beauty, and what other condition produces ugliness? Here the great aesthetic doctrine of the Greeks immediately suggests itself. Beauty is a kind of harmony.[1] This, indeed, seems to be the answer and is widely accepted as such. We are conscious of beauty when our imagination is active and its activity is characterized

---

[1] The principles of order, symmetry, proportion, and harmony were first emphasized by the Pythagoreans and constitute the dominant note of the teaching on the subject by Plato and Aristotle, except as it is overshadowed in the former by his doctrine of Ideas.

by internal harmony. Especially clearly is this asserted by Professor R. G. Collingwood.[1]

The beauty of a work of art depends, in large part at least, upon its power to stimulate the imagination, but only so far as it stimulates and directs it in a self-harmonious activity. It is not necessary that imagination should harmonize with the real world except so far as features of the real world are given in the stimulus and so cannot be separated from the artistic whole. What is necessary is that the artistic whole (the object of artistic appreciation and thought) shall indeed be a whole, that it shall have a significant meaning without self-contradiction, that it shall suggest harmonious trains of ideas. Its personalities must be concrete individuals, whatever their complexities and distractions; the very distractions must be such as "belong" to the person and situation depicted. The imagery must be "fitting." Where function is suggested it must be matched by quality and form that are suited to it. Balance, harmony, proportion—these words are so familiar in the vocabulary of art that they are almost synonymous with beauty. Yet we must not overlook the first requisite of all: the thing of beauty must have power to stimulate, to suggest. And this means that there must be scope, variety, novelty, mystery, the half-revealed that calls aloud for our imagination to complete it.

In brief, when we state the conditions which an object must fulfil to be beautiful, or which a process of imagination must fulfil in order to present beauty, we find ourselves stating again what we have described as the ultimate form of will of the finite individual as such—the will to penetrate and grasp its world in a continuous activity that is harmonious and yet ever new. For whether in play or in practical affairs, in intellectual or aesthetic activity, this is the only kind of activity which is finally and fully satis-

[1] R. G. Collingwood: *op. cit.*

fying. When the process of imagination falls short of these demands beauty turns to ugliness. If variety is lacking, if that which is so familiar that the end is known from the beginning is presented again for our imagination, it is a burden and a bore. If there are jarring notes, contradictory suggestions that do not fit into a larger whole, failures in connection between the parts so as to destroy unity, then aesthetic charm is lost, if not actually turned to pain. The aesthetic imagination, then, presents us with experience of the beautiful when, in the pursuit of its own particular end (the following up of this suggestion or that, the creative expansion of this or that thought), it works in apparent harmony with the ultimate end of all cognitive activity, the long, long will to go on, gathering all the world, actual and potential, into the orbit of its grasp.

In imagination it is, of course, the *potentialities* of the world of which we lay hold. But these, nevertheless, though they abstract in some way from the concrete actuality or totality of things, are a grappling with the real, a penetration of its might-have-beens, a working out of its possibilities, even though they postulate a Lilliput or a two-dimensional geometry. We only abstract from reality in the sense of the *given* to pursue it in the realm of the *hypothetical*. About all true art and beauty there is a certain seriousness. It may be gay and fanciful, but it tends to lose its quality if it becomes flippant. Art must be genuine, true to itself, to its own intrinsic nature. It is an expression of something that is very real in human personality, and its world is real. Such vaguely expressed requirements we hear from every artist who seeks to tell what art means to him. They can hardly be put more plainly. But what they mean becomes intelligible when we realize that artistic expression has its sanction and validity in its conformity to the most general and fundamental demand of the human spirit—the will to fill the world with its work and gather the world into its mind. It is this that saves art and the appreciation of the beautiful from triviality, though only an incomplete cognitive activity and divorced from practical goods. And it not only saves them from being trivial, but exalts them to the realm of the spiritual.

This must be said even of the lower forms of art, such as humour and the imaginative exercise in games and other forms of play.[1] They are rightly admired by the great majority of people above the pleasures of appetite and such mere instinctive satisfactions as the gratification of self-display. It is only prejudice and confusion that ever leads anyone to doubt their value or rate them lower than mere practical goods and comforts. The principal source of this confusion is that these ministrations to physical needs are, up to a certain point, necessary as a basis for many or all of the higher values. But this does not make them *intrinsically higher*. So far as these ministrations are not necessary to the higher values, i.e. so far as they are mere comforts and luxuries, they are lower in the value scale. A secondary source of confusion is the prejudice arising from recognition of a tendency in some quarters to over-emphasize sport as against other higher values. But in the straightforward comparison of values (apart from questions of untoward consequences of either over-emphasis of the one or neglect of the other) play (at the imaginative level) and humour are distinctly higher in the value scale than creature comforts and luxuries. This, I think, will be generally recognized. Few, for example, will deny that it is a sound judgment of value that prefers the activity of games to the enjoyment of harmless creature comforts and an unsound

[1] So far as play is mere aimless physical activity for its own sake, it is on the lowest level of value, for it neither deals purposively with the actual nor penetrates the potentialities of the possible. So far as it allies itself with motives of health, exercise, self-display, etc., it realizes merely biological values. It is only when it becomes imaginative that it has aesthetic value.

judgment that prefers these to the humour of any book or play that deserves the name of art. Yet here we are comparing the lowest order of aesthetic values with the highest types of pleasure (considered as intrinsic values and not as means) in which there is no spiritual (aesthetic, intellectual, or moral) element present.

Now when we speak of the beauty (or other value) of *objects* it must be remembered that objects only have value as means or, if they have intrinsic value, it is as possessors of the capacity to condition immediately the presentation of value to some subject. A picture, a poem, a landscape, or a symphony, therefore, may be said to have beauty, or be beautiful, in the sense that, or to the degree that, they have the power to stimulate in persons those reactions of appreciation and imagination through which beauty is presented in experience.[1] The beauty itself is a feature of the qualitative character of the perspective of the world presented in the total experience. It is non-spatial, as is the sensum, and only attached to, or a quality of, any particular sensory or physical or mental object in the perspective in the sense that such object appears to be the immediate objective condition of its presentation. Nevertheless, just

[1] This interpretation has received the weighty endorsement of the Provost of Oriel. "The view to which I find myself driven in the attempt to avoid the difficulties that beset both a purely objective and a purely subjective point of view, is one which identifies beauty with the *power* of producing a certain sort of experience in minds, the sort of experience which we are familiar with under such names as aesthetic enjoyment or aesthetic thrill." In judging an object to be beautiful "one is in effect saying 'the object has it in it to produce aesthetic enjoyment in anyone sufficiently capable of feeling such.' "—W. D. Ross: *op. cit.*, pp. 127 and 129. It is unfortunate, however, that Dr. Ross should "identify" beauty with this power, for this involves the divorcing of beauty from the aesthetic experience and the denial that beauty is an intrinsic value. What is needed to avoid these incongruities is the recognition of beauty as the aesthetic value *quale* which is object of aesthetic feeling, and that the sensory-physical object only *has* beauty in the sense of having the power to condition the experiencing of this *quale*.

as we project the sensum in perception in the spatial position where we believe the physical object to be to which we refer it, so we tend to project the aesthetic quality upon the physical or mental object which appears to condition our awareness of it. The beauty seems to belong to the picture and the music almost as intimately as the colour or sound; and only a little less close seems to be the connection between the words of a poem and their beauty. It is only reflection upon the variability of our aesthetic experiences of the same object that forces a rejection of this notion.

But we best preserve our natural way of speaking of these things if we recognize that what we mean by saying that an object is intrinsically beautiful is that it has the capacity (immediately, not merely as a means to the presentation of something else which has that capacity), when contemplated in the appropriate way, to stimulate the kind of mental activity whereby we experience beauty. This capacity different objects possess in different degrees for different persons and for the same person at different times. But still, as Dr. Ross says, there is a very definite sense in which one may say "The object has it in it to produce aesthetic enjoyment in anyone sufficiently capable of feeling such." This capacity of the object is sometimes a capacity to stimulate the mind to a vivid and continuous process of self-consistent imagination. According to the degree in which we find it can do that we judge it to be beautiful. But, as pointed out earlier, the object may only stimulate the kind of activity we have called appreciation; and we have now to examine the question as to the further conditions which must obtain if this activity is to produce positive rather than negative aesthetic experience.

In regard to appreciation, of course, much less depends on the aesthetic capacity of the mind, and more on the aesthetic character of the object, than in the case of imagination. Yet the person of truly artistic spirit is capable of seeing beauty in most unlikely places and, if he possesses the required technique, is capable of expressing it on canvas, or in some other form, so that others are able to see it. For the most part, this feat is performed by giving prominence, in the representation, to certain features which have meant beauty to the artist so that their suggestiveness is sufficiently plain to stir more sluggish imaginations. So far as the beauty is such as depends upon appreciation, however, its possession by an object must depend upon what it offers to sensory apprehension to provide material for that type of contemplation. But even here artistic treatment can greatly enhance the capacity of an object for presentation of beauty.

The characteristics of the object, whether an object of art or of nature, which possesses this capacity to stimulate and maintain the act of appreciation vary according to the sense appealed to and the type of beauty concerned. A full analysis of these conditions would fill many volumes. In a very general way, however, we may say that there are four requirements to be filled. In the first place the object must be able to *stimulate* that non-practical interest in sheer quality and form which we have called appreciation. The artistic soul who is looking for beauty may discover it where there is no such stimulus obvious. But the wideness of the aesthetic appeal of an object certainly depends on this capacity to entice the individual into the aesthetic attitude. Thus brightness and contrast of colours and simple tuneful sounds are universally effective. The dullest Philistine can appreciate a sunset. This capacity to stimulate is, of course, only the first requisite of beauty and the most stimulating objects often lack the other requirements, or have them only in small degree. Further, because they require so little stimulation, trained and aesthetically sensitive persons are apt to rate the importance of this factor low. Nevertheless, *some* capacity to stimulate the aesthetic activity is obviously

BEAUTY

necessary—perhaps it is possessed by every sense datum. But, since sense data possess this capacity in such different degree, it is the object which possesses it (together with other necessary qualifications) in high degree that receives wide recognition as beautiful.

The other conditions may be more briefly mentioned. The second is variety. The object can only hold aesthetic attention so long as it has new beauties to reveal or old ones that reveal themselves more fully. When we have exhausted its beauty it becomes boring to have to attend to it. So far as the beauty of a thing depends on sheer appreciation therefore—attention to quality and form—it must have variety and depth (which is a form of variety) if it is to have much beauty. The third principle is very important. It is the requirement of harmony. In the case of sound this is well understood. In the case of colour its nature is not so clear, but its existence is plain. In the case of shape it is well recognized and its principles fairly fully known. The importance of harmony in the aesthetic object cannot be exaggerated. Without it stimulus and variety are in vain. Indeed, without harmony they only present us with ugliness. The fourth requirement is akin to the third and does not strictly concern mere appreciation. But it must be added because aesthetic contemplation constantly tends to include more than appreciation, i.e. to develop imagination. So we need to add to the aesthetic requirements of an object that so far as it does stimulate imagination it must stimulate and direct it with internal harmony. It is because of failure here that otherwise beautiful objects lose much of their appeal; although the lover of beauty may often overcome this defect by abstracting the really beautiful features from the concrete setting which adversely affects the imagination.

These four requirements plainly reduce to two—the two fundamental requirements of all the higher values—an activity directed upon the real with an object that is ever new and an activity that is internally harmonious. Awareness of quality and form, even though abstracted from their further meaning regarding existence and practice, is awareness of reality. The activity of appreciation is thus a perfectly genuine process of further grasp or penetration of our world; and it has its own peculiar effectiveness because of the limitation of the interest involved. But the remarkable feature of these conditions is the fact that this activity only presents us with a value experience (with beauty) when the object is such that appreciation of it is an activity that maintains its own peculiar internal harmony. If beauty depended merely on the simple act of attending to form and quality in abstraction from the practical then this condition should not exist. The fact that it does exist shows that the presentation of value (even sheer sensory value) depends on an activity in which the will to the nearer end is in harmony with that to a remoter or more ultimate end —the will to harmonious self-expression. Value here too seems to require for its appearance a harmonious operation of the more immediate and more fundamental forms of will.

The explanation of aesthetic value, both perceptual and conceptual, falls into line, then, with the general conditions of value experience which we have found elsewhere. It also brings further corroboration of the statement that the higher values of human life are concerned with the will of the individual to a continuous yet always self-harmonious activity which increasingly lays hold of, or moulds the processes of, the world in which it finds itself. Value is felt whenever activity is directed to an end that appears to fulfil this aim. And every value, beauty included, makes its demand upon the will. It calls upon us to continue the activity in which it is discovered. It demands the recognition that this is what we *ought* to do. This is the claim of every aesthetic experience to validity. The question is whether, in the light of the variability of our experience of beauty, it can be justified.

Before we pass on to the discussion of this final problem for our theory of aesthetics, however, it will be well to say what little needs must be said about the place of pleasure in aesthetic experience. There are four different sources of the hedonic tone which tends to mingle with the experience of the beautiful: (a) that arising from the nature of the sense data which stimulate the aesthetic activity; (b) that arising from the ease and harmony of the activity itself (for easy and harmonious activity of any kind is pleasant); (c) that arising when the activity of the moment appears also to fulfil some practical end—though any partial diversion of attention to such ends will lessen the aesthetic experience; (d) that inevitably associated with aesthetic value because the activity appears progressively to fulfil the ultimate end of the self. Yet pain may enter into an experience of positive aesthetic value if the activity becomes too intense; the degree of aesthetic value is then probably very high, the experience intensely beautiful, though painful. We say that it is painfully beautiful, an exquisite pain! The occasion of such intensity is probably always that of concomitant emotional excitement; and it is to these inadequately satisfied emotional tendencies that the pain is due. Or again, the emotions excited in an aesthetic experience may be "painful" emotions, as in witnessing tragedy. Then the pain of these emotions will be felt simultaneously with the aesthetic experience of harmoniously active imagination stimulated by the scenes witnessed. Tragedy is enjoyed, in spite of the painful emotions it stirs, because of its powerful effect upon the imagination and the consequent rich aesthetic experience.

But far the greater part of our positive aesthetic experience is purely pleasant, the sources of the pleasure being the four enumerated above. Indeed, if the hedonic tone arising from any of these four sources becomes negative it is apt to mar the aesthetic experience, for it interrupts the activity of appreciation or imagination, directing cognitive activity to practical ends. It is important not to confuse the hedonic tone and the aesthetic, however. The beauty of a picture, or of music, does not depend upon, nor consist in, the sensory pleasantness of the colours or sounds, nor upon any pleasure in extraneous ends which the beautiful object may serve. Indeed, the beauty may even be enhanced by certain elements of sensory unpleasantness, or by a recognition of the disutility of the aesthetic object. Yet the limits of this are narrow. Any very distinct unpleasantness, and any disutility that is related to the function which is part of the meaning of an object (as in architecture), is apt to mar the aesthetic experience simply because it forces a breakdown of the imaginative activity stimulated by the object. Consequently, positive aesthetic experience tends to be accompanied by almost exclusively pleasant hedonic tone.

We come then, finally, to the question of the objectivity of aesthetic value, a fact which is, in some sense, universally admitted, but one extremely difficult to define and explain. On the one hand we are faced with the fact that the beauty of an object is so obviously relative to the interest and capacity of the observer, that opinions on aesthetic questions differ so widely. On the other hand, every aesthetic experience, as given, is equally real at the time. Wherever beauty appears it makes its claim to be admired; it is felt as something that *ought* to be cherished. And, as different things present to us different degrees of beauty, the more beautiful makes the greater claim upon us as something that is more *worthy* of attention and preservation. This is the subjective standard of beauty, a standard that is an integral feature of the aesthetic experience. If it be unreal then all objective standards are unreal, for it is only because of this claim to validity which is integral to every aesthetic expe-

BEAUTY

rience that we have any thought of an objective standard at all.

The validity of the subjective standard can only be maintained if we can show that its apparent variability is due to our own misunderstanding of its meaning and claim; and this, on the theory here developed, can be maintained. In the first place, the misunderstanding is due, as in the case of the sensa, to the supposition that the quality belongs to the thing (in the case of beauty, the sensory-physical or conceptual object) independently of its relation to any mind. Qualities, as we have tried to show, belong to perspectives; and a perspective is a select arrangement of the world from a particular point of view. A value appearing in a perspective, therefore, declares a certain validity of the perspective, which can only mean a certain rightness of the attitude or activity which constitutes the point of view and maintains the perspective. Now if, as we have maintained, the value is presented in the perspective through the harmony of the immediate activity with the ultimate aim of the finite individual as such, then the rightness of this activity and attitude must be recognized. Beauty enters into our experience of the world whenever we engage in those distinctive kinds of contemplative activity we have called appreciation and imagination in a manner which is in accord with the ultimate aim of all our activity. It makes its demand upon the subsidiary forms of the will that that activity should be maintained. It gives to the perspective, and to the attitude of mind that maintains it, the stamp of validity.

But in the interpretation of this experience of aesthetic validity there are three sources of error. In the first place the value may be attached to the wrong object. The aesthetic activity must needs be directed upon some object and the meaning of the validity is the worth of maintaining that activity upon that object. But the object is always complex, is affected by its place in the perspective in relation to other objects and by those features of the perspective which are the media through which it is observed. Consequently, failure to understand all the conditions of the perspective must lead to many mistaken judgments on the question of what objects "possess" beauty in the sense of possessing the capacity to present beauty when aesthetically contemplated. And similarly, mistakes will be made regarding the comparative beauty of different objects. It is only by the understanding of aesthetic technique—both that of the different arts and what may be called the aesthetic technique of nature, or the natural conditions of beauty—that such mistakes can be avoided. But in so far as accuracy of understanding is achieved we are able to formulate objectively valid judgments regarding aesthetic objects. Such judgments cannot be of the form: All persons will, on all occasions, find this object beautiful and that object even more beautiful than this. The other two sources of error make it impossible to formulate valid judgments of that kind. Our statements about the beauty of objects must rather take the form suggested by Dr. Ross: "The object has it in it to produce aesthetic enjoyment in anyone sufficiently capable of feeling such." Even in this form comparative statements about the beauty of different objects can only be very tentative on account of the different capabilities of different individuals. But this aspect of the problem is connected with the other two sources of error.

The second source of error in aesthetic judgment is the failure to distinguish clearly between different types of value experienced at the same time. Especially does confusion arise from the mingling of pleasure and pain with aesthetic experience. We are very apt to ascribe the greater beauty to the object we have aesthetically contemplated with the greater pleasure, although this pleasure may have been due to non-aesthetic sources, as outlined above. Purely emotional interest, extraneous in its source, adding to the intensity of appreciation and imagination on some occasions and detracting from it on others, also deceives us. Moral and truth values also affect aesthetic judgment illegitimately. Much homely poetry owes its wide appeal to its sound philosophy of life rather than to its aesthetic character, but is popularly adjudged "beautiful." It is even said to be beautiful *because* it is good and true; which is a plain confusion. So, too, pictures of children and animals sell well, not merely because of their aesthetic charm but because of their appeal to sentiment. Obviously a sound aesthetic judgment must be able to distinguish beauty from these other forms of value which may or may not be felt together with it; and such sound judgment requires a capacity for aesthetic abstraction which is only achieved with training.

At this point, however, a word of caution needs to be sounded. Beauty cannot be entirely abstracted from other values in those cases where the meanings that have to be grasped in order to appreciate the beautiful also have significance for other values. This is especially the case in architecture and in the beauty of other essentially useful things. These things must stimulate the imagination by their meaning. So if an attempt has been made to secure aesthetic value at the plain cost of lessening their value in the ways in which they are primarily meant to be of value, then this element of disvalue will tend to be felt as the meaning of the thing is grasped, and it necessarily adversely affects the activity of aesthetic appreciation and admiration. In the same way a picture, poem, or drama, which depends for its beauty on its capacity to stimulate the imagination of those who grasp its meaning, has its effectiveness destroyed if its meaning is such as to provoke rebellion at its falsity (e.g. if it is not true to the life it claims to depict) or at its vulgarity or false sense of moral values. The line here is difficult to draw and it is impossible to lay down fixed canons. But there is no doubt that many works of art destroy their own beauty by thus offending good sense.

The third source of error in aesthetic judgment is the failure to recognize that beauty, being relevant only to a particular perspective, depends as much for its appearance upon the subjective activity which formulates that perspective as upon the objects included in it. Every appearance of beauty is a private appearance to a particular subject. Its validity is immediately for that subject alone. Every value makes its claim upon the will of the individual, appealing to the subsidiary form of will to conform to the higher. As a leading of the agent on to the realization of more ultimate goals it is always, if properly interpreted, valid. It is a call to the realization of his own true nature. But because every individual occupies a different point of view the way to the higher goal will not be the same from every point of view. Because individuals live in the same world, and because the nature of each bears the common stamp of their ultimate common origin and their largely common history, the way to the realization of the higher goals must have an essential similarity in all cases—a similarity which makes possible the laying down of certain broad principles for the pursuit of valid ends. But because of individual differences the same objective situation cannot be equally valuable, and valuable in the same way, for all.

This means, for aesthetics, that when we pronounce this more beautiful than that our judgments can only hold good for those with an aesthetic capacity similar to ours and who contemplate the object from a similar point of view. It may be true that the objects possess these respectively different capacities for beauty for anyone capable of taking advantage of them. But that is all. Yet even so there is a sense in which absolutely valid aesthetic judgments regarding objects are possible. Experience reveals the possibility of increasing the capacity for enjoyment of the beautiful by cultivation.

BEAUTY 271

And those who have thus passed through a series of stages in their capacity for aesthetic appreciation can understand the viewpoint of those still at the lower stages—if they have not forgotten. Their experience thus justifies the defining of varying levels of aesthetic capacity among individuals and the types of object most valuable to those at these different levels. They are able to advise others how to train their aesthetic capacity and those who follow such advice may find it justified by experience. Thus, tentatively and erringly, but nevertheless with growing success, we are able to formulate certain broad canons of taste in art and realize that there is truth in the conviction that these canons are approximations to the statement of ultimate validities.

Those with a deeper understanding of these things may be guides to the rest of us in the discovery of greater aesthetic values. When they tell us what is best we are wise to study it, contemplate it aesthetically as best we can, practice and cultivate our capacities on the acknowledged best. But for each of us there is a limit. And it is folly to pretend aesthetic enjoyment where there is none. The social ideal should be the cultivation of the aesthetic capacity of all as fully as possible and the provision of an abundance of the objects of beauty suited to all levels. In his pursuit of the aesthetic goal each must appreciate what he can. Aesthetic capacity can never be developed by trying to appreciate what is entirely beyond one. It is by being true to the subjective standard that we approach the objective, for as we exhaust the beauty of certain forms and develop our capacity to the point where it is fit to appreciate the higher our own subjective standard changes and leads us on. We only learn to appreciate the more beautiful by enjoying to the full what we can; and the teacher of music or any other art who ignores this truth may develop a technician but not an artist. In beauty, as in all the realms of value, the subjective standard reveals its own inherent validity in that when we adhere to it faithfully and intelligently it gradually discloses a standard which is more and more genuinely objective. In the higher ranges of aesthetic experience there will always be differences of opinion and there is no authority there that can guide. But the development of aesthetic culture, with all its vagaries and backslidings, shows a genuine progress. And that progress is only made as each of the pioneers seeks to be intelligently true to beauty as he sees it. The validity of the subjective standard and the reality of the objective are both vindicated in that the one points the way to the other.

CHAPTER XI

MORAL VALUES

WHEN we begin to think of moral values it is very important to keep clear the distinction drawn in an earlier chapter between value as a quality and as a validity or obligation. Moral value is immediately felt, as a quality, in the experience of conscience. The sense of guilt and the less vivid, but equally definite, sense of moral approval, both of our own actions and of those of others, is the foundation of the whole structure of ethical thought. Yet when we say that an act or a state of affairs is morally right, or that an action or character is morally good, we do not merely mean that we have a sense of moral approval in regard to it, or that other people have such a sense of approval. If pressed for the relation between the sense of moral approval and the rightness or goodness of that which is approved then the latter is offered as the ground of the former; i.e. we approve of things *because* we believe them to be right or good. The rightness or goodness is regarded as being independent of our approval and—except upon certain authoritarian notions—independent of any human approval. Right and good are questions of validity; they determine an ought—including that which our conscience ought to approve.

Yet it is the experience of conscience that gives these terms their distinctive meanings as defining a *moral* validity.[1]

[1] "The so-called 'voice of conscience' is a basic form of the primal consciousness of value; it is perhaps the most elemental way in which the sense of value gains currency among men. . . . Conscience is the revelation of moral values in actual consciousness, their entrenchment within the reality of human life. . . . But this is possible, only provided that values themselves are an existent *prius*. They are, then, simply the 'condition of the possibility of conscience.' "—Nicolai Hartmann: *Ethics*, Vol. I, p. 202.

Apart from conscience acts and characters and social conditions might be referred to as pleasant, useful, lawful, customary, etc., and the reverse. And they might even be described as right or wrong, or good or bad, in any of these senses. But the genuinely moral issue would not arise. That which is pleasant, useful, lawful, or customary may or may not be moral; and it is only the fact of conscience that sets up this further standard. For though conscience never claims that it, of itself, constitutes the standard implied in the terms right and good it is, nevertheless, only from conscience that we derive the notion that there is such a standard. Like every felt value quality it makes its appeal to the will. It presents an obligation. It characterizes something as valid or invalid. It calls for acknowledgement that something ought to be or ought not to be. Simply to be aware of this value quality, the feeling of conscience, is to make this acknowledgement. Though it is a far cry from this mere recognition of what ought to be and the active response which seeks to fulfil the obligation.

The distinction between the feeling of conscience as a quality (a feeling element more or less satisfactory or troublesome) and the validity it calls on us to acknowledge points to the further fact that conscience always presents this validity as something independent of the state of feeling, as something that we cannot rid ourselves of by ridding ourselves of the feeling. If it be true that "there is nothing either good or bad but thinking makes it so," then conscience is the greatest liar in our experience. For the claim of conscience is always to discover good and evil, not to make them. Any suggestion of the ultimate relativity of moral questions is a flat rejection of the essential meaning of moral experience. It explains that experience by explaining it away, which explains nothing—as an argument that proves too much proves nothing.

Yet, in spite of the claim of conscience to discover that

which is objectively real, its vacillations, hesitations, changes and contradictions are all too common and give rise to the moral scepticism of the proverb just quoted. It is here, in the realm of the moral conscience, that the distinction between the subjective standard and the objective standard presents the question of the reality of value experience in its most acute form. Conscience is frequently forced to acknowledge its mistakes in the past and yet it constantly maintains its unchallengeable authority in the present. It may hesitate and be far from sure that it is right. Yet it insists on being obeyed. To deny that its claim is valid is to declare the essential feature of our moral experience unreal. Yet to assert that its presentation of duty is always final and objective is to fly in the face of experience. Here, as in the case of the appearances of truth and beauty, the contradiction can only be explained away if it can be shown that the error is due to our blindness to other elements of moral value presented in the same situation and to misinterpretations of the perspective in which the value experience occurs, so that the element of value in it is related in thought to the wrong data. If it is true that deeper moral insight and fuller understanding of the conditions of the moral perspective would eliminate errors, and if it is further true that, not only is a more intelligent understanding of the conditions necessary to a truer moral judgment, but also, that faithfulness to the moral judgment as at present formulated is necessary to the progressive deepening of moral insight, then the claim of the subjective standard to authority in each succeeding situation is vindicated. But if we are to show that this is the case then we must begin with an analysis of the conditions of the moral perspective.

Now there is a distinction between the notions of the right and the good which should be kept clear. A careful analysis of the usage and significance of the two terms has been made by Dr. W. D. Ross.[1] The "right," as he shows, may be conveniently defined as "something that ought to be done." It is the "morally obligatory." It is used to describe an act which produces or maintains some state of affairs which ought to be produced or maintained. What is right in any particular case is therefore describable in terms of objectively observable events. The "morally good," however, is not equivalent to the "morally obligatory." "The only acts that are morally good are those that proceed from a good motive," but it can never be morally obligatory to act from a good motive, for we cannot produce our motives by choice in that way. Action-from-a-certain-motive may therefore be described as good or bad according to the nature of the motive concerned. This is the element of truth in the famous Kantian formula that there is nothing good without qualification save the good will.

The nature of what we mean by moral goodness is shown most clearly by consideration of our habits of praise and blame, both in regard to ourselves and others. It would be generally recognized, for instance, that a philanthropic subscription has no moral value, even though it is large enough to involve some sacrifice in other directions, if the motive is merely a demonstration of wealth or the making of a show of generosity. Neither can any other action be called morally good, however good its consequences or however well its principle harmonizes with recognized standards, unless the motive is one that the moral conscience approves. On the other hand, lack of success does not make an action wrong if the motive is good. We do not feel that anyone can be blamed if he has done the best he could in the circumstances. As a notable example, the British public is, at the moment of writing, generally consoling itself for the fall of Addis Ababa by reflection that, as a nation, they have striven to prevent the wrong by every

[1] W. D. Ross: *op. cit.*, pp. 4–5, 46–7.

means possible without creating a greater evil. Even if a person's opinion on a question of right and wrong is one that we feel should be condemned we recognize that he cannot be blamed for acting in accordance with that opinion if he has had no reasonable opportunity of greater enlightenment. Thus it is generally admitted to be foolish to censure the savage for his polygamy or his blood feud. What we do demand as conditions of moral approval of any action is that the individual should make all possible effort to see clearly what is his duty in the circumstances and to secure the successful fulfilment of the moral obligations he thus recognizes. Of all the features in the moral perspective, therefore, it is to the *motive* that moral value rightly attaches. Yet there is much confusion in popular thought due to lack of critical clearness on this point. Praise and blame are given without reflection on the nature of the motive involved; and also many a sensitive soul has felt mortified in conscience for some failure for which he was in no way at fault.

That which is felt in the experience of conscience is usually not very intense or vivid so long as the value is positive. The negative experience may, of course, be very poignant and lead to all forms of self-mortification and even suicide. But the good conscience is unexcited and calm. Though the highest of the values it is least able to appeal by reason of any intensity of enjoyment it may offer. If the appeal of value experience to the will depended solely on the emotional force that could be aroused by contemplation of the value quality of an objective then, apart from a certain driving power of the negative experience of a guilty conscience, the effectiveness of the experience of moral value would be almost *nil*. Indeed, if value as quality were all that we considered in our value judgments, it would be the part of wisdom not to cultivate a sensitive conscience. It is certainly possible to develop a large measure of psychic blindness in matters of conscience, as it is in regard to aesthetic and intellectual values. But in these latter cases this means a net loss in positive feelings of value. In regard to conscience, however, it would mean a net gain. The more keenly alive an individual is to moral values the less is he apt to be satisfied with himself. A deep moral truth is expressed in the lines of the hymn: "And they who fain would serve Thee best are conscious most of sin within."

In the greater part of our activity we are scarcely aware of a moral issue, even where one is definitely involved. We go about the ordinary duties of the day, which we recognize that it would be wrong to neglect, without any flattering feelings of a vivid good conscience. It is, indeed, only in the moral crises of life that moral value and disvalue are keenly experienced. So long as we are treading beaten paths the right or wrong of our way is usually taken for granted with little effect upon conscience. We tend to become aware of the moral issue where new decisions have to be made, new purposes formulated, in which moral values are involved. And where the decision to do right is difficult, runs contrary to inclination or desire, there the satisfaction of the good conscience is apt to be keenest. For this reason we are always inclined to praise more highly the moral action which involves sacrifice or a great effort at self-control.

The Austrian pioneers in the realm of value theory, attempting the task of constructing a scale of moral worthiness of actions, were clearly influenced by this feeling. Thus Meinong constructed a table of values indicating by symbols the relative merit of moral deeds. The most worthy type is that which involves the willing of a small good to another person at great cost to the self, and the cases vary by degrees to that where a great evil is willed to another for the sake of a small good to the self.[1] And Ehrenfels argues that

[1] A. von Meinong: *Psychologisch-ethische Untersuchungen zur Werttheorie*, p. 132.

"where goals of equal ethical value are the object of striving, an increase in the ethical valuation follows an increase in the sacrifice which is made."[1] Such principles of value judgment are far from being satisfactory in operation; yet, nevertheless, they do point to a very important fact of our value experience—the fact that the peculiar positive, moral, value *quale* is felt most keenly where the moral decision constitutes a genuine moral achievement. It is the operation of the will, in despite of other motives, in pursuit of an objective to which conscience directs it that is most clearly felt to have moral value. Where no such deliberate act of will is needed, as when the right action is performed as a matter of course in accordance with set habits, the moral value of the motive tends to be overlooked. Indeed, reflection on such cases leads us to attribute moral value to them only in the secondary sense that they are the expression of a character, or habits, the acquirement of which has involved moral decisions requiring some effort of will. This, however, does not place such actions any lower in the value scale.

Recognition of the important part played by conflict in our moral experience has led some thinkers, notably Spinoza and Kant, to regard it as essential to any awareness of moral value. Thus Spinoza, who regarded moral evil as an error due to mental confusion and passion, believed that if it were possible for an individual to have nothing but "clear ideas" and the "active emotions" which are the wholesome correlates of clear, rational knowledge, then, though he would always enjoy the highest good, he would not know the meaning of good and evil. Similarly, Kant attributes our experience of moral obligation to the fact that the "good will" is subject to the solicitation of impulses and desires that tend to lead it astray. The holy will, on the other hand, such as must belong to God—a will con-

[1] C. von Ehrenfels: *System der Werttheorie*, II, p. 51.

taining no tendency to action not in accord with righteous principles—would be presented with no experience of obligation at all.

This, however, is too narrow a reading of moral value. Goodness does not merely consist in avoiding evil. So the reality of moral value cannot be confined to the cases where there is an overcoming of temptation. All that is needed to account for the peculiar vividness of our sense of moral approval in cases where we recognize that real temptation has been overcome is the realization that moral value is essentially associated with *achievement*. Spiritual victory in some moral crisis of the soul is a very important achievement. But there is also real achievement in the steady performance of recognized duties and continuous alertness to opportunities of social usefulness which characterize the lives of a great many people who scarcely feel tempted to do otherwise. The happiness which such people find in their activities involves a value experience which is essentially moral in its nature, though their modesty prevents them dwelling on the thought of it as such. Even such an assertion as that "there is more joy in Heaven over one sinner that repenteth than over ninety and nine just persons that need no repentance," when interpreted in the light of its context, is found to emphasize both sides of the truth here involved. The repentance of the sinner is an occasion of rejoicing because it is a real moral achievement. But this evidence of a divine discontent is set in sharp contrast to the smug self-satisfaction of the conventional "just person" whose life is devoid of any active good work, even in the face of an obvious need of it.

This connection of moral value with positive activity, rather than with the mere negative avoidance of evil, is again shown in the universal recognition of the virtue of industry. It would be easy to heap up quotations from the most ancient Egyptian and Babylonian inscriptions, from the sayings of Confucius and from the Vedic hymns, Homeric poems and Hebrew scriptures to show how universal and primitive is the moral approval of the industrious person. It is a virtue which has been emphasized so much in the past, and one which brings with it so many extrinsic rewards that tend to develop a prostitution of it, that we have of late been growing somewhat sceptical of its intrinsic goodness. Many anthropologists, and even some writers on ethics, suggest that the preference of certain peoples for idleness and ease rather than a vigorous effort at the improvement of the material and intellectual conditions of their lives is in no way a moral question. Yet even such people themselves recognize the moral value of industry. I have found that the Australian aboriginal, for example, though he regards the white man as excessively vigorous, and views laziness as a most venial sin, nevertheless recognizes a moral issue as involved in the attitude of the individual to life's tasks and opportunities.

From this initial study of the general conditions of the experience of moral value, therefore, it is plain that, like all our higher values, it is associated with what we have recognized as the ultimate form of the will of the individual as such—the will to a continuous and self-harmonious activity in the cognitive grasp and conative control of the world in which he lives. Moral value is distinctive of the conative aspect of this activity and we have seen, in three characteristic features of moral experience, the tendency to find moral value in sheer, active self-expression. These three features are (1) the high evaluation of the moral decision requiring great effort of will; (2) the complementary moral stigma attaching to smug moral satisfaction which fails to exert itself in works of practical goodness or to awaken to the possibilities of developing to a higher spiritual level; (3) the universal recognition of industry as a virtue. In none of these cases is the mere conative activity the sole condition of their moral value. Their significance lies, however, in that they bring out so clearly the fact that it is with the *active expression of will* that morality has to do, and that moral value claims the greatest possible continuity and fullness of this self-expression.

In asserting that the moral judgment is based upon qualities *felt* in the experience of conscience we are forced to take issue with Dr. W. D. Ross, who has expressed the contrary view.[1] So far as aesthetic judgment is concerned Dr. Ross agrees that "All predications of beauty seem to rest on the opinion that the judges, or someone else, has derived aesthetic enjoyment from the object." But "In my attitude towards the things I call good," he argues, "my opinion that they are good seems to be the primary thing, and my feeling to be consequent upon this." "This is a matter of psychological analysis and it is difficult to be certain about it. But after a good deal of reflection I feel pretty clear that if I delight in contemplating a virtuous action, for instance, it is because I think the action to be good, and not vice versa. If we think that feeling is here the primary thing, I suppose that the most natural name for it would be 'approval'; but if we ask ourselves what approval is we find that the basic element in it is not feeling at all but the judgment that an object is good."

Now this is a vitally important point for the whole theory of value here developed, unless moral value is to be regarded as somehow an exception. The notion of validity we have interpreted as the acknowledgment of the claim upon the will made by a value quality immediately experienced or felt. Dr. Ross does not feel very confident about the problem of psychological analysis involved, but we would agree that his introspective deliverance is correct so far as the great majority of our moral judgments are concerned. Most of our moral judgments are secondary rather than primary.

[1] W. D. Ross: *op. cit.*, p. 131.

MORAL VALUES 283

Probably the majority are of the type Professor McDougall[1] has called "imitative" rather than "original," i.e. they merely follow the lines laid down for us by others, are merely conventional, instead of based upon our own personal experience of approval and disapproval. But even of the "original" judgments, where our own feelings are certainly involved, Dr. Ross doubts whether the feeling is basic. We would suggest that in the developed moral consciousness it usually is not, but that the reason for this is that such a mind forms its moral judgments by reference to established principles and classifications formulated in past reflection and moral decision. The judgment may be "original" in McDougall's sense of the term; i.e. the person has made that principle his own and genuinely feels its moral importance. But it is not original in the sense of being a new formulation of the moral outlook for that person.

Now the judgment that is original in the sense of being new to the person concerned (a new formulation of the moral issue) if it is more than merely an imitative adoption of opinions expressed by others, will, I would contend, always be based on "feeling."[2] We may be helped to our first formulations of such judgments by suggestions from others; and we certainly need to reflect upon the nature of the data about which we judge; but there could be no formulation of a *moral* judgment unless the experience of the peculiar *quale* we know as conscience, positive or negative, entered into the experience. This must, I think, be true in every case of the new formulation of a moral principle and acceptance of it as such, however much one is helped to the formulation of such principles by the educative influence of the moral tradition. The usual course of our moral experience is, I think, correctly analysed by McDougall

[1] W. McDougall: *An Introduction to Social Psychology*.
[2] In the broad sense of the term, which is inclusive of all immediate awareness of value qualities.

in the distinction mentioned above. We begin by imitatively accepting certain notions of right and wrong without feeling strongly about them. But when an occasion arises where an action so describable touches closely our experience (directly, or sympathetically through its effect on others near to us) for good or ill, then feeling is aroused. Thenceforth the judgment is original in the sense of being genuinely our own. It is the fact of moral feeling that makes this difference. Thereafter our approval and disapproval is tinged with feeling. The judgment of right and wrong on the basis of principle may still be the basis for the feeling on each particular occasion. But it is the fact that moral feeling has entered into the adoption of the principle that stamps that principle for us as a genuinely *moral* principle instead of being merely a pale imitation of the moral opinions of others. Indeed, we may go further and say that though in the case of imitatively adopting any particular principle as moral we may have no moral feeling at first so far as it, in particular, is concerned, yet, *unless we had had some moral feeling in regard to some moral issue at some time we would not understand what was meant in describing it as moral.*

The primacy of felt value quality in the moral judgment would seem then to be clear in regard to the fundamental moral insights of every individual. But it is still clearer in regard to the progressive development of moral insight in the race. This has recently been strongly emphasized by Professor Bergson.[1] He emphasizes the large degree to which our sense of moral obligation is an experience of social pressure, instinctively felt, and our ethical arguments in support of our moral convictions a mere rationalization of beliefs that are forced upon us by our social relations. But the moral geniuses of the race who have contributed to its larger moral vision have, as he points out, not reached their views of wider horizons, their deeper insights, by any pro-

[1] Henri Bergson: *The Two Sources of Morality and Religion.*

cess of reasoning from previously accepted premises. They express an inspiration they have felt, as does the artist; though the moral inspiration is not aesthetic, but something unique. Bergson describes the feeling as an "emotion," but it would seem to be more exact to speak of it as a value quality. It is something distinctive in experience and has influence upon the will, as the mere rational grasp of an idea has not. "No amount of speculation can create an obligation or anything like it: the theory may be all very fine, I shall always be able to say that I will not accept it. . . . But if the atmosphere of the emotion is there, if I have breathed it in, if it has entered my being, I shall act in accordance with it, uplifted by it; not from constraint or necessity, but by virtue of an inclination which I should not want to resist." "Beyond instinct and habit there is no direct action on the will except feeling." "When music weeps, all humanity, all nature, weeps with it. In point of fact it does not introduce these feelings into us; it introduces us into them, as passers-by are forced into a street dance. Thus do pioneers in morality proceed. Life holds for them unsuspected tones of feeling like those of some new symphony, and they draw us after them into this music that we may express it in action."[1]

Moral goodness then is a character ascribed to an action by reason of its association in experience with a certain felt moral value. The action is believed to be good because it appears to be a response to the appeal or claim of the value *quale* felt. The motive or aim, from which the overt act springs, is thus the psychological element most immediately characterized by the *quale*. It is the *motive* that is judged as good. In a secondary sense the objective is also judged as good, and the act which achieves it is judged as right. We have no distinctive term for the quality itself in abstraction from the things qualified by it, as we have in the case

[1] Henri Bergson: *op. cit.*, Chapter I.

of beauty, for the term "goodness" like the term "truth" refers to the validity of the claim rather than to the experienced *quale* that presents it. The importance of the objective validity in both these cases overshadows that of the qualitative character enjoyed in a way that is not the case with aesthetic experience. So we have to use the cumbersome phrase "moral value quality" to indicate that which is actually felt in the experience of moral approval.

This moral value quality ascribed to a motive, like every value quality ascribed to anything, stamps it as objectively valuable. The subjective value experience, like all value experience, asserts a claim upon the will that is authoritative and one that is felt to be valid for all persons in the same circumstances. Yet the errors of conscience are all too familiar. In every war there are men who fight with a good conscience on both sides. In every religious persecution there are some among the persecutors who firmly believe in the righteousness of their actions. Probably no person of keen and earnest thoughtfulness to-day but has changed his conscientious convictions on some important moral questions. This mutability of our experience of moral value and our view of what seem to us to be objective moral standards becomes plainer with increasing knowledge. It has led many earnest souls to surrender their own attempt to formulate objective standards and to decide that the right thing to do is to leave that task to an institution, such as the church. They make an intellectual sacrifice to save their moral sanity.

Such sacrifice is shown to be unnecessary when we recognize the true function of subjective value experience. Like all our value qualities the experience of conscience is the guide of the immediate and subsidiary will to the purpose of the more ultimate and higher will. The value perspective needs to be analysed with care; and we need to recognize that we can never be certain that all sources of error have been eliminated. There is always danger in the adoption of very rigid rules. Law and logic can never be adequate in the decision of complex moral questions. The humble, good-hearted person with a clear head and genuine sympathetic insight will make mistakes; but they are less likely to be serious than are the mistakes of the person who seeks to apply rigidly fixed principles to every case. Every moral problem is a new value perspective. An intelligent understanding of the conditions of the perspective, and a readiness to follow the lines indicated by the values that appear in it, is the way of practical moral wisdom, and leads to least regrets.

Even where errors are made, providing the person has been faithful to his own subjective standard of right and wrong his own moral character does not suffer. Indeed, one can point to cases where moral disintegration has resulted from a refusal or neglect to do some action believed to be a duty, though of a kind which a more enlightened conscience would recognize as wrong. The classical case is Hamlet. Faced with the duty, as he understood it, of committing an assassination to avenge his father's death, he hesitated and postponed the deed, not out of fear, but because of a certain repugnance to the act. And the master dramatist depicts the steadily growing demoralization of his lofty spirit because of this failure. As an example of another kind we might point to Saul of Tarsus, persecuting the Christians as a matter of bitter conscientious duty, though finding it hard to "kick against the pricks." It was a mistake—an example of the unwisdom referred to above of riding principles too hard. But, convinced that it was a duty, he did it, though it would have been much easier to have contented himself with cursing the heretics, as did most of his orthodox friends. Had he failed in that supposed duty, mistaken as it was, it is hardly conceivable that he could ever have become the great apostle to the Gentiles.

Thus, important though it is that we should avoid mistakes of conscience, the essence of moral goodness lies in the adherence of the individual to his own subjective standard—to "the light as he sees it"—rather than in the performance of tasks or duties that are right by an objective standard. To place the emphasis on the consequences of the act, or to measure it by a set of accepted principles, is to miss the spirit of the moral life, to regard moral value as chiefly a means to the social good, or to an arbitrarily ordered service of God, instead of seeing that it intrinsically belongs to the soul whose development it guides. The moral salvation of the individual is not by "works of the law," but by faithfulness to the good as the spirit discerns it. This deeper insight is brought out in the doctrine of "bhakti" in which the religious thought of India reaches its finest expression. It is also the truth expressed by the Christian doctrine of justification by faith.

Yet though the subjective standard sets for us the immediate goal, and though the essence of the moral life consists in thoughtful faithfulness to that goal, the subjective standard itself has no meaning apart from the objective standard which shines through it. It is to the clarification of that objective standard, therefore, that ethical thought must chiefly devote itself. Here there is a double problem, first, the question of what is objectively "good," and second, that of what is objectively "right." Moral goodness, as we have seen, refers to the motive. The question of the goodness of the motive is therefore that of the scale of the value to which the act of will responded. Was this act of will a response to the highest value presented in the subject's perspective? Did he ignore the higher value and choose a lower which was more immediate or more intense? Such judgments passed on another person's motives are notoriously difficult. For practical purposes they are sometimes necessary, but fortunately such questions do not need to be answered in order to make our own moral problems clear. It is necessary, however, that we decide for ourselves as to the nature of our own motives; and this task is much simpler. Yet it is not altogether simple, for it is possible to be psychically blind, in particular cases, to elements of value with which we are normally familiar. And further, as is disclosed by the fact of moral progress in the individual and the race, there are values that may remain undiscovered for half a life-time, or the whole of it, values that the race had to wait for its spiritual geniuses to discern and reveal to it. To those highest values it is very easy to be psychically blind and, as Professor Bergson shows in the work to which we have already referred, the ordinary mortal is only awakened to their appeal through contact, more or less direct, with those great personalities, the saints and sages, prophets and founders of religions, who have embodied in their lives their own insights and thus revealed to the common man the unsuspected values latent in his own soul.

But the morally good can only be described and discussed as it manifests itself in the overt act; and this describable act, as we have already pointed out, is not appropriately called "good," but "right." Dr. Ross has done good service for Ethics in pointing out that, though it is not the consequences of the act that in themselves are regarded as morally right and wrong, neither is it the bare action itself apart from its consequences. Questions of right and wrong concern the effective operation of acts. "An act is not right because it, being one thing, produces good results different from itself; it is right because it is itself the *production of a certain state of affairs. Such production is right in itself*, apart from any consequence."[1] This brings out what we may regard as the second point in which the conditions of moral value are found to coincide with those of our other forms of higher value. The first of these was the fact that the

[1] Henri Bergson: *op. cit.*, pp. 46–7 (italics ours).

value of experience arises in the course of the active self-expression of the individual. The second is the requirement that this activity should be concerned with the real world outside the self. Even the imaginative activity involved in aesthetic experience, we saw, only presents beauty when it has that self-harmonious character which links it to the genuine potentialities of the real; there is a kind of "unreality" in art whereby it loses beauty. In the case of moral experience this requirement, however, is clear, even apart from the question of internal harmony. An act is only right so far as it affects the affairs of the world. An act of will, motive or intention is only good so far as it is directed toward the achievement of some effect upon the world. Moral value, in brief, is concerned with the active impact of the self upon the malleable processes of the world in which it lives.

Now in the spheres of aesthetic and intellectual values we found the further requirement that active self-expression should be self-harmonious. Discord and contradiction present negative values; self-consistent activity presents positive value. In these three requirements we found an adequate explanation of the conditions of these two forms of value experience. So we must inquire whether this third condition holds good also in the realm of moral experience and whether, taken together with the other two conditions, it is sufficient to explain that experience. Briefly: Does the moral conscience require that our purposive activity shall be self-harmonious? And does it require anything more than this?

The answer to the former question is certainly in the affirmative. It is essentially the ethical theory of the Greeks, and was thought by them to be adequate. For Plato "justice," the term he used for the ideal good both of man and the state, is a harmony produced by the reign of reason over the turbulent spirited and appetitive tendencies of the soul. The four cardinal virtues are harmonies. Wisdom is the harmony of reason; Courage and Temperance are the harmony of the spirited and appetitive factors respectively with reason; Justice is the harmony of the whole. The same ideal of internal harmony dominates the ethical teaching of Aristotle. It is manifested clearly in his emphasis upon the importance of settled habit and the necessity of discipline, and in his conception of virtue as a mean between two extremes. The Stoic doctrine of the life according to Nature, because of the religious metaphysic that entered into the concept of Nature, became equivalent to a life according to reason. That this, in turn, meant a life of internal harmony of purposive activity is shown in the emphasis upon the necessity of controlling emotion as the great disturber of the soul. It is shown too in the Stoic picture of the "wise man," possessor of all the cardinal virtues in the highest degree and meeting the smiles and buffetings of fortune alike with imperturbable calm. Even Epicurus, with his doctrine of pleasure as the only good, raises a genuinely ethical edifice on this unlikely foundation, and shows himself true to the Greek spirit, in his teaching that the truest and fullest pleasure or happiness is to be found in the well-ordered life; so that Seneca tells us that there is little practical difference between the laws of virtue recognized by the Stoics and the Epicurean precepts for acquiring pleasure.

It requires little reflection upon the experience of conscience to recognize the reality of this demand for internal harmony. Conscience is not at rest unless there is peace within the soul; and if there is internal peace then conscience not only ceases to disturb but active self-expression is fraught with the positive joy of interested contentment. The difficulties in the way of securing this internal harmony arise, of course, from the complexity of will or conative tendency within the self. Appetitive impulses, the desires connected with the psychological values (which include the natural tendencies to love and loyalty associated with the family, nation, and other social groups) and also the intellectual and aesthetic interests, all press toward their own particular objectives and conflict is inevitable. What our study of the moral consciousness has so far revealed is that there is a peculiar sense of disvalue that attaches itself to failure to co-ordinate these motives in accordance with the scale of values with which they are concerned—the guilty conscience. And there is a mild but distinctive satisfaction in achieving that co-ordination—the satisfaction of the good conscience. Further, that whenever there presents itself a conflict of motives in which differences in value scale are involved there is felt a demand upon the will so to adjust itself that the lower motive shall give way to the higher.

In the light of our general theory of value the presentation to consciousness of these distinctive value elements (both quality and validity) is certainly to a large extent intelligible as the interaction of the various subsidiary specific conative tendencies with the ultimate will of the finite individual to self-harmonious self-expression. As such the relation between the moral values on the one hand, and the intellectual and aesthetic on the other, becomes clear. Appreciation and imagination, we have already pointed out, are incomplete cognitive acts. They have their place in the fulfilment of the ultimate will to self-expression but, necessarily, are a less complete fulfilment than that of the complete cognitive act of truth-seeking. Thus the moral conscience, which requires the completest possible self-expression that is also self-harmonious, has usually felt that, though it is impossible for there to be too much beauty, beauty should not be purchased at the expense of truth, still less at the expense of the moral conscience itself which is concerned with activity in the full sense—both cognitive and conative together.

With regard to truth the position is similar. Knowing is

an act of the self which always points beyond itself to deeds, either as possible or impossible. That knowledge is worth while for its own sake the clearest-sighted moral thinkers have never doubted; and one of the greatest, Aristotle, made it the highest of all goods. But the pursuit of knowledge must itself, occasionally, come before the bar of conscience; i.e. where it involves actions destructive of other values. The careful control and limitation of vivisection, which the modern moral conscience demands, and its refusal to allow vivisection of criminals as in the ancient Hellenic world, are cases in point. Knowledge has a spiritual value. But the pursuit of knowledge is an activity which must be made to conform harmoniously with the total expression of the self, or the moral conscience condemns it. As for the *telling* of truth, the demand for harmony inevitably requires it. Apart altogether from the social consequences of lying, the lie involves a breach of one's own personal integrity at which the moral consciousness inevitably revolts. It is emphatically and obviously not a case of harmonious self-expression. Yet it is only a dull or ultra-rigid morality that would say that it must always be wrong. Cases do arise where it seems the lesser of two evils—where it makes the smaller of two necessary discords in harmony of self-expression and therefore becomes the way of completest possible harmony—something which the moral conscience, in the circumstances, approves, after all, as good.

The will to self-harmonious self-expression therefore offers a fairly complete explanation of the presentation of our value experience. Yet when we think of the finest forms of moral conduct we cannot help but feel that it is ultimately inadequate. The sense of social obligation, the high value which is almost everywhere placed on altruism, and some, if not all, forms of self-sacrifice seem scarcely explicable as determined by the harmony of the will to self-expression with any form of will that is *subsidiary* to it. Harmonious self-expression may be an ultimate requirement of the moral conscience; but the question is whether the forms of will that need to be harmonized with it are all subsidiary to it, or whether there is not some demand that is independent of this ultimate demand of the finite self, and above it. A morality responsive to nothing higher would be a morality of personal integrity and self-expression. That there *is* such a morality there is no doubt; but the question is whether this principle is adequate to explain the whole of our moral experience.

If the principle of personal integrity, the rational good, the Greek ideal of the harmony of the soul, is ever inadequate it is in reference to our wider social obligations and the occasional need of high personal self-sacrifice for the sake of others. How far then can it account for the element of altruism in our recognized moral obligations? It is certainly at this point that the Greek ethic was weakest. It arose amid a social structure based on slavery and was developed by the leisured class which benefited from that institution. Yet there was among the philosophers no prophet to condemn this injustice. Plato's metaphysic, which posited an objective standard of the good in an eternal Idea, provided a basis for the doctrine of equality of human rights in its recognition of the ideal form of man among the eternal ideas. Yet he never drew the inference. And Aristotle, who teaches that the highest good is the exercise of the distinctive human capacity of reason, instead of inferring from this the wrong of debasing men to the level of cattle, made it an argument in defence of that practice.

But though the Greeks did not find in the principle of personal integrity a basis for the wider and finer forms of altruism it does not follow that it is not there. Many modern thinkers have thought that it is, that human nature itself so contains the seeds of altruism that the consistent rational cultivation of human personality cannot fail to produce these finer fruits—and that without any reference to a supra-human source of obligation. This faith in humanity has received much encouragement from the psychological recognition of the wide ramifications of the parental and herd instincts in man and from observation of the importance of "mutual aid" in biological evolution. The suggestion that in these tendencies we have the origin of the notion of duty was made by Charles Darwin in *The Descent of Man*: "Any animal whatever, endowed with well-marked social instincts, the parental and filial affections being here included, would inevitably acquire a moral sense, or conscience, as soon as its intellectual powers had become as well, or nearly as well, developed as in man."[1] Long before Darwin, however, Bishop Butler in his famous sermon *Upon the Social Nature of Man* had declared that "There is a natural principle of *benevolence* in man; which is in some degree to *society*, what *self-love* is to the individual." Prince Kropotkin, Professor McDougall and other recent writers have emphasized the same fact. It is clear, therefore, that there can be no internal harmony within a personality that does not give due place to these altruistic tendencies. The only question is whether this instinctive basis of altruism is sufficient to explain our highest moral experience—the felt obligation to *universal* justice and those occasional acts of high devotion wherein life itself is made subservient to a worthy cause.

In another work I have examined in some detail the nature of the parental and herd instincts and sought to show their limitations.[2] They enter into many of our sentiments of love and obtain, by association of ideas, a certain degree of extension beyond their ordinary, natural objects. But it is impossible to regard them as the basis of all our altruistic ideals. I shall not repeat this argument here but shall support it with another from the recent work of Professor Bergson.[3]

[1] Chapter IV.
[2] *The Mind in Action*, pp. 99–105 and 131–42.   [3] *Op. cit.*

There is a lower type of morality, he points out, the compulsive power of which is derived from the influence of the group upon the mind of the individual. So far as it is altruistic in tendency it plainly depends upon those natural instincts we have already referred to; and the power of social pressure is such that the individual will sometimes passionately and enthusiastically sacrifice himself for the group. But, Bergson points out, the group is always a *limited* group. It is *constituted* by *differentiation* from others. However large it grows, it can never be the whole, or it would cease to be a group. There can therefore be no mental transition from obligation to the group to obligation to those outside it. We can never pass from a limited family, or tribal, or national morality, by any natural or rational process, to a universal morality. The notion of a universal obligation must be derived from some entirely different source.

It has always been felt that in the notion of a universal obligation and equality of human rights there is something supremely rational; and consequently many attempts have been made to derive these notions from some purely intellectual contemplation of the notion of the good. Professor G. E. Moore, for example, sets out to prove that nothing can be an ultimate rational end for any individual that is not a part of "Universal Good."[1] He begins with an appeal to the moral consciousness to show that good is a simple objective notion like yellow (not a complex object such as the fulfilment of a desire) and something which must not be confused with pleasure. The force of this argument plainly depends upon our recognition of good as a validity independent of our personal wishes. But Professor Moore then uses the term, so defined, to show that any statement that a thing is "good for me" must mean, simply, and absolutely, that the thing is good without qualification, or that my having it is good without qualification, i.e. that it is

[1] G. E. Moore: *Principia Ethica*, especially pp. 9–19, 97–9.

a part of "Universal Good." This alleged refutation of Egoism, however, rests on a conception of the good which no Egoist would accept. But suppose the Egoist failed to see the *petitio principii* and was thus convinced that it was entirely illogical to think of anything as good which was not a part of "Universal Good." Would he then be persuaded to forsake the pursuit of selfish goals and devote himself altruistically to social welfare? Or would he say: "Logic be hanged! I am going to look out for myself"? Plainly even if by sounder arguments we could show that the pursuit of Universal Good alone is rational, that demonstration is insufficient of itself to move the will. And since humble souls who could never follow a subtle argument devote themselves unselfishly to Universal Good there must be a motive to it that they find elsewhere.

A different kind of attempt to trace universal altruism to reason, and one which tries to avoid the last mentioned objection to Professor Moore's theory by seeking to show that reason is *directive* of motives, is made by Professor L. T. Hobhouse. At the human level, he points out, the felt impulses which move us tend to become correlated by general principles of action and directed toward ends involved in more comprehensive views of life. This, of course, is no more than the enlightened formation of sentiments (most important of which is that of self-respect) that is widely recognized in the psychology of the moral life; but it does not explain the passage beyond the kind of altruism that is limited to the group. Professor Hobhouse, however, tries to overcome this limitation. Reason, his argument runs, must needs be self-consistent. It is the principle of interconnection persistently applied to the discovery of the objective order. But "in so far as we think a thing *good for ourselves* here and now" we are disposed to act in such a way as to secure or preserve it. "If an end is genuinely conceived as good it means that we have at least some feeling for it."[1] "If this analysis is correct a judgment of the form 'this is good' is an assertion, but something more than an assertion. *Unless qualified by some saving clause that makes it 'good for someone else, but not for me,'* 'good from your point of view but not from mine,' it is the expression of a practical attitude or disposition."[2] Then, because reason is an organic principle requiring consistency within itself and tending to objectivity, "the rational good forms a connected whole in which no part is isolated but in the end every element involves each other. This postulates a harmony of feeling with feeling . . . a harmony of all experience of all sentient beings with this body of feeling."[3] "That is to say, it is the function of the rational impulse in practice to embrace this world in a single system of purposes, just as it is the function of the rational in recognition to embrace the world of experience in a single system of thought."[4]

The fallacy in this argument is in the lines italicized. An impulse that is initially egoistic cannot by any *rational* process pass over into one that is altruistic. If I pass from the notion "This is good for me" to the notion "This is good," there is no logical connection whatever between the two judgments. The mere dropping of the qualifying phrase "for me" changes the meaning of the judgment without replacing it by the phrase "for someone else, but not for me." So even if reason were able to carry impulse and feeling with it, as it passes from one inference to another, in the way that Hobhouse supposes, it would not be by a rational process but only by a logical error that we would pass from egoism to altruism. And mistakes of that kind we do not often make, for the reference to self is usually all too plain a part of our notions of the goodness of our objects of desire.

It would be fruitless to pursue the argument further. There

[1] L. T. Hobhouse: *op. cit.*, pp. 78–9 (italics ours).
[2] *Op. cit.*, p. 81 (italics ours).   [3] *Op. cit.*, pp. 98–9.   [4] Pages 100–1.

is no passage from Egoism to Altruism. Neither is there any passage from the limited altruistic tendencies of human nature, which have their roots in the instincts of the family and social life and which require to be organized into the harmoniously integrated self, to that lofty altruism which recognizes the brotherhood of man, the equality of human rights, and the moral necessity of self-sacrifice when the occasion calls for it.

The principle of personal integrity will carry us far in the explanation of the moral life. It is the root of most of those special obligations which Mr. Bradley so aptly summed up in the conception of "my station and its duties."[1] It is the source of those particular principles which have so much puzzled moral philosophers by their apparent claim to absolute validity, and which yet seem to need to allow of occasional exceptions; e.g. the obligations to tell the truth, keep promises, pay debts. These are not merely social obligations, important though they are in that regard, but are part of the general felt need of self-consistency in our actions. But the morality that moves on this level, while it perhaps never deserves our censure, and while it always earns our respect, never kindles our enthusiasm or fires us with noble ideals. Its value quality is felt as a very important element in our higher value experience. It controls and gathers up into itself the values of beauty and truth. But it in turn, together with these other spiritual values, is caught up into, rather than made subservient to, that loftiest of all our values, manifested clearly in the spiritual leaders of the race and spasmodically appearing in lesser personalities inspired by them, the value found in devotion[2] of the self to a good that is universal.

[1] F. H. Bradley: *Ethical Studies*.
[2] This high evaluation of devotion has found expression in the works of a number of important German thinkers. Thus August Messer, in *Deutsche Wertphilosophie der Gegenwart*, quotes Arvid Grotenfeld with

There can be no doubt that it is not to the moral philosophers but to the prophets of religion that humanity owes the inspiration of this higher ideal. On this point Professor Bergson is very emphatic. "In all times there have arisen exceptional men, incarnating this morality. Before the saints of Christianity, mankind had known the sages of Greece, the prophets of Israel, the Arabants of Buddhism, and others besides. It is to them that men have always turned for that complete morality which we had best call absolute morality."[1] But it is only in the teaching of the founder of Christianity that the ethic of universal brotherhood and high devotion became sufficiently clear, emphatic, and consistent to make any deep impression on the general moral outlook. Yet when once that ideal was clearly presented it found a wide response in the human soul. To all who have directly or indirectly come under its influence, and who are in earnest about matters of the moral life, the supreme ethical principle is the brotherhood of man. Even where religious authority is repudiated and the religious origin of the ideal ignored it is nevertheless recognized as supreme. For the leaders of the French revolution, for the modern Communist and Humanist, society is universal and moral good is social good; and no fair-minded observer can deny how genuinely many of the leaders of these movements manifest the high devotion that is the implication of their creed.

No modern writer has shown deeper insight in his analysis of these higher virtues than Professor Hartmann. He speaks approval. "The unconditionedly valuable is not the attainment of a certain objective cultural level, nor of a moral insight or faith existing as objective historical reality. It is rather the *seeking* after the ideal and *devoted working* for it. This means, finally, that it is the measure of devotion to the ideal and of possession by it, the measure of 'Gottinnigkeit,' in the most general sense, that man inwardly attains. It is the movement of the human spiritual life that belongs to the temporal and at the same time participates immediately in the eternal."

[1] Henri Bergson: *op. cit.*, pp. 25–6.

of "the transformation which the ancient ethos underwent through Christianity," introducing a "new class of moral values," fundamental among which is that of "brotherly love." Yet, strangely, he regards this Christian doctrine as limited in its vision to those near by and in need, thus missing the import of the parable of the Good Samaritan as an answer to the question "Who is my neighbour?" overlooking the significance of the command to "love your enemies," and forgetting the commission to carry the Gospel to all the world and the end of the age. Higher still than "brotherly love" he puts the "love of the remote," a term derived from Nietzsche who, in his complete misunderstanding of Christian teaching on the matter, thought he had discovered it. Hartmann accepts Nietzsche's claim and then describes the virtue in words which re-echo the thought of St. Paul. "It is an ethos of love, but of another love than that for one's neighbour, a love for the man who is to be, as he is conceivable in Idea by the living. It is a love which knows no return of love, which radiates only, gives only, devotes, overcomes, sacrifices, which lives in the high yearning which cannot be fulfilled for the one who loves, but which knows there is always a future and that indifference to it is sin."[1] If beside this we put Hartmann's picture of its twin and complementary ideal, "radiant virtue,"[2] a virtue which comes down to earth from the vision of distant horizons and pours out its spiritual goods, of its own fullness, to everyone who knows how to partake, we have a picture of the Ideal that was the gift of Christianity to the world. It is an ideal that is interpretable as the morality of personal integrity and true and complete self-expression caught up into the larger life of the will to universal good—for all mankind and every sentient creature.

This finer flower of the life of Christendom, that is found among orthodox and heterodox alike, is no mere dancing

[1] Hartmann: *op. cit.*, Vol. II, p. 317.   [2] *Op. cit.*, pp. 332 ff.

to a tune piped by a Galilean peasant some nineteen hundred years ago. It is rather that through his teaching and inspiring example the world has become conscious of a value that was nowhere clearly recognized before. That value, once felt, makes its claim upon the will, a claim that is recognized as higher in scale than the goods of personal integrity and self-expression, of truth, and of beauty. It does not contradict these other values (the lower moral good, the beautiful, the true), but gathers them up in itself, co-ordinates, and resolves such conflicts as may arise among them, in the same way as they, in turn, do this for the still lower goods we call pleasures. But above all, it eliminates from the notion of the good, from the concepts of obligation and validity, all peculiar reference to the private personal self. From this higher standpoint nothing can ever be truly good that is merely a good "for me" if it is purchased at the cost of a greater good for some other, no matter how distant. On the other hand, if by the sacrifice of some private good I can bring a greater good to others, then that sacrifice is my duty; and in doing my duty, though I may not find happiness, I shall find my highest good. In particular instances this doctrine is hard to believe and harder still to practice; yet when we reflect upon our experience of values and their claims upon the will we know it in our hearts to be true.

Thus, though we have approached the ethical problem from a different angle, and with a different metaphysical view of the self, the conclusion of our study of moral values might be stated in the words of Mr. F. H. Bradley. "What we have left is this—the end is the realization of the good will which is superior to ourselves; and again the end is self-realization. Bringing these two together, we see the end is the realization of ourselves as the end which is above ourselves."[1] This interpretation of the moral goal has usually

[1] F. H. Bradley: *op. cit.*, p. 162 (second edition).

been criticized as insufficiently concrete. In the setting of an Idealistic metaphysic this criticism, I think, is sound. But in the light of our analysis of the self in earlier chapters it may be affirmed that the ideal end receives definite shape. The self to be realized is one in harmony with the form of the Eternal Will; and its guide in the process of realization is objectively given in the fixed potentialities of the value scale. But this is the theme of our last chapter.

CHAPTER XII

CONCLUSION

THIS examination of our value experience has brought to light three facts which are of deep significance for our understanding of the meaning of life. The first of these is that of the relation between value and will. Value is a phenomenon of the complexity of will due to the fact that we have general and relatively permanent aims which can only be realized by a multiplicity of purposive activities; and the limitations of the finite intelligence are such that the whole scheme cannot be kept in mind at once; and, indeed, since some of the goals were set by our racial origins they can only be understood in proportion as they are realized. It is this situation that gives the value quality its function. When the present, attentive, purposive activity is so directed upon an objective that its aim is in apparent harmony with that of the more ultimate and general will upon which it depends, and of which it is a particular expression, then value experience is positive; and when the primary and subsidiary forms of will are not thus in harmony value experience is negative. Thus the felt value constrains and guides the otherwise free activity of the subsidiary form of will, encouraging it in one direction and discouraging it in another according to its consistency with the more fundamental and larger aims of the self. These more ultimate and general aims thus, though not clearly formulated or always kept in mind, nevertheless, because of their effect upon the value *quale*, tend to control the direction of the immediate purposive activity. Even a goal which has never been explicitly thought of may thus gradually define itself within experience. Tentatively and erringly, but with increasing sureness of touch, the highly particularized atten-

CONCLUSION 305

tive purpose of the present moment may, and does, feel its way to the realization of the larger goals set by the more permanent forms of will within the complex constitution of the self.

The second significant fact derived from our study is that of the objective value scale and, in particular, its association with the varying levels of will concerned in the values experienced. Thus the healthy functioning of the sense organ is an end fixed within the purposive structure of the organic whole and is subsidiary to the healthy functioning of the organism as a whole; and in accordance with this relation we recognize a difference in the objective value scale between the mere pleasures of sense and those of the larger organic welfare and function. Again, the will to physical self-maintenance is subsidiary to the will to full self-expression, and in accord with this we recognize that all pleasures are lower in the value scale than the spiritual values of the aesthetic, intellectual, and practical life. The differences in scale, which are objective facts of the value continuum, are thus co-ordinate with the hierarchy of forms of will which is concerned in their presentation. And the higher, or more fundamental, forms of will tend to become explicit as they are implicitly operative in the presentation of value.

Thus the finite self is revealed as primarily a form of will directed toward an ever-increasing cognitive grasp and conative control of its world in accordance with the essential requirement of an inner harmony of its own activity.

This we may call briefly the will to self-expression. It finds its first specific expression in the building up and maintenance of the physical organism, a process in which are developed many subsidiary conative tendencies or forms of will which become what Professor Ward called the "psychoplasm"[1] handed on from generation to generation. These tendencies are of four types: (*a*) those tending to activities

[1] James Ward: *Psychological Principles*.

U

directly affecting the maintenance of the organism as a whole and yielding, notably, the pleasures of appetite; (*b*) tendencies set to maintenance of the particular organs of sense, so that when further subsidiary vital processes occur in those organs there is a distinctive type of pleasure-unpleasure, lower in the value scale; (*c*) tendencies to distinctive types of activity (e.g. play, social intercourse) which primarily subserve biological ends but also serve to some extent the more ultimate goal of self-expression, so that the "psychological" pleasures arising from them are viewed as higher than the biological pleasures. But when mere physical maintenance is assured, and there is capacity for activity beyond that which can find adequate expression even in the activities of type (*c*), then the highest values of self-expression are discovered in (*d*) activities which subserve directly and purely the ultimate will to self-expression; these are the aesthetic and truth values and the moral values of self-expression and personal integrity.

Thirdly, we have found that beyond any activity subservient to the ultimate will of the finite individual as such (the will to self-expression defined above) there is another value makes its appearance, and one that is universally acclaimed the highest of all by all who have experience of it. It is found in the making of the individual life of the self-subservient to the good of the whole. It is evident that this value has to some extent been known throughout the spiritual history of the race, so far as the records of that history can inform us. For it alone can account for the preaching of social justice from the Pyramid Age to the present day, and for the admiration of genuine altruism by civilized man and primitive savage. But the full and proper nature of the goal was slow to define itself. Mankind felt its way to a knowledge of this ideal, helped by the spiritual geniuses who from time to time appeared. But it was not until the birth of Christianity that its meaning as a universal

CONCLUSION 307

brotherly love was clearly and decisively emphasized. To-day, though we fall sadly short of it in practice, the supreme value of that principle is widely recognized both within and outside the ranks of the professed adherents of the Christian religion. The finer spirits have awakened everywhere to the reality of a form of will within themselves that seeks something more than a good "for me" *plus* a limited circle that tends to be gathered within the larger self by the influence of biological impulses concerned with the family and the herd. It seeks the good of the race and of every individual in it. It recognizes the essential equality of the rights of every individual so far as he is able to bear the responsibility that needs must go with every right. It counts the self as no more than one in the sharing of privileges. And it finds its truest joy in selfless devotion to the larger good.

These three facts, taken together, are immensely significant both for Ethics and Metaphysics, and in these concluding pages we must seek to indicate briefly what they mean. For Ethics they mean the supremacy of the altruistic and humanitarian ideal. While reinterpreting the notion of "good" we must endorse the Utilitarian principle of "the greatest good of the greatest number." Morality must transcend the boundaries of race and nation, caste and creed. This principle would sound trite were it not for certain reactionary tendencies manifest in Europe to-day. And it is in view of these tendencies that importance is to be attached to a second principle that emerges. The higher goods for each individual become his only through his *own* self-expression. We cannot *confer* these values on others. We can only create the conditions in which they will have scope and encouragement to pursue those objectives through which they will discover them. There is no such thing as an objective that we have not chosen of ourselves; and it is only by faithfully and intelligently pursuing the good (i.e. the good objective) as we find it that we can feel our way to higher goods. There can therefore be no higher goods conferred on any people save by freedom, the only limits to freedom that can rightly be applied either to adult or child being those suggested by the known incapacity or unwillingness of the individual to bear safely the responsibility which freedom, like every right and every power, brings with it.

It would be beyond the scope of this book to develop fully the implications for ethical theory and practice of our general theory of value; but there are some points on which something must be said to guard against misinterpretation. The value scale and value quality (positive or negative) define questions of obligation. The psychological values are higher than the biological; the spiritual are higher than the psychological; there are degrees of the value scale, *within* the sphere of the spiritual, which accord with the completeness of self-expression obtained in the activity concerned and with the harmony of self-expression with the will to universal good. But in every objective there is a complexity of values, some of which are intrinsic (immediate potentialities), while to others it (the objective) is only a more or less necessary and more or less certain means. It is this complexity that constitutes the difficulty of the value judgment. We have to try to be sure that we are aware of all the values involved, their kind and scale, quality, and intensity, their duration, permanence, propinquity, purity, and inclusiveness, as well as our own subjective preferences or those of other people concerned. Often an objective of great intrinsic value has to be set aside because it would be inclusive, as a means, of greater disvalues. As stated above, it is with the distinctions of quality and scale (of good and bad, higher and lower) that the moral issue is concerned. It is these that distinguish the objectives whereby, in its progressive activity, harmony is maintained within the soul—including the harmony of the will to self-expression with the will to universal good. The validities of conscience are thus one with those of the whole scale of values. Thus the fundamental general moral obligation is to be faithful to conscience; and because of the complexity of our value experience the derivative obligation to the most intelligent possible examination of its problems is only second in general importance.

But within the whole sphere of values there is a wide scope for subjective preferences into which questions of obligation do not enter—except the obligations to widen rather than narrow the scope of the preferences of others. Having once decided that the value qualities concerned in any choice of objectives (both intrinsically and as a means) are indifferent as to quality (positive or negative) and scale we may exercise preference without obligation on questions of the kind of value and such matters as their relative intensity, duration, permanence, propinquity, purity, and inclusiveness. Some of these questions, particularly permanence and inclusiveness, frequently have moral implications from the effect of the objective as a means; but so far as such implications are absent there is no ethical objection to the choice, for example, of a more intense and briefer pleasure to a less intense but more permanent one. Or again, providing moral obligations are given due attention there is no difference in value scale between careers or hobbies devoted to the intellectual, aesthetic or practical forms of self-expression. There is room in life for the exercise of "taste" or preference in many matters according to individual capacity and acquired interest and opportunity. And though the will to universal good must be recognized as supreme, yet that "good" is itself so complex and relative to individual capacity that, even at the level of the highest moral values, there is, as Professor Hartmann has shown,[1] no clearly defined *summum bonum* which can be regarded

[1] Hartmann: *op. cit.*, Vol. II, pp. 66–70.

as the distinctive apex of the value scale and a measure for the relative worth of the other loftier virtues.

Apart from the fact that so often we are not sure of all the implications and possibilities in a situation our greatest difficulties in value judgment arise where a choice must be made between values of the same scale and quality which cannot both be realized. It is here that we have to consider the various dimensions of the value qualities of an objective —their inclusiveness, purity, permanence, duration, propinquity, and intensity. No general rules can be laid down, but usually consideration and preference need to come in the above order, although a marked difference in intensity of the value qualities concerned will, for example, require that it should be given greater prominence. The inclusiveness of the value concerned is of particular importance as embodying, among other considerations, the principle of the "greatest good of the greatest number." This principle is, however, not so simple in its application as Utilitarians have usually assumed. The recognition of distinctions of scale, and of dimensions of value which are only very roughly objectively commensurable, makes the computation of the "greatest" good no simple matter. Yet more or less effectively it is done and must be done. The difficulty of doing it for others, however, is yet another reason for the retention and extension of those democratic forms of social order so much under criticism to-day.

Turning to the metaphysical implications of the three facts regarding our value experience enumerated at the beginning of this chapter we find that we have in them the key to several problems which remained unsolved at the conclusion of our discussion of the self and the world in Chapter v. We have found that value is experienced when one form of will operates in apparent harmony with a more ultimate will from which it is derived and to which it is subsidiary. And we have found that the will of the

CONCLUSION

individual to full and harmonious expression (a form of will indicated as the most fundamental and highest feature of the strictly finite self by the fact that it determines the scale of all our egoistic values and the form of our aesthetic and intellectual values and the moral values of personal integrity and self-expression) discovers a new value experience when it makes its objective the disinterested realization of the good of others; and in that value experience the self discerns a new obligation transcending all its formerly recognized duties. Through this experience of value *quale* and obligation the self becomes aware, in the depths of its own being, of a hitherto latent, or at least unrecognized, will to universal good. Then it becomes plain that this value discovered only in man's higher spiritual development is a value felt through harmony of the will to self-realization with the will to realization of the good of all.[1]

Thus we see that the will to self-realization is subservient to, derivative from, the higher will to the universal good. But the will to self-realization is the very foundation of the finite self. It is the root from which has developed the whole complex of conative tendencies that form the inherited psycho-plasm and is handed on with them from generation to generation. It and its derivatives simply *constitute the individuality* of the self. This form of will can itself be derivative from no other than the Eternal Will which is the ultimate form of will from which all finite wills, all finite selves, are derived. The will to universal good can be neither more nor less than the form of the Eternal Will immanent in the

---

[1] It is important to remember that the value qualities thus *discovered* through this complex interaction of will are not *produced* by it. They are objective features of reality, the determinate potentialities for the experience of which must therefore be resident in the structure of the Eternal Object. And as the rational structure of the self is, as we have seen, adapted to the discovery of the spatial structure of the Object, so too the volitional structure of the self is adapted to the discovery of the valuational structure of the Object.

finite self. Its presence through the long history of biological evolution may then be taken to account for the most marvellous of all the developments in animate nature—the origin and evolution of mutual aid. And with the development, at the human level, of consciousness of self and other selves it gives its unique sense of value to the unselfish deed until man at last awakens to find in this higher will the ultimate meaning of life.

It is, as Bergson points out, the great religious teachers of mankind who first clearly grasped the nature of this ultimate moral value; and it is through religion that the recognition of it has become a part of the cultural inheritance of the race. People who have grown up under the influence of this ideal, have been taught to acknowledge it before they have understood it. It has grown familiar to them in thought before they have felt its appeal in practice; and they grow into the adoption of it so naturally that they are apt to take it for granted as a part of human nature. Thus, in these days when science has made us suspicious of the supernatural, it is very easy, even for those to whom the ideal is a powerful incentive, to regard it as a product of evolution—thus reversing the true relation. But the prophets and seers who discovered it for themselves never believed that they had invented it. They could not even think that it was a part of the nature with which they were born. To them it was a revelation. It was the will of God.

In this the prophets and seers were undoubtedly right, as our whole analysis of will and value has shown. The highest moral experience and genuine religious experience are essentially one. Stripped of the accretions of magic and myth religion is, as Professor John Baillie describes it, "a moral trust in reality," "an apprehension of reality through, and in terms of, our moral values."[1] One can grasp the

[1] John Baillie: *The Interpretation of Religion*, p. 318.

CONCLUSION 313

moral ideal and serve it without recognizing its metaphysical significance. Yet that is only because we have been so helped and nurtured from childhood in the atmosphere of the ideal that it is a part of ourselves and affects our motives even though it does not seem to belong essentially to anything that transcends our finite selves. One wonders, however, whether the race can long retain its vision of the supreme values if it forgets entirely how that vision is revealed. And it is certainly true that the ideal must lose in significance and vitality if it is thought a mere product of social evolution and therefore something that may yet be outgrown. So, though the finest flowers of morality may bloom without the support of religious conviction, it seems hardly possible that they should bloom so well, still less that they should be able to propagate their seed forever. The modern tendency to divorce ethics and religion is therefore one fraught with social danger as well as metaphysically unsound. There is a needed strength given to the moral life if one can but see that "the presence of the Ideal is the reality of God within us."[1]

At this point we can take up again the question left unanswered in our discussion of the self and the world. We saw reason there to believe that the Eternal Will was the source of our rational character and of the intelligible form of the processes of space-time. But since the world of finite beings is such a mixture of good and evil we found it impossible, from any examination of their external relations to each other, to say whether the Will from whose act they must ultimately have issued was good. To this question our highest value experience supplies an emphatic and affirmative answer. The Eternal Will is the all-benevolent will. Immanent in us it defines for us our highest duty. Directly or indirectly it is the source of everything in life we find worth while. And though it is indirectly the source, too, of

[1] A. S. Pringle-Pattison: *The Idea of God in Modern Philosophy*, p. 246.

our pains, and directly the source of the higher sense of sin, these very disvalues function, as do the values, as guides to the finite mind and will toward the realization of all that is best.

This is not, in itself, a complete explanation of the problem of evil—of the pain and disvalue, error and sin—within the world. But it does enable us to assert, on the basis of immediate experience, that the Will that gave us our finite being was a will that seeks without favour the fullest good of all. Each individual is at the same time the instrument and the end of that seeking. That will to the universal good, which we recognize as not the product of our own spirit, but a high, a Holy Spirit, immanent within us, could not be seeking the good of man through us if the Eternal Will, whose form it must express, were indifferent to our good. It is this elementary fact of the higher religious experience that has led all great religious teachers, in spite of the obvious evil of the world, to declare that God is good.[1] In our knowledge of that Will which is the source of our finite existence, the light of our spiritual ideals, the law of our rational life, we have a knowledge of a Being that is adequate to the religious notion of God. This Being is personal because inclusive of our personalities and the transcendent completion of them. While we cannot say with certainty that He is omnipotent, and thus far have not ground to call Him infinite, we certainly must regard Him as eternal; and we know that His purpose, manifested in us and through us and toward us, is one of universal love.

But the Eternal Will is not the Absolute. It is rather what Greek philosophers and Christian theologians have called the *Logos*. In our earlier analysis we found it necessary to postulate also an Eternal Object, of distinctive nature and capable of diversification into the multiple qualities and

---

[1] If Gotama and Lao-tse are exceptions it is in a denial of the existence, not of the goodness, of God.

CONCLUSION 315

forms of space, sense, and value. And besides these notions, static and merely potential when thus conceived in abstraction, we had to recognize that Reality involves the active process of Time or Mind. But each of these three types of entity is incomplete without the other. They are not so many distinct and independent reals. The nature of each is complementary to the other. The Eternal Will and Time, in relation to the Eternal Object, are only the abstract forms into which we have analysed enduring structure and the concrete active process of the world and the life it contains. The analysis has its advantage in enabling us to see the unity of that process as a whole—the Universal Will expressing itself creatively in free creatures of almost infinite variety. We see in that Will the source of finite spirits who find an increasing value in their own lives as they grow into a completer harmony with the form of the Original Will. The concrete process of Time, when thus recognized as the expression of a Universal Will, is seen as the Universal Mind in which all finite minds live and move and have their being—immanent within them, transcendent beyond the totality of them. But the complement of the Universal Mind, as subject, is the Eternal Object, distinctive and determinate, but infinitely rich in the potentialities of its diverse self-revelation. Subject and Object in their complementary character together form the Absolute, a Being that we can only call Spiritual or Personal.

He is infinite in the sense that He is not limited by anything outside Himself, but not in the sense that there is nothing determinate (and determination implies limitation) within Himself. But if the determinacy of His nature as reason, and the fixity of the conditions of His self-revelation to finite spirits as spatial medium, sense and value, constitute limitations of His omnipotence and providence they are limitations inherent in His own nature and conditions essential to the life and development of finite spirits.

If there is trouble and disorder among the finite individuals who share His life it is because it is of the essence of His nature as Mind that they should all be free. The freedom of finite individuality is the condition of the actuality and complexity of will; the actuality and complexity of will is the condition of the realization of value and disvalue; and the occasional realization of disvalue is the condition of the advance to higher values. These conditions are rooted in the nature of the Eternal, are beyond the control of Will, and as such are beyond description as morally good or evil. But that which is of deepest significance for the meaning of the finite life in all this that may be known of the nature of the Whole—and that of which there is the clearest and most immediate certainty—is that the Eternal Will is one of universal and disinterested love. If, beyond that, the human sufferer seeks a further consolation in his pain it may perhaps be found in the thought that, since all immediate experience is ultimately and finally real, and since the finite mind is but a part of the Universal Mind, the Absolute shares with us the immediate *quale* of our joys and sorrows, though not the errors of our interpretation of them due to our finite point of view.

It is the knowledge that the Eternal Will is good that transforms our conception of the Absolute into what religion means by God. It is truth that needs no philosophical reasoning to understand or prove. It is given in its clearness to the moral insight that discovers within the soul a will that "seeketh not its own." For when that will is discovered it is not man's natural thought to believe that it is entirely his own will. It requires the sophistication of the modern man, priding himself on his racial self-achievement of an ascent from Simian ancestry, even to think it is his own. A deeper and somewhat humbler reflection will always carry us back to the first thought of the spiritual leaders of the race who made the discovery. The conclusion they drew might be put in words from Robert Bridges' *Testament of Beauty*—that throughout the range of our experience of value, and especially in this highest insight of all,

"God is seen as the very self-essence of love,
Creator and mover of all as active Lover of all,
Self-expressed in not-self, without which no self were."

INDEX

Absolute, the, 66, 68, 101 ff., 131, 314-16
Activity factor in perception, 50
Act of awareness, 25, 58, 102-3, 16 ff.
Aesthetic "appreciation," 253, 261
ALEXANDER, S., 24, 30, 52, 55, 64, 116, 129, 249, 250
Altruism, 293 ff., 306
Appreciative theory of value, 193, 195
ARISTOTLE, 195, 247, 256, 291, 293, 294
Attention, 31
AUGUSTINE, 131, 195
AVELING, F., 25, 92

BAILLIE, JOHN, 131, 312
BALDWIN, J. M., 109
BALFOUR, A. J., 156
BENTHAM, J., 196
BERGSON, H., 28, 284 ff., 289, 295, 300, 312
BERKELEY, 20
Body and mind, 141
BRADLEY, F. H., 71, 101, 104, 299, 302
BRENTANO, F., 196
BROAD, C. D., 21
BURNS, C. D., 116
BUTLER, JOS., 195, 196, 295

CARRITT, G. F., 249
Causal agency (psychological), 97
Causation, 63 ff.
CLUTTON-BROCK, A., 162
Cognition, 75, 102, 228, 241
COLLINGWOOD, R. G., 250-7
Common sense, 21
Complication, 48, 176
COMTE, AUGUST, 31
Conation, 75, 82 ff., 130, 132, 140

Conscience, 173, 273, 286, 291, 309
Consciousness, function of, 80 ff.
Continua, sense and value, 119, 130, 156, 167, 176, 180, 226
Contradiction, 229, 234, 242
Creation, 131
Creationism, 143, 148
CROCE, B., 196, 250, 251

DARWIN, CHARLES, 295
DESCARTES, 15, 19, 43, 67, 70
Devotion, 299
DEWEY, JOHN, 43, 226
DRAKE, D., 24, 34 ff., 43, 119
Duty, two principles of, 191, 309

EATON, H. O., 169
EDDINGTON, A. S., 135
Egoism, refutation of, 297
EHRENFELS, C. von., 196, 279
Elective theory of value, 192 ff.
Entropy, 126, 130, 132, 142
Epicureans, 131, 291
Error in valuation, 194, 267 ff., 316
Eternal Object, 128, 180, 311, 314
Evil, 133 ff., 314
Expectation, 235 ff.

Feeling, 82 ff., 283
FITE, W., 247
Freedom, 135, 137, 151-3, 303, 316

Gestalt, psychology, 47, 61
God, conclusions concerning, 314-17
GOTAMA, 153, 314

HALDANE, J. S., 85 ff.
Harmony of ends, 220-4, 290
HARTMANN, N., 150, 154, 163, 169, 185, 186, 273, 300, 309
Hedonic tone, objectivity of, 58

INDEX

Hedonism, 161, 196
Heisenberg theory, 131, 135
HOBHOUSE, L. T., 206, 297
HOCKING, W. E., 218
HOLT, E. B., 23
Hormic processes, 221
HUME, DAVID, 25, 60, 64, 65, 93, 112

Idealism, 101 ff.
Illusion, 17, 21, 101, 105
Images, 120
Imagination, 252
Immortality, 147, 175
Industry, 281
Intelligibility, principles of, 66, 68
Interest theory of value, 197 ff.
Introspection, 31, 74

JAMES, WILLIAM, 23, 26, 43
JEANS, Sir JAMES, 133, 137, 138
JENNINGS, H. S., 90

KANT, I., 19, 60, 63, 65, 66, 67, 75, 101, 195, 196, 250, 276, 279
KROPOTKIN, Prince, 295

LAIRD, J., 89 ff., 182, 192, 194
LAO-TSE, 314
LEIBNIZ, 16, 70
LIPPS, T., 250
LOCKE, JOHN, 52
Logos, 314

MACH, E., 43
MALEBRANCHE, 16
Mathematical principles, 137–8
McDOUGALL, W., 37, 38, 215, 221, 283, 295
Mechanism, 35, 41
MECHNIKOV, I., 91
MEINONG, A. von., 149, 278
MESSER, AUGUST, 153, 299
Mind, 16, 22, 78, 129, 140, 142, 315

MITCHELL, Sir WILLIAM, 121
MONTAGUE, W. P., 109, 133
MOORE, G. E., 16, 102, 109, 167, 171, 296
Moral achievement, 280
Motion, 55, 60, 64, 107, 130, 132
MÜNSTERBURG, H., 183, 206
Mutual aid, 295, 312

New Realism, 23, 43
NIETZSCHE, F., 301
NUNN, T. P., 221

Original moral judgments, 283
Other minds, 116 ff.
Ought-to-be and Ought-to-do, 185

Pan-objectivism, 24
PARKER, DE WITT, 196, 202 ff.
PATON, H. J., 206, 208
Perceptual object, 108
Personal identity, 93 ff.
Personal integrity, 294 ff.
PERRY, R. B., 196 ff.
Perspectives, 106, 122, 176 ff., 189, 194, 267, 275, 286, 288
Philosophy, scope and method of, 13–15
PLATO, 131, 193, 195, 206, 256, 291, 294
Play, 219, 223, 259
Pleasure as a value, 59, 159, 222, 250, 265
PRALL, D. W., 251, 252, 254
PRINGLE-PATTISON, A. S., 131, 313
Projection, 120
Promises, 299
Psychic blindness, 37, 254, 277, 289
Psychic fusion, 37 ff.
Pythagoreans, 256

Quantum, 135

RADIN, PAUL, 108
Realism, 101–2

Reality and experience, 100 ff.
definition of, 109 ff.
degrees of, 110 ff.
Religion, 70, 131, 134, 139, 300, 312
Representative Perception, 19
RHINE, J. B., 147
Right and Good, 276, 289
ROSS, W. D., 182, 184, 191, 260, 268, 276, 282, 289
RUSKIN, JOHN, 250
RUSSELL, B., 23, 43, 119

Satiety, 162
Self, 98, 130, 305
SENECA, 291
Sensa, 21, 46, 118 ff., 175
Sensation, conditions of, 77
SMITH, N. KEMP, 52, 55, 61
SOCRATES, 167
Soul, 98, 103, 142 ff.
Space, 47 ff., 130, 135
Specious present, 27, 238
SPINOZA, 16, 70, 153, 195, 203, 279
Stoics, 195, 291
STOUT, G. F., 31, 50, 61, 70, 76, 89, 117, 119, 221, 229
Subconscious processes, 80–2
Subjective and Objective, definition of, 113
Subjective activity, 25, 30, 33, 34
Subjectivist theory of value, 193 ff.
Substance, 65 ff., 98, 131, 145

TAYLOR, A. E., 101, 247
Telepathy, 147
TENNANT, F. R., 102, 143
Time, 26, 61, 122, 125 ff., 131, 315
Timological theory, 192
Totality, 61 ff.
Traducianism, 143, 148
Tragedy, 265
Truth, criteria and standards of, 232–3, 238, 240, 245, 248
Truth, definition of, 233, 236, 238

Truth-value, 232, 247
TYLOR, E. B., 75

Unconscious activity, 80
Unity of consciousness, 36–7
Universals, 239–40
URBAN, W. M., 68, 182, 184, 188, 195, 196
Utilitarian principle, 307, 310

Validity, 182 ff., 194, 212, 225, 248, 264, 266, 270, 273 ff., 286
Value experience as objective process, 57, 154
Value experience, function of, 208, 210, 226, 304
Value experience, its relation to conation, 76, 83, 149
Value, general analysis of, 158 ff.
intrinsic, 171, 260
potentiality, 166 ff.
quality, 232, 260, 277, 282 ff., 308
reality of, 106, 211
scale, 158, 163 ff., 187, 227, 288, 292, 305, 308
subjective and objective standards of, 174, 179 ff., 188–95, 225, 266, 271, 275, 288
Valuing and evaluation, 183
Vitalism, 85 ff.

WARD, JAMES, 31, 305
WHITEHEAD, A. N., 29, 65, 128, 167
WILDE, OSCAR, 250
Will, primacy of, 84 ff.
primary and subsidiary, 206 ff., 224, 264, 286, 304
subconscious effects of, 207
to activity or self-expression, 219, 225, 231, 247, 257, 281, 292, 305, 311
to universal good, 293, 302, 305, 311

ZENO, 29

For Product Safety Concerns and Information please contact our EU representative GPSR@taylorandfrancis.com
Taylor & Francis Verlag GmbH, Kaufingerstraße 24, 80331 München, Germany

www.ingramcontent.com/pod-product-compliance
Lightning Source LLC
Chambersburg PA
CBHW071803300426
44116CB00009B/1183